Flexible Pattern Matching in Strings

String matching problems range from the relatively simple task of searching a single text for a string of characters to searching a database for approximate occurrences of a complex pattern. Recent years have witnessed a dramatic increase of interest in sophisticated string matching problems, especially in information retrieval and computational biology.

This book presents a practical approach to string matching problems, focusing on the algorithms and implementations that perform best in practice. It covers searching for simple, multiple, and extended strings, as well as regular expressions, exactly and approximately. It includes all of the most significant new developments in complex pattern searching.

The clear explanations, step-by-step examples, algorithms pseudo-code, and implementation efficiency maps will enable researchers, professionals, and students in bioinformatics, computer science, and software engineering to choose the most appropriate algorithms for their applications.

Gonzalo Navarro obtained his Ph.D. in computer science at the University of Chile in 1998 and was appointed Assistant Professor in 1999. His interests include design and analysis of algorithms, information retrieval, text searching, text compression, approximate text searching, and searching in metric spaces. He has co-authored more than 80 papers on these topics, and has been a program committee member of several international conferences, as well as program committee chair of SPIRE'2001. He is a member of the ACM and the Chilean Computer Science Society.

Mathieu Raffinot received his Ph.D. in theoretical computer science at the University of Marne-la-Vallée in 1999. Since October 2000 he has worked as a CNRS bioinformatics researcher at the Laboratoire Génome et Informatique. His interests include design and analysis of algorithms, pattern matching, and computational biology. He is the co-author of numerous articles in international conferences and journals in computer science and bioinformatics, and he works as a consultant for bioinformatics companies, including Gene-IT, the provider of the software application LASSAP.

T0212548

Flexible Pattern Matching in Strings

Practical On-Line Search Algorithms for
Texts and Biological Sequences

GONZALO NAVARRO

University of Chile

MATHIEU RAFFINOT

*Centre Nationale de
Recherche Scientifique,
Marne-La-Vallee, France*

CAMBRIDGE
UNIVERSITY PRESS

CAMBRIDGE UNIVERSITY PRESS
Cambridge, New York, Melbourne, Madrid, Cape Town, Singapore, São Paulo

Cambridge University Press
The Edinburgh Building, Cambridge CB2 8RU, UK

Published in the United States of America by Cambridge University Press, New York

www.cambridge.org
Information on this title: www.cambridge.org/9780521813075

First published 2002
Reprinted 2004
This digitally printed version 2007

A catalogue record for this publication is available from the British Library

Library of Congress Cataloguing in Publication data

Navarro, Gonzalo, 1969–
Flexible pattern matching in strings : practical on-line search algorithms for texts and
biological sequences / Gonzalo Navarro, Mathieu Raffinot.
  p. cm
Includes bibliographical references and index.
ISBN 0-521-81307-7
1. Computer algorithms. 2. Database searching. I. Raffinot, Mathieu, 1973– II. Title.

QA76.9 .A43 N38 2002
005.74–dc21   2001043704

ISBN 978-0-521-81307-5 hardback
ISBN 978-0-521-03993-2 paperback

This book was partially supported
by ECOS-CONICYT project C99E04

A Betina, Martina, mis padres y hermana,
quienes, cada uno a su tiempo y manera,
me han hecho feliz.
A París, por lo mismo.

A toute ma famille, à Pía Marcela del
Campo Rojas, à Matthieu Latapy, aux
oursins, et bien sûr, au Pisco Sour.

Contents

1

Introduction

1.1 Why this book? Our aim and focus

String matching can be understood as the problem of finding a pattern with some property within a given sequence of symbols. The simplest case is that of finding a given string inside the sequence.

This is one of the oldest and most pervasive problems in computer science. Applications requiring some form of string matching can be found virtually everywhere. However, recent years have witnessed a dramatic increase in interest in string matching problems, especially within the rapidly growing communities of information retrieval and computational biology.

Not only are these communities facing a drastic increase in the text sizes they have to manage, but they are demanding more and more sophisticated searches. The patterns of interest are not just simple strings but also include wild cards, gaps, and regular expressions. The definition of a match may also permit slight differences between the pattern and its occurrence in the text. This is called "approximate matching" and is especially interesting in text retrieval and computational biology.

The problems arising in this field can be addressed from different viewpoints. In particular, string matching is well known for being amenable to approaches that range from the extremely theoretical to the extremely practical. The theoretical solutions have given rise to important algorithmic achievements, but they are rarely useful in practice: A well-known fact in the community is that simpler ideas work better in practice. Two typical examples are the famous Knuth-Morris-Pratt algorithm, which in practice is twice as slow as the brute force approach, and the well-known Boyer-Moore family, whose most successful members in practice are highly simplified variants of the original proposal.

It is hard, however, to find the simpler ideas in the literature. In most current books on text algorithms, the string matching part covers only the classic theoretical algorithms. There are three reasons for that.

First, the practical algorithms are quite recent, the oldest one being just a decade old. Some recent developments are too new to appear in the established literature or in books. These algorithms are usually based on new techniques such as bit-parallelism, which has appeared with the recent generation of computers.

The second reason is that in this area the theoretical achievements are dissociated from the practical advantages. The algorithmic community is interested in theoretically appealing algorithms, that is, those achieving the best complexities and involving complicated algorithmic concepts. The development community focuses solely on algorithms known to be fast in practice. Neither community pays much attention to what the other does. Only in the last few years have new algorithms emerged that combine aspects of both theory and practice (such as BNDM), and the result has been a new trend of fast and robust string matching algorithms. These new algorithms have also not yet found a place in the established literature.

Finally, the search for extended patterns, of much interest nowadays, is largely unrepresented in the established literature. There are no books dealing with such new search problems as multiple or approximate pattern matching.

These reasons make it extremely difficult to find the correct algorithm if one is not in the field: The right algorithms exist, but only an expert can find and recognize them. Consider the case of software practitioners, computational biologists, researchers, or students who are not directly involved in the field and are faced with a text searching problem. They are forced to dig into dozens of articles, most of them of theoretical value but extremely complicated to implement. Finally, they get lost in an ocean of choices, without the background necessary to decide which is better. The typical outcomes of this situation are (a) they decide to implement the simplest approach, which, when available, yields extremely poor performance and affects the overall quality of development; and (b) they make a (normally unfortunate) choice and invest a lot of work in implementing it, only to obtain a result that in practice is as bad as a naive approach or even worse.

The aim of our book is to present, for a large class of patterns (strings, sets of strings, extended strings, and regular expressions) the existing exact and approximate search approaches, and to present in depth the most practical algorithms. By "practical" we mean that they are efficient in practice and that a normal programmer can implement them in a few hours. Fortunately, these criteria normally coincide in string matching. We focus on *on-line* searching, which means that we do not build data structures on the text. Indexed searching, although based on on-line searching, would deserve a complete volume by itself.

This book is intended to be of use to a large audience. Computer scientists will find everything needed to understand and implement the fastest search algorithms. If they want to go further in studying text algorithms, we give precise links and research references (books, proceedings, articles) to many related problems. Computational biologists will be able to enter in depth in the pattern matching field and find directly the most simple and efficient algorithms for their sequence searches.

We have implemented and experimented with all the algorithms presented in this book. Moreover, some are ours. We give experimental maps whenever possible to help the reader see at a glance the most appropriate algorithms for a particular application.

This book is not a complete survey on text algorithms. This field is too large for a single book. We prefer to focus on a precise topic and present it in detail. We give a list of related recent books in Section 7.2.

1.2 Overview

Chapter 2: String matching

A *string* is a sequence of characters over a finite alphabet Σ. For instance, ATCTAGAGA is a string over $\Sigma = \{A, C, G, T\}$. The string matching problem is to find all the occurrences of a string p, called the pattern, in a large string T on the same alphabet, called the text. Given strings x, y, and z, we say that x is a prefix of xy, a suffix of yx, and a factor of yxz.

We present string matching algorithms according to three general approaches, depending on the way the pattern is searched for in the text.

The first approach consists in reading all the characters in the text one after the other and at each step updating some variables so as to identify a possible occurrence. The **Knuth-Morris-Pratt** algorithm is of this kind, as is the faster **Shift-Or**, which is extensible to more complicated patterns.

The second approach consists in searching for the string p in a window that slides along the text T. For every position of this window, we search backwards for a suffix of the window that matches a suffix of p. The **Boyer-Moore** algorithm uses this approach, but it is generally slower than one of its simplifications, **Horspool**. And when it is not, it is slower than other algorithms of other approaches.

The third approach is more recent and leads to the most efficient algorithms in practice for long enough p. As with the second approach, the search is done backward in a window, but this time we search for the longest suffix of the window that is also a factor of p. The first algorithm using this approach was **BDM**, which, when p is short enough, leads to the simpler and more efficient **BNDM**. For longer patterns, a new algorithm, **BOM**, is the fastest.

We give an experimental map to easily choose the fastest algorithm according to the length of the pattern and the size of the alphabet.

The three approaches represent a general framework in which the most efficient algorithms fit. There exist other algorithms, for instance, those based on hashing, but they are not efficient enough. We give references to these algorithms in the last section.

Chapter 3: Multiple string matching

A set of strings $P = \{p^1, p^2, \ldots, p^r\}$ can be searched for in the same manner as a single string, reading the text once. Many search algorithms for searching a single string have been extended to search a set, with more or less success. This chapter is a survey of the most efficient algorithms. Surprisingly, many of them have just been published as technical reports and it is quite difficult for a nonexpert to know of their existence.

All three approaches to search for a single string lead to extensions to a set of strings. The first one leads to the well-known **Aho-Corasick** algorithm and, when the sum of the pattern lengths, $|P|$, is very small, to the **Multiple Shift-And** algorithm.

The second one leads to the famous **Commentz-Walter** algorithm, which is not very efficient in practice. The extension of the **Horspool** algorithm, **Set Horspool**, is efficient for very small sets on large alphabets. A last algorithm, **Wu-Manber**, mixes the suffix search approach with a hashing paradigm and is usually fast in practice.

The third approach permits an extension of **BOM**, the **SBOM** algorithm, which becomes very efficient when the minimum pattern length grows. Similarly to **Shift-Or**, **BNDM** leads to **Multiple BNDM** when $|P|$ is very small.

We give experimental maps that permit choosing which algorithm to use depending on the total pattern size $|P|$, the minimum length, and the size of the alphabet.

Chapter 4: Extended string matching

In many applications, the search pattern is not just a simple sequence of characters. In this chapter we consider several extensions that appear normally in applications and show how to deal with them. All these extensions can be converted into regular expressions (Chapter 5), but simpler and faster particular algorithms exist for the ones we consider here.

The simplest extension is to permit the pattern to be a sequence of classes (sets) of characters instead of just characters. Any text character in the class will match that pattern position. It is also possible for the classes to appear in the text, not only in the pattern.

A second extension is bounded length gaps: Some pattern positions are designated to match any text sequence whose length is between specified minimum and maximum values. This is of interest in computational biology applications, for example, to search for PROSITE patterns.

A third extension is optional and repeatable characters. An optional pattern character may or may not appear in its text occurrence, while a repeatable character may appear one or more times.

Problems arising from these three extensions and combinations thereof can be solved by adapting **Shift-Or** or **BNDM**. Both algorithms involve bit-parallelism to simulate a nondeterministic automaton that finds all the pattern occurrences (see Section 1.3). In this case we have more complex automata, and the core of the problem is finding a way to simulate them. Extending **Shift-Or** leads to an algorithm unable to skip text characters but whose efficiency is unaffected by the complexity of the pattern. Extending **BNDM**, on the other hand, is normally faster, but the efficiency is affected by the minimum length of an occurrence, the alphabet size, and the sizes of the classes and gaps. No classical algorithm can be extended so easily and obtain the same efficiency.

Finally, we show that a small set of short strings can be searched for using a similar approach, and give references to other theoretical algorithms that search specific kinds of extended strings.

Chapter 5: Regular expression matching

Regular expressions give an extremely powerful way to express a set of search patterns, containing all the previous types of problems we have considered so far. A regular expression specifies simple strings and concatenations, unions, and repetitions of other subexpressions. The algorithms addressing them are more complex and should be used only when the problem cannot be expressed as a simpler one.

Searching for a regular expression is a multistage process. First, we need to parse it to obtain a more workable tree representation. We show at the end of Chapter 5 how to do this. We then use the tree representation throughout the chapter.

The second stage is to build a nondeterministic finite automaton (NFA) from the pattern. The NFA is a state machine which has some states active that change as we read text characters, recognizing occurrences when states designated as "final" are reached. There are two interesting ways to obtain an NFA from a regular expression. Thompson's algorithm obtains an NFA whose number of transitions is proportional to the length of the regular expression and which satisfies some regularity properties that are of interest. Glushkov's algorithm produces an NFA that has the minimum number of states and other interesting regularities.

The NFA can be used directly for searching (we call this algorithm **NFA-Thompson**), but this is slow because many states can be active at any time. It can also be converted into a deterministic finite automaton (DFA), which has only one active state at a time. The DFA is appealing for text searching and is used in one of the most classical algorithms for regular expression searching. We call this algorithm **DFAClassical**. Its main problem is that the size of the DFA can be exponential on that of the NFA, which makes the approach workable only for small patterns. On longer patterns, a hybrid approach that we dub **DFAModules** builds an NFA of small DFAs and retains a reasonable efficiency.

Another trend is to simulate the NFAs using bit-parallelism instead of converting them to DFAs. We present two relatively new approaches, **BP-Thompson** and **BPGlushkov**, which are based on simulating the respective NFAs using their specific properties. We show that **BPGlushkov** should always be preferred over **BPThompson**.

A third approach, also novel, permits skipping text characters. The algorithm **MultiStringRE** computes the minimum length ℓmin of an occurrence of the regular expression and computes all the prefixes (of that length) of all the occurrences. It then conducts a multistring search (Chapter 2) for all those strings. When one such prefix is found, it tries to complete the occurrence. An extension of it, **MultiFactRE**, selects a set of strings of length ℓmin such that some of these strings must appear inside any occurrence (the set of prefixes is just one option). Finally, **RegularBNDM** extends **BNDM** by simulating Glushkov's NFA.

Choosing the best algorithm is a complex choice that depends on the structure of the regular expression. We give simple criteria based on properties of the pattern to decide which algorithm to use.

Chapter 6: Approximate matching

Approximate matching is the problem of finding the occurrences of a pattern in a text where the pattern and the occurrence may have a limited number of differences. This is becoming more and more important in problems such as recovering from typing or spelling errors in information retrieval, from sequence alterations or measurement errors in computational biology, or from transmission errors in signal processing, to name a few.

Approximate matching is modeled using a distance function that tells how similar two strings are. We are given the pattern and a threshold k, which is the maximum allowed distance between the pattern and its occurrences. In this chapter we concentrate on the Levenshtein (or edit) distance, which is the minimum number of character insertions, deletions, and substitutions needed to make both strings equal. Many applications use variants of this distance.

We divide the existing algorithms into four types. The first is based on dynamic programming. This is the oldest approach and still the most flexible one to deal with distances other than edit distance. However, algorithms of this kind are not among the most efficient.

The second type of algorithm converts the problem into the output of an NFA search, which is built as a function of the pattern and k, and then makes the automaton deterministic. The resulting algorithms behave reasonably well with short patterns, but not as fast as newer techniques.

Bit-parallelism is the third approach, and it yields many of the most successful results. The algorithms **BPR** and **BPD** simulate the NFA, while **BPM** simulates the dynamic programming algorithms. **BPM** and **BPD** are the most efficient of the class, but **BPR** is more flexible and can be adapted to more complex patterns.

Finally, the fourth approach is filtration. A fast algorithm is used to discard large text areas that cannot contain a match, and another (nonfiltration) algorithm is used to check the remaining text areas. These algorithms are among the fastest, but their efficiency degrades quickly as k becomes large compared to the pattern length m.

Among the many filtration algorithms, we present the two most efficient ones. **PEX** splits the pattern in $k + 1$ pieces and resorts to multistring searching of them, as at least one must appear unaltered in any occurrence. **ABNDM** is an extension of **BNDM** that simulates the NFA of approximate searching.

We present an experimental map comparing these algorithms. In general, filtration approaches work better for low k/m values. **ABNDM** is best for small alphabet sizes (such as DNA) while **PEX** is best for larger alphabets (such as proteins or natural language). For larger k/m values, and also to verify the text areas that the filters cannot discard, the best algorithms are the bit-parallel ones.

There are some developments for approximate searching of other types of patterns. For multiple pattern matching with errors, the main algorithms are **MultiHash**, which works only for $k = 1$ but is efficient even when the number of patterns is large; **MultiPEX**, which takes $k+1$ strings from each pattern and is the most efficient choice for low k/m values; and **MultiBP**, which superimposes the NFAs of all the patterns and uses the result as a filter, this being the best choice for intermediate k/m values.

For matching extended strings and regular expressions with errors, there are a few approaches: one based on dynamic programming for regular expressions, one based on an NFA of DFAs permitting errors, and a bit-parallel one based on **BPR**. This last one is the most attractive because of the combination of simplicity and efficiency it offers.

1.3 Basic concepts

1.3.1 Bit-parallelism and bit operations

The *bit-parallelism* technique takes advantage of the intrinsic parallelism of the bit operations inside a computer word. That is, we can pack many values in a single word and update them all in a single operation. By taking advantage of bit-parallelism, the number of operations that an algorithm performs can be cut down by a factor of up to w, where w is the number of bits in the computer word. Since in current architectures w is 32 or 64, the speedup is very significant in practice.

Let us introduce some notation to describe bit-parallel algorithms. We use exponentiation to denote bit repetition, for example, $0^3 1 = 0001$. A sequence of bits $b_\ell \ldots b_1$ is called a *bit mask* of length ℓ, which is stored somewhere inside the computer word of length w. We use C–like syntax for operations on the bits of computer words, that is, "|" is the bitwise OR, "&" is the bitwise AND, "$\wedge$" is the bitwise XOR, "$\sim$" complements all the bits, and "$<<$" ("$>>$") moves the bits to the left (right) and enters zeros from the right (left), so that, for example, $b_\ell b_{\ell-1} \ldots b_2 b_1 << 3 = b_{\ell-3} \ldots b_2 b_1 000$.

We can also perform arithmetic operations on the bits, such as addition and subtraction. These operate on the bits as if they formed a number. For instance, $00010110 + 00010010 = 00101000$ and $10010000 - 1 = 10001111$.

We may have to use many computer words to store a given set of values, and in this case the operations described have to be applied over this entire representation. This is quite trivial for most operations, but the arithmetic ones need some care because we have to consider the propagation effects. For example, imagine that we have to simulate $Z \leftarrow X + Y$ or $Z \leftarrow X - Y$, where $X = X_t \ldots X_1$ and $Y = Y_t \ldots Y_1$ are each represented using t computer words. Figure 1.1 shows the algorithm for both operations.

Add$(X = X_t \ldots X_1, Y = Y_t \ldots Y_1)$
1. $carry \leftarrow 0$
2.   **For** $i \in 1 \ldots t$ **Do**
3. $Z_i \leftarrow X_i + Y_i + carry$
4.   **If** $Z_i < X_i$ OR $(Y_i = 1^w$ AND $carry = 1)$ **Then** $carry \leftarrow 1$
5.   **Else** $carry \leftarrow 0$
6.   **End of for**
7.   **Return** $Z = Z_t \ldots Z_1$

Subtract$(X = X_t \ldots X_1, Y = Y_t \ldots Y_1)$
8. $carry \leftarrow 0$
9.   **For** $i \in 1 \ldots t$ **Do**
10. $Z_i \leftarrow X_i - Y_i - carry$
11.   **If** $Z_i > X_i$ OR $(Y_i = 1^w$ AND $carry = 1)$ **Then** $carry \leftarrow 1$
12.   **Else** $carry \leftarrow 0$
13.   **End of for**
14.   **Return** $Z = Z_t \ldots Z_1$

Fig. 1.1. Algorithms for adding and subtracting unsigned numbers stored in multiple machine words. The first word, Z_1, is the least significant. We ignore the final overflow in the operation, but the overflow information is contained in the variable *carry*.

1.3.2 Labeled rooted tree, trie

Most of the data structures presented in this book are based on classical strings and rooted trees. A *rooted tree* is a set of nodes linked together with unidirectional links. The source node of each link is called the *parent* and the target is called a *child*. One special node has no parent; this node is denoted *root*. The rest of the nodes of the tree have exactly one parent each. Nodes with no children are called *leaves*.

For our purpose, it is convenient to attach a *label* to each link, which is normally a character of the alphabet Σ. An example of such a tree is shown in Figure 1.2.

When the labeled rooted tree is associated to a set of strings, it is called a *trie*. A complete presentation of the trie structure is given in Chapter 3.

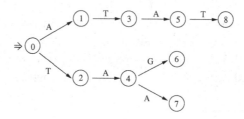

Fig. 1.2. A labeled tree. State 0 is the root. Each node, except the root, has a unique parent.

An algorithm that uses a labeled rooted tree performs computations over the nodes in a specific order. In *prefix order*, the algorithm performs the computation first over a node and then over its children (if any). In *postfix order*, the computation over the node is done after those over the children. For instance, for the tree in Figure 1.2, the nodes we compute over in prefix order are 0, 1, 3, 5, 8, 2, 4, 6, 7, and in postfix order they are 8, 5, 3, 1, 7, 6, 4, 2, 0. The specific order in which sibling nodes are processed is not relevant.

Another frequently used order is the *transversal order*. The *level* of a node is its distance, in terms of the number of intermediate nodes, to the root. In transversal order the nodes are processed in increasing level order. Inside a level, the order has generally no importance, but sometimes we impose one to simplify the algorithms. Two transversal orders are shown in Figure 1.3. The dashed arrows represent the way the nodes are processed.

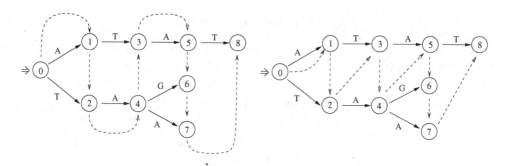

Fig. 1.3. Tree traversals. State 0 is the root. The traversals are shown in dashed arrows.

1.3.3 *Automata*

The term *automaton* has many meanings in computer science. For our purposes, a finite automaton, which we call simply an automaton, is a finite set of *states* Q, among which one is *initial* (state $I \in Q$) and some are *final* or *terminal* (state set $F \subseteq Q$). Transitions between states are labeled by elements of $\Sigma \cup \{\varepsilon\}$. These are formally defined by a transition function $\mathcal{D}$, which associates to each state $q \in Q$ a set $\{q_1, q_2, \ldots, q_k\}$ of states of Q for each $\alpha \in \Sigma \cup \{\varepsilon\}$. An automaton is then totally defined by $A = (Q, \Sigma, I, F, \mathcal{D})$.

In practice, we distinguish two general types of automata, depending on the form of the transition function. If the function $\mathcal{D}$ is such that there exists a state q associated by a given character α to more than one state, say $\mathcal{D}(q, \alpha) = \{q_1, q_2, \ldots, q_k\}$, $k > 1$, or there is some transition labeled by ε, then the automaton is called a *nondeterministic finite automaton* (NFA), and the transition function $\mathcal{D}$ is denoted by the set of triples $\Delta = \{(q, \alpha, q'), q \in Q, \alpha \in \Sigma \cup \{\varepsilon\}, q' \in \mathcal{D}(q, \alpha)\}$. Otherwise, the automaton is called a *deterministic finite automaton* (DFA), and $\mathcal{D}$ is denoted by a partial function $\delta : Q \times \Sigma \to Q$, such that if $\mathcal{D}(q, \alpha) = \{q'\}$, then $\delta(q, \alpha) = q'$. We give examples of both types of automata in Figure 1.4.

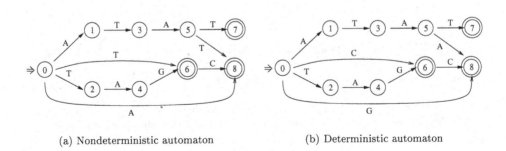

(a) Nondeterministic automaton   (b) Deterministic automaton

Fig. 1.4. Two automata. In both, the state 0 is initial and the double-circled states are terminal. The left automaton is nondeterministic since from the state 0 by T we reach 2 and 6. The right one is deterministic because for a fixed transition character all the states lead to at most one state.

A string is *recognized* by the automaton $A = (Q, \Sigma, I, F, \Delta)$ or $A = (Q, \Sigma, I, F, \delta)$ if it labels a path from an initial to a final state. The *language recognized* by an automaton is the set of strings it recognizes. For instance, the language recognized by the automaton in Figure 1.4 (a) is the set of strings: A in state 8, ATAT in states 7 and 8, T in state 6, TC in state 8, TAG in state 6, and finally TAGC in state 8.

In NFAs, we accept that some transitions are labeled with the empty string ε, and they are called ε-transitions (or empty transitions). This means that we do not have to read a character to go through the transition. If we are at the source state of the ε-transition, we can simply jump to its target state. This can also be seen as reading an empty string. These transitions are generally used to simplify the construction of the NFA, but there always exists an equivalent automaton, recognizing the same language without ε-transitions.

Both in NFAs and DFAs, if a string x labels a path from I to a state s, we say that s is *active* after reading x. DFAs have at most one active state at a time, while NFAs may have many.

The two automata shown in Figure 1.4 have a simple form, in the sense that the transitions do not form cycles. Such automata are called *acyclic*, whether they are deterministic or not. However, we can easily conceive of *cyclic* automata. These automata are useful for regular expression matching. The two automata of Figure 1.5 are cyclic. The language recognized by a cyclic automaton can be infinite. For instance, the automaton of Figure 1.5 (a) recognizes TAG, but also TA·GAA·G, TA·GAA·GAA·G, TA·GAA·GAA·GAA·G, and so on.

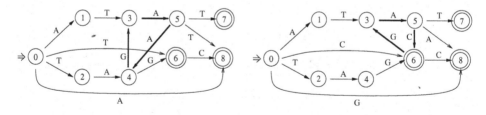

(a) Nondeterministic cyclic automaton   (b) Deterministic cyclic automaton

Fig. 1.5. Two cyclic automata. In both, the state 0 is initial and the double-circled states are terminal. The cycles are marked in bold.

1.3.4 Complexity notations

We will generally describe the efficiency of our pattern matching algorithms in terms of the number of character comparisons and other basic operations, depending on the size of the pattern, m, and of the text, n. We do not usually give a precise function of n and m, only its growth rate or *complexity order*. The O notation is used to express this idea.

Definition *A function $g(n)$ is said to be $O(f(n))$ if there exist two constants C and n_0 such that $g(n) \leq C \times f(n)$ for all $n > n_0$.*

For instance, $2n^2 + 3n + \log\log n$ is $O(n^2)$, $n\log n + 120n + \log n$ is $O(n\log n)$, and $n^4 + 3n^3 + 15n^2 + n$ is $O(n^4)$. A deeper presentation of complexity notations and their meanings can be found in [Sed88, CLR90].

This notation permits us to compare algorithms of different complexities. For example, if algorithm **A** takes time $O(n)$ and algorithm **B** takes time $O(n\log(m)/m)$, then we know that for large enough m algorithm **B** will be faster than algorithm **A**. We do not know how large is "large enough." Moreover, when both algorithms have the same complexity we do not know which is better.

Sometimes a finer analysis can be done, comparing the exact number of text inspections, table accesses, register accesses, and so on, that are performed by each algorithm. These values are not only more complex to obtain, but they also do not guarantee that we can predict which algorithm is better on a given computer: Not only may the accesses have different costs depending on the architecture, but also caching and pipelining effects complicate any prediction.

The O notation is independent of the architecture, but its predictive power is limited. In many cases we must resort to empirical measures to determine which algorithm is better depending on the instance.

Two complexities are usually studied in the analysis of an algorithm. Its *worst-case* complexity corresponds to the maximum cost over every possible input. Its *average-case* or *expected-case* complexity refers to averaging the cost over all the inputs. This involves assuming a probabilistic distribution of the data. In this book we assume that the pattern and text characters are independent and uniformly distributed over a finite alphabet.

2

String matching

2.1 Basic concepts

The string matching problem is that of finding all the occurrences of a given pattern $p = p_1 p_2 \ldots p_m$ in a large text $T = t_1 t_2 \ldots t_n$, where both T and p are sequences of characters from a finite character set Σ. Given strings x, y, and z, we say that x is a prefix of xy, a suffix of yx, and a factor of yxz.

Many algorithms exist to solve this problem. The oldest and most famous are the **Knuth-Morris-Pratt** and the **Boyer-Moore** algorithms. These algorithms appeared in 1977. The first is worst-case linear in the size of the text. This $O(n)$ complexity is a lower bound for the worst case of any string matching algorithm. The second is $O(mn)$ in the worst case but is sublinear on average, that is, it may avoid reading some characters of the text. An $O(n \log_{|\Sigma|} m / m)$ lower bound on the average complexity has been proved in [Yao79].

Since 1977, many studies have been undertaken to find simpler algorithms, optimal average-case algorithms, algorithms that could also search extended patterns, constant space algorithms, and so on. There exists a large variety of research directions that have been tried, many of which lead to different string matching algorithms.

The aim of this chapter is not to present as many algorithms as possible, nor to give an exhaustive list of them. Instead, we will present the most efficient algorithms, which means the algorithms that for some pattern length and some alphabet size yield the best experimental results. Among those that have more or less the same efficiency, we will present the simplest.

The algorithms we present derive from three general search approaches, according to the way the text is searched. For all of them, a *search window* of the size of the pattern is slid from left to right along the text, and the pattern is searched for inside the window. The algorithms differ in the way

15

in which the window is shifted. The general scheme is shown Figure 2.1, together with our favorite running example on English, which we will show for all our algorithms.

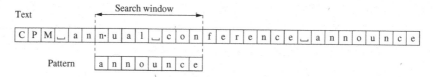

Fig. 2.1. The search is done in a window that slides along the text. The search window has the size of the pattern.

In general, strings that are searched for in natural language texts are simpler than in DNA sequences because the former contain fewer intrinsic repetitions. To show all the tricky cases that could appear, we also show the behavior of all our algorithms when searching for the string ATATA in the sequence AGATACGATATATAC.

The three search approaches are presented below.

Prefix searching (Figure 2.2) The search is done forward in the search window, reading all the characters of the text one after the other. For each position of the window, we search for the longest prefix of the window that is also a prefix of the pattern. The **Knuth-Morris-Pratt** algorithm uses this approach.

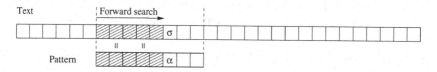

Fig. 2.2. First approach: We search for a prefix of the pattern in the current window.

Suffix searching (Figure 2.3) The search is done backwards along the search window, reading the longest suffix of the window that is also a suffix of the pattern. This approach enables us on average to avoid reading some characters of the text, and therefore leads to sublinear average-case algorithms. The most famous algorithm using this technique is the **Boyer-Moore** algorithm, which has been simplified by Horspool and by Sunday.

Factor searching (Figure 2.4) The search is done backwards in the search window, looking for the longest suffix of the window that is also

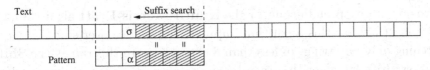

Fig. 2.3. Second approach: We search for a suffix of the pattern in the current window.

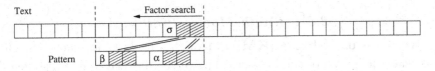

Fig. 2.4. Third approach: We search for a factor of the pattern in the current window.

a factor of the pattern. As with suffix searching, this approach leads to sublinear expected algorithms, and even to optimal algorithms. The main drawback is that it requires a way to recognize the set of factors of the pattern, and this is quite complex.

These three approaches lead to algorithms that are efficient in several cases, depending on the size of the pattern and the size of the alphabet. An experimental map of their relative performances is given in Section 2.5.

2.2 Prefix based approach

Suppose that we have read the text up to position i and that we know the length of the longest suffix of the text read that corresponds to a prefix of the pattern p. When this length is $|p|$ we have an occurrence. The main algorithmic problem is to find an efficient way to compute this length when we read the next character of the text. There exist two classical ways to solve this problem:

- The first is to find a mechanism to effectively compute the longest suffix of the text read that is also a prefix of p, preferably in amortized constant time per character. This is what the algorithm of Knuth, Morris, and Pratt, **KMP**, does [KMP77].
- The second is to maintain a kind of set of all the prefixes of p that are also suffixes of the text read, and update the set at each character read. The bit-parallelism technique enables managing such a set in an efficient way if the pattern is short enough. This leads to the **Shift-And** and **Shift-Or** algorithms [WM92b, BYG89b].

We do not give pseudo-code for the **Knuth-Morris-Pratt** algorithm, nor a deeper study, for this algorithm improves in practice over suffix or factor searching only for strings of less than 8 characters. In this range, the **Shift-And** or **Shift-Or** algorithms can be run on any computer, and are at least twice as fast and much simpler to implement.

2.2.1 Knuth-Morris-Pratt idea

The **Knuth-Morris-Pratt** (**KMP**) algorithm updates for each text character read the length of the longest prefix of the pattern that is also a suffix of the text. The mechanism is based on the following observation. Let us complete Figure 2.2 of the general prefix matching approach with a representation of what what we would like to obtain. This is shown in Figure 2.5. The string $v\beta$ is a new potential prefix of the pattern that could be the new longest prefix of p that is also a suffix of $t_1 \ldots t_{i+1}$. We observe that v is a suffix of u, and also a prefix. We call it a *border* of u. Also, the character β has to be equal to t_{i+1} (σ on the figure).

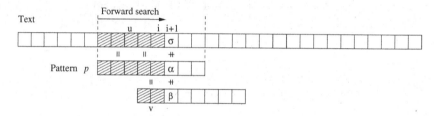

Fig. 2.5. The shift in the **Knuth-Morris-Pratt** algorithm. The string v is a suffix of the prefix u, and also a prefix. The character β differs from α, which differs from the text character σ, on which the prefix search failed.

The original idea, due to Morris and Pratt [MP70], is

- Precompute the longest border $b(u)$ for each prefix u of the pattern.
- Now, in the current position, let u be the longest prefix of p that is a suffix of $t_1 \ldots t_i$. We read the character $\sigma = t_{i+1}$ of the text. If $\sigma = p_{|u|+1}$ (denoted α in Figure 2.5), then the new longest prefix is $up_{|u|+1}$. However, if $\sigma \neq p_{|u|+1}$, then we compare σ with $p_{|b(u)|+1}$. If $\sigma = p_{|b(u)|+1}$, then $b(u)p_{|b(u)|+1}$ is the new longest prefix of p that is a suffix of $t_1 \ldots t_{i+1}$. If $\sigma \neq p_{|b(u)|+1}$, then we compare it with $\sigma = p_{|b(b(u))|+1}$ and so on, until one border is followed by σ, or until there are no more borders (the empty border ε does not have a border), in which case the new longest prefix is the empty string ε.

Knuth proposed the following improvement. We know that if the comparison of $\sigma = t_{i+1}$ with $p_{|u|+1}$ fails, the letter that follows any border of u must differ from $p_{|u|+1}$ if it is to match σ. So at the precomputing phase, we can precompute for each *proper* prefix u of p ($p = uw$, $w \neq \varepsilon$) the longest border v that satisfies $p_{|u|+1} \neq p_{|v|+1}$.

The **KMP** algorithm is $O(n)$ in the worst and average case for the searching phase. For the preprocessing phase, the goal is to compute two things: first, for each proper prefix u of the pattern, the longest border v such that $p_{|u|+1} \neq p_{|v|+1}$; and second, for the pattern itself, its own longest border. Now, if we read the pattern $p_1 \ldots p_m$ character by character, and if we want to compute at each position p_{i+1} the length of the longest border of $p_1 \ldots p_{i+1}$, we want, in fact, to compute the longest suffix of $p_1 \ldots p_{i+1}$ that is also a prefix of p. It turns out that we are applying the **KMP** algorithm for searching p itself. The preprocessing phase of **KMP** can also be done with **KMP**, and its complexity is $O(m)$.

We do not explain **KMP** further. Details can be found in [KMP77, CR94]. Many studies and variants exist. We give in Section 2.6 the most important bibliographic references.

2.2.2 Shift-And/Shift-Or algorithm

The idea of the **Shift-And** and the **Shift-Or** algorithms is much simpler than that of **KMP**. It consists in keeping a set of all the prefixes of p that match a suffix of the text read. The algorithms use bit-parallelism to update this set for each new text character. This set is represented by a bit mask $D = d_m \ldots d_1$.

We first explain the **Shift-And** algorithm, which is easier to explain than **Shift-Or**.

We put a 1 in the j-th position of D (the j-th position of D is said to be *active*) if and only if $p_1 \ldots p_j$ is a suffix of $t_1 \ldots t_i$. If the size of p is less than w, then this array will fit in a computer register. We report a match whenever d_m is active.

When reading the next text character t_{i+1}, we have to compute the new set D'. A position $j + 1$ in this set will be active if and only if the position j was active in D, that is, $p_1 \ldots p_j$ was a suffix of $t_1 \ldots t_i$ and t_{i+1} matches p_{j+1}. This new set is easy to compute in constant time using bit-parallel operations.

The algorithm first builds a table B, which stores a bit mask $b_m \ldots b_1$ for each character. The mask in $B[c]$ has the j-th bit set if $p_j = c$.

We initially set $D = 0^m$, and for each new text character t_{i+1} we update D using the formula

$$D' \leftarrow ((D << 1) \mid 0^{m-1}1) \ \& \ B[t_{i+1}] \tag{2.1}$$

Intuitively, the "$<<$" shifts the positions to the left to mark at step $i + 1$ which positions of p were suffixes at step i. We also mark the empty string ε as a suffix, so we OR the new bit mask with $0^{m-1}1$. Now, we keep from these positions only those such that t_{i+1} matches p_{j+1}, by AND-ing this set of positions with the set $B[t_{i+1}]$ of positions of t_{i+1} in p.

The cost of this algorithm is $O(n)$, assuming that the operations in formula (2.1) can be done in constant time, in practice when the pattern fits in a few computer words.

The **Shift-Or** algorithm is a tricky implementation of **Shift-And**. The idea is to avoid using the "$0^{m-1}1$" mask of formula (2.1) in order to speed up the computation. For this, we complement all the bit masks of B and use a complemented bit mask D. As the shift "$<<$" operation will introduce a 0 to the right of D', the new suffix coming from the empty string is already in D'.

Shift-And $(p = p_1 p_2 \ldots p_m, \ T = t_1 t_2 \ldots t_n)$
1. Preprocessing
2. For $c \in \Sigma$ **Do** $B[c] \leftarrow 0^m$
3. For $j \in 1 \ldots m$ **Do** $B[p_j] \leftarrow B[p_j] \mid 0^{m-j}10^{j-1}$
4. Searching
5. $D \leftarrow 0^m$
6. For $pos \in 1 \ldots n$ **Do**
7. $D \leftarrow ((D << 1) \mid 0^{m-1}1) \ \& \ B[t_{pos}]$
8.   **If** $D \ \& \ 10^{m-1} \neq 0^m$ **Then** report an occurrence at $pos - m + 1$
9. **End of for**

Fig. 2.6. **Shift-And** algorithm.

The **Shift-And** and the **Shift-Or** algorithms can be seen as the simulation of a nondeterministic automaton that searches for the pattern in the text (Figure 2.7). Formula (2.1) is then related to the moves in the nondeterministic automaton for each new text character: Each state gets the value of the previous state, but only if the text character matches the corresponding arrow.

The "$\mid 0^{m-1}1$" after the shift allows a match to begin at the current text position. This corresponds to the self-loop at the beginning of the automaton.

Fig. 2.7. Nondeterministic automaton recognizing all prefixes of the pattern "announce".

The automaton point of view is also valid for **KMP**, which can be seen as an economical method to compute a deterministic automaton that searches for the pattern in the text. The difference between **KMP** and **Shift-Or** is that the former uses a deterministic automaton that the latter simulates with bit-parallelism. However, **Shift-Or** is in practice twice as fast as **KMP**, is simpler to implement, and can handle extended strings (Chapter 4).

Example using English We search for the string "announce" in the text "annual_announce".

$$B = \begin{cases} \text{a} & 0\,0\,0\,0\,0\,0\,0\,1 \\ \text{c} & 0\,1\,0\,0\,0\,0\,0\,0 \\ \text{e} & 1\,0\,0\,0\,0\,0\,0\,0 \\ \text{n} & 0\,0\,1\,0\,0\,1\,1\,0 \\ \text{o} & 0\,0\,0\,0\,1\,0\,0\,0 \\ \text{u} & 0\,0\,0\,1\,0\,0\,0\,0 \\ * & 0\,0\,0\,0\,0\,0\,0\,0 \end{cases}$$

$D = 0\,0\,0\,0\,0\,0\,0\,0$

1.	Reading a	$0\,0\,0\,0\,0\,0\,0\,1$
		$0\,0\,0\,0\,0\,0\,0\,1$
	$D =$	$0\,0\,0\,0\,0\,0\,0\,1$

2.	Reading n	$0\,0\,0\,0\,0\,0\,1\,1$
		$0\,0\,1\,0\,0\,1\,1\,0$
	$D =$	$0\,0\,0\,0\,0\,0\,1\,0$

3.	Reading n	$0\,0\,0\,0\,0\,1\,0\,1$
		$0\,0\,1\,0\,0\,1\,1\,0$
	$D =$	$0\,0\,0\,0\,0\,1\,0\,0$

4.	Reading u	$0\,0\,0\,0\,1\,0\,0\,1$
		$0\,0\,0\,1\,0\,0\,0\,0$
	$D =$	$0\,0\,0\,0\,0\,0\,0\,0$

5.	Reading a	$0\,0\,0\,0\,0\,0\,0\,1$
		$0\,0\,0\,0\,0\,0\,0\,1$
	$D =$	$0\,0\,0\,0\,0\,0\,0\,1$

6.	Reading l	$0\,0\,0\,0\,0\,0\,1\,1$
		$0\,0\,0\,0\,0\,0\,0\,0$
	$D =$	$0\,0\,0\,0\,0\,0\,0\,0$

7.	Reading _	$0\,0\,0\,0\,0\,0\,0\,1$
		$0\,0\,0\,0\,0\,0\,0\,0$
	$D =$	$0\,0\,0\,0\,0\,0\,0\,0$

8.	Reading a	$0\,0\,0\,0\,0\,0\,0\,1$
		$0\,0\,0\,0\,0\,0\,0\,1$
	$D =$	$0\,0\,0\,0\,0\,0\,0\,1$

9.	Reading n	$0\,0\,0\,0\,0\,0\,1\,1$
		$0\,0\,1\,0\,0\,1\,1\,0$
	$D =$	$0\,0\,0\,0\,0\,0\,1\,0$

10.	Reading n	$0\,0\,0\,0\,0\,1\,0\,1$
		$0\,0\,1\,0\,0\,1\,1\,0$
	$D =$	$0\,0\,0\,0\,0\,1\,0\,0$

11.	Reading o	$0\,0\,0\,0\,1\,0\,0\,1$
		$1\,0\,0\,0\,1\,0\,0\,0$
	$D =$	$0\,0\,0\,0\,1\,0\,0\,0$

12.	Reading u	$0\,0\,0\,1\,0\,0\,0\,1$
		$0\,0\,0\,1\,0\,0\,0\,0$
	$D =$	$0\,0\,0\,1\,0\,0\,0\,0$

13.	Reading n	$0\,0\,1\,0\,0\,0\,0\,1$
		$0\,0\,1\,0\,0\,1\,1\,0$
	$D =$	$0\,0\,1\,0\,0\,0\,0\,0$

14. Reading c
$$
\begin{array}{l}
0\,1\,0\,0\,0\,0\,0\,1\\
0\,1\,0\,0\,0\,0\,0\,0\\
\hline
D=\quad 0\,1\,0\,0\,0\,0\,0\,0
\end{array}
$$

15. Reading e
$$
\begin{array}{l}
1\,0\,0\,0\,0\,0\,0\,1\\
1\,0\,0\,0\,0\,0\,0\,0\\
\hline
D=\quad 1\,0\,0\,0\,0\,0\,0\,0
\end{array}
$$
The last bit is set; we mark an occurrence.

Example using DNA We search for the string ATATA in the sequence AGATACGATATATAC.

$$
B=\left\{
\begin{array}{|c|c|}
\hline
A & 1\,0\,1\,0\,1\\
\hline
T & 0\,1\,0\,1\,0\\
\hline
* & 0\,0\,0\,0\,0\\
\hline
\end{array}
\right.
$$

$D = 0\,0\,0\,0\,0$

1. Reading A
$$
\begin{array}{l}
0\,0\,0\,0\,1\\
1\,0\,1\,0\,1\\
\hline
D=\quad 0\,0\,0\,0\,1
\end{array}
$$

2. Reading G
$$
\begin{array}{l}
0\,0\,0\,1\,1\\
0\,0\,0\,0\,0\\
\hline
D=\quad 0\,0\,0\,0\,0
\end{array}
$$

3. Reading A
$$
\begin{array}{l}
0\,0\,0\,0\,1\\
1\,0\,1\,0\,1\\
\hline
D=\quad 0\,0\,0\,0\,1
\end{array}
$$

4. Reading T
$$
\begin{array}{l}
0\,0\,0\,1\,1\\
0\,1\,0\,1\,0\\
\hline
D=\quad 0\,0\,0\,1\,0
\end{array}
$$

5. Reading A
$$
\begin{array}{l}
0\,0\,1\,0\,1\\
1\,0\,1\,0\,1\\
\hline
D=\quad 0\,0\,1\,0\,1
\end{array}
$$

6. Reading C
$$
\begin{array}{l}
0\,1\,0\,1\,1\\
0\,0\,0\,0\,0\\
\hline
D=\quad 0\,0\,0\,0\,0
\end{array}
$$

7. Reading G
$$
\begin{array}{l}
0\,0\,0\,0\,1\\
0\,0\,0\,0\,0\\
\hline
D=\quad 0\,0\,0\,0\,0
\end{array}
$$

8. Reading A
$$
\begin{array}{l}
0\,0\,0\,0\,1\\
1\,0\,1\,0\,1\\
\hline
D=\quad 0\,0\,0\,0\,1
\end{array}
$$

9. Reading T
$$
\begin{array}{l}
0\,0\,0\,1\,1\\
0\,1\,0\,1\,0\\
\hline
D=\quad 0\,0\,0\,1\,0
\end{array}
$$

10. Reading A
$$
\begin{array}{l}
0\,0\,1\,0\,1\\
1\,0\,1\,0\,1\\
\hline
D=\quad 0\,0\,1\,0\,1
\end{array}
$$

11. Reading T
$$
\begin{array}{l}
0\,1\,0\,1\,1\\
0\,1\,0\,1\,0\\
\hline
D=\quad 0\,1\,0\,1\,0
\end{array}
$$

12. Reading A
$$
\begin{array}{l}
1\,0\,1\,0\,1\\
1\,0\,1\,0\,1\\
\hline
D=\quad 1\,0\,1\,0\,1
\end{array}
$$
The last bit is set; we mark an occurrence.

13. Reading T
$$
\begin{array}{l}
0\,1\,0\,1\,1\\
0\,1\,0\,1\,0\\
\hline
D=\quad 0\,1\,0\,1\,0
\end{array}
$$

14. Reading A
$$
\begin{array}{l}
1\,0\,1\,0\,1\\
1\,0\,1\,0\,1\\
\hline
D=\quad 1\,0\,1\,0\,1
\end{array}
$$
The last bit is set; we mark an occurrence.

15. Reading C
$$
\begin{array}{l}
0\,1\,0\,1\,1\\
0\,0\,0\,0\,0\\
\hline
D=\quad 0\,0\,0\,0\,0
\end{array}
$$

2.3 Suffix based approach

The main difficulty in the suffix based approach is to shift the window in a safe way, which means without missing an occurrence of the pattern.

We present the **Boyer-Moore** (**BM**) algorithm [BM77] and then the **Horspool** simplification [Hor80]. We do not give any pseudo-code for the first, nor a deeper study, for although **BM** improves over the algorithms of the other two general approaches, it is never the fastest.

2.3.1 Boyer-Moore idea

The **Boyer-Moore** algorithm precomputes three shift functions d_1, d_2, d_3 that correspond to the following three situations. For all of them, we have read a suffix u of the search window that is also a suffix of the pattern, and we have failed on a text character σ that does not match the next pattern character α (Figure 2.3).

First case The suffix u occurs in another position as a factor of p. Then a safe shift is to move the window so that u in the text matches the next occurrence of u in the pattern. This situation is shown in Figure 2.8. The idea is to compute for each suffix of the pattern the distance to the position of its next occurrence backwards in the pattern. We call this function d_1. If the suffix u of p does not appear again in p, then u is associated by d_1 to the size m of the whole pattern.

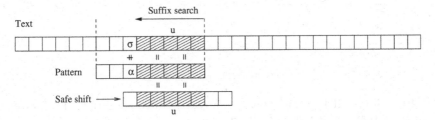

Fig. 2.8. First shift function d_1 of the **Boyer-Moore** algorithm. The pattern is shifted to the next occurrence of u.

Second case The suffix u does not occur in any other position as a factor of p. This does not mean that we can safely skip the whole search window, for the situation shown in Figure 2.9 can occur. A suffix v of u can also be a prefix of the pattern. To manage this case, we compute a second function d_2 for all suffixes of the pattern. It associates to each suffix u of p the length of the longest prefix v of p that is also a suffix of u.

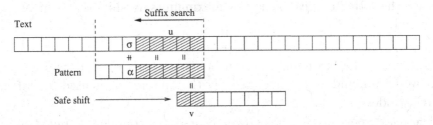

Fig. 2.9. Second shift function d_2 of the **Boyer-Moore** algorithm. No other occurrence of u exists in p. The pattern is shifted to the longest prefix of p that is also a suffix of u.

Third case The backward search has failed on the text character σ. If we shift the window with the first function d_1 and this letter is not aligned with a σ in the pattern, we will perform an unnecessary verification of the new search window. This case is shown in Figure 2.10. The third function, d_3, is computed to ensure that the text character σ will correspond to a σ in the pattern for the next verification. It associates to each character σ of the alphabet the distance of its rightmost occurrence to the end of the pattern. If a character σ does not occur in p, it is associated with m.

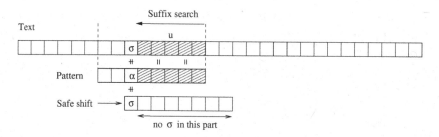

Fig. 2.10. Third shift function d_3 of the **Boyer-Moore** algorithm. The pattern is shifted to the next occurrence of σ in p.

To shift the window after we read u and failed on σ, the **Boyer-Moore** algorithm compares two shifts:

- the maximum between the shifts given by $d_1(u)$ and $d_3(\sigma)$, since we want to align u with its next occurrence in the pattern, knowing that the σ of the text has to match another σ in the pattern;

- the minimum between the result of the previous maximum and $m - d_2(u)$, since the latter expression is the maximum safe shift that can be performed.

However, if the beginning of the window has been reached, which means that we have found an occurrence, only the function d_2 is used to shift the search window.

The search part of **BM** has $O(mn)$ worst-case complexity, but it is sub-linear on average. Many variations have been designed to make it linear in the worst case. The most important references are given in Section 2.6.

The main inconvenience of **BM** is the computation of the functions d_1, d_2, and d_3. They can be computed in $O(m)$ time, but that is difficult [Ryt80]. We now present a simplification that leads to algorithms that are more efficient than **BM** itself in numerous cases.

2.3.2 *Horspool algorithm*

The **BM** algorithm was first simplified by Horspool [Hor80], who assumed that, for a reasonably large alphabet, the shift function d_3 will always yield the longest shift. Horspool just considered a small modification of d_3 that is easy to compute and yields longer shifts. The resulting algorithm works as follows (Figure 2.11).

For each position of the search window, we compare its last character (β in the figure) with the last character of the pattern. If they match, we verify the search window backward against the pattern until we either find the pattern or fail on a text character (σ in the figure). Then, whether there was a match or not, we shift the window according to the next occurrence of the letter β in the pattern. Pseudo-code for the **Horspool** algorithm is given in Figure 2.12.

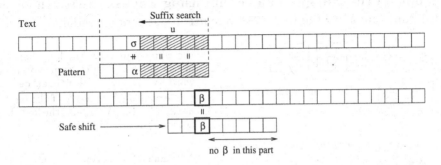

Fig. 2.11. **Horspool** algorithm. The pattern is shifted according to the last character of the search window.

Horspool $(p = p_1 p_2 \ldots p_m,\ T = t_1 t_2 \ldots t_n)$
1.   Preprocessing
2.   **For** $c \in \Sigma$ **Do** $d[c] \leftarrow m$
3.   **For** $j \in 1 \ldots m-1$ **Do** $d[p_j] \leftarrow m - j$
4.   Searching
5. $pos \leftarrow 0$
6.   **While** $pos \le n - m$ **Do**
7. $j \leftarrow m$
8.   **While** $j > 0$ AND $t_{pos+j} = p_j$ **Do** $j \leftarrow j - 1$
9.   **If** $j = 0$ **Then** report an occurrence at $pos + 1$
10. $pos \leftarrow pos + d[t_{pos+m}]$
11.   **End of while**

Fig. 2.12. **Horspool** algorithm.

We notice that:

- The verification also could have been done forward. Many implementations use a built-in memory comparison instruction.
- The main loop can be "unrolled," which means that we can first shift the search window until its last character matches the last character of the pattern, and then perform the verification.

The variant of Sunday Instead of shifting the window using its last character, we may use the next character after the window, which leads on average to longer shifts. This algorithm has been proposed by Sunday [Sun90]. Although the shifts are longer, the lower number of memory references of the *unrolled* **Horspool** algorithm makes it faster in general.

Example of the Horspool algorithm using English We search for the string "announce" in the text "CPM_annual_conference_announce".

$$m = 8, \ d = \left\{ \begin{array}{|c|c|c|c|c|c|} \hline a & c & n & o & u & * \\ \hline 7 & 1 & 2 & 4 & 3 & 8 \\ \hline \end{array} \right.$$

1. $\boxed{\text{CPM\_annu}}$ al_conference_announce

   u $\neq$ e, $d[\text{u}] = 3$

2. CPM $\boxed{\text{\_annual\_}}$ conference_announce

   _ $\neq$ e, $d[\_] = 8$

3. CPM_annual_ $\boxed{\text{conferen}}$ ce_announce

   n $\neq$ e, $d[\text{n}] = 2$

4. CPM_annual_co $\boxed{\text{nference}}$ _announce

   The last character [nferenc$\boxed{\text{e}}$] of

the window matches the last character of the pattern. We continue the backward verification [nferen$\boxed{\text{ce}}$] , [nfere$\boxed{\text{nce}}$] , and it fails on the next character. We re-use the last character of the window, $d[\text{e}] = 8$.

5. CPM_annual_conference $\boxed{\text{\_announc}}$ e

   c $\neq$ e, $d[\text{c}] = 1$

6. CPM_annual_conference_ $\boxed{\text{announce}}$

   The last character [announc$\boxed{\text{e}}$] of the window matches the last character of the pattern. We verify backward the window and find the occurrence.

Example of the Horspool algorithm using DNA We search for the string ATATA in the sequence AGATACGATATATAC.

$$m = 8, \ d = \left\{ \begin{array}{|c|c|c|} \hline A & T & * \\ \hline 2 & 1 & 5 \\ \hline \end{array} \right.$$

1. $\boxed{\text{AGATA}}$ CGATATATAC

   The last character [AGAT$\boxed{\text{A}}$] of the window matches the last character of the pattern. We continue the

backward verification [AGA$\boxed{\text{TA}}$] , [AG$\boxed{\text{ATA}}$] , and it fails on the next chararacter. We re-use the last character of the window, $d[\text{A}] = 2$.

2. AG $\boxed{\text{ATACG}}$ ATATATAC

   G $\neq$ A, $d[\text{G}] = 5$

3. AGATACG ┌ATATA┐ TAC

The last character ┌ ATAT A ┐ of the window matches the last character of the pattern. We verify backward the window and find the occurrence. We then shift by re-using the last character of the window, $d[A] = 2$.

4. AGATACGAT ┌ATATA┐ C

The last character ┌ ATAT A ┐ of the window matches the last character of the pattern. We verify backward the window and find the new occurrence. We then shift by re-using the last character of the window, $d[A] = 2$. Then, $pos > n - m$ and the search stops.

2.4 Factor based approach

The factor based approach leads to optimal average-case algorithms, assuming that the characters of the text are independent and occur with the same probability.

The idea for moving the search window with this approach is elegant and simple. It is shown in Figure 2.13. Suppose that we have read backward a factor u of the pattern, and that we failed on the next letter σ. This means that the string σu is no longer a factor of p, so no occurrence of p can contain σu, and we can safely shift the window to after σ.

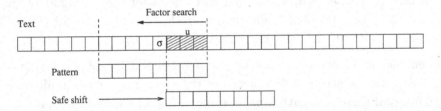

Fig. 2.13. Basic idea for shifting the window with the factor search approach. If we failed to recognize a factor of the pattern on σ, then σu is not a factor of the pattern and the window can be safely shifted after σ.

The main drawback to this approach is that it requires recognizing the set of factors of the pattern. We first present the **Backward Dawg Matching (BDM)** algorithm [CCG+94]. This algorithm uses a suffix automaton, which is a powerful but complex structure. We will not describe it in this chapter for two reasons:

(i) When the pattern is short enough, of size less than w, the suffix automaton can be simulated efficiently with bit-parallelism. This algorithm, **Backward Nondeterministic Dawg Matching** [NR00], is faster than **BDM**, simpler to implement, and applicable to extended patterns (Chapter 4).

(ii) When the pattern is longer, the **Backward Oracle Matching** algorithm [ACR01], based on a modification of the factor based approach, leads to the same experimental times as **BDM**, but with a much simpler automaton, called the *factor oracle*.

2.4.1 Backward Dawg Matching idea

The **Backward Dawg Matching** algorithm uses a suffix automaton to perform the factor search, and it also improves the basic search approach. We begin with a general description of the *suffix automaton* and then explain the main parts of the algorithm.

Suffix automaton We need to recognize whether a given word u is a factor of the pattern p. There exist many indexing structures that enable us to determine whether u is a factor of p in $O(|u|)$ time. The most classic structure is the *compact suffix tree* [McC76]. However, in this structure, the transitions are coded as factors of the pattern, and to pass through a transition we need access to an arbitrary part of the pattern. The *suffix automaton* has the same efficiency, but its transitions are labeled with single characters. This speeds up the search and the pattern matching algorithms that use it. The interested reader can find a complete survey of the suffix automaton in [CH97, CR94]. We simply recall its three basic properties:

Pr_1 It enables us to determine whether a string u is a factor of a string p in $O(|u|)$ time. A string u is a factor in the suffix automaton built on p if and only if there is a path labeled u beginning at the initial node.

Pr_2 It enables us to recognize the suffixes of the pattern on which it is built. If a path beginning at the initial node reaches a terminal state of the automaton built on p, it means that the label of this path is a suffix of p.

Pr_3 It can be built on $p = p_1 p_2 \ldots p_m$ in $O(m)$ time with an *on-line* algorithm, which means that the characters p_j can be added one after another into the structure, updating at each step j the suffix automaton of the prefix $p_1 \ldots p_{j-1}$ to obtain that of $p_1 \ldots p_j$.

Search algorithm The **BDM** algorithm [CCG+94] makes use of the properties of the suffix automaton. The general approach of Figure 2.13 is possible using the suffix automaton. Moreover, property Pr_2 enables a tricky improvement.

To search a pattern $p = p_1 p_2 \ldots p_m$ in a text $T = t_1 t_2 \ldots t_n$, the suffix automaton of $p^{rv} = p_m p_{m-1} \ldots p_1$ is built. The algorithm searches backwards along the window for a factor of the pattern using the suffix automaton.

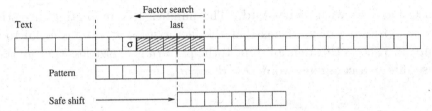

Fig. 2.14. Basic search of the **BDM** algorithm with the suffix automaton. The variable *last* stores the beginning position of the longest suffix of the part read that is also a prefix of the pattern.

During this search, if a terminal state is reached that does not correspond to the entire pattern, the position in the window is stored in a variable *last*. Due to property Pr_2, this corresponds to finding a *prefix* of the pattern starting at position *last* inside the window and ending at the end of the window since the suffixes of p^{rv} are the reverse prefixes of p. Since we stored the last prefix recognized backwards, we have the *longest* prefix of p in the window. This backward search ends in two possible ways:

(i) We fail to recognize a factor, that is, we reach a letter σ that does not correspond to a transition in the suffix automaton of p^{rv}. We then shift the window so that its new starting position corresponds to the position *last*. We cannot miss an occurrence because in that case the suffix automaton would have found its prefix in the window. This situation is shown in Figure 2.14.

(ii) We reach the beginning of the window, thus recognizing the pattern p. We report the occurrence, and we shift the window exactly as in the previous case.

The algorithm is $O(mn)$ time in the worst case. However, it is the optimal $O(n \log_{|\Sigma|} m/m)$ on average under the assumption that the text characters are independent and have the same occurrence probabilities.

2.4.2 Backward Nondeterministic Dawg Matching algorithm

The **Backward Nondeterministic Dawg Matching** (**BNDM**) algorithm uses the same search approach as **BDM**, but the factor is searched using bit-parallelism. Compared to the original **BDM** algorithm, **BNDM** is simpler, uses less memory, has more locality of reference, and is easier to extend to more complex patterns (Chapter 4).

The idea is to maintain a set of positions on the reverse pattern that are the beginning positions of the string u read in the text. This set is stored with 0 and 1 as with **Shift-And**. The number 1, representing an active state at position j of p, means that the factor $p_j \dots p_{j+|u|-1}$ is equal to u. Figure 2.15 shows this relationship. If the pattern is of size less that w, then the set fits in a computer word $D = d_m \dots d_1$.

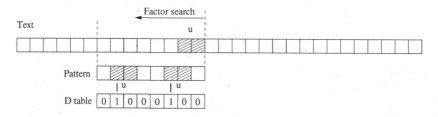

Fig. 2.15. Bit-parallel factor search. The table D keeps a list of the positions in p where the factor u begins.

We need to update the array D to D' after reading a new character σ of the text. A state j of D' is active if it corresponds to the beginning of the string σu in the pattern; that is, if

- u began at position $j+1$ in the pattern, which means that the $(j+1)$-th position in D is active, and
- σ is in position j in the pattern.

If we precompute a table B exactly as for **Shift-And** that associates to each letter of p the set of its positions in p with a bit mask, then we obtain D' from D by the following formula:

$$D' \leftarrow (D << 1) \ \& \ B[\sigma] \qquad (2.2)$$

However, there is a problem with the initialization. We would like to mark in the initial table D that each position of D matches the empty string, which means D should be 1^m. But in that case, the first shift will give $(D << 1) = 1^{m-1}0$ and we will miss the first factor, which corresponds to the entire word. The simplest solution would be to take D of size $m+1$, initialized to 1^{m+1}. However, it reduces to $w-1$ the maximum length of the string that can be searched. Instead we split formula (2.2) into two parts.

We first perform the operation $D'_1 \leftarrow D \ \& \ B[\sigma]$ and verify the match, and then we perform the register shift $D' \leftarrow D'_1 << 1$. The initialization is then $D = 1^m$. A string read in the text is a prefix of p if the first position is active, that is, if in D'_1 the position d_m is active.

The **BNDM** algorithm is the same as **BDM**, except that the factor search is done with the bit-parallelism technique. Each time the bit d_m is active,

BNDM $(p = p_1 p_2 \ldots p_m,\ T = t_1 t_2 \ldots t_n)$

1. **Preprocessing**
2.   **For** $c \in \Sigma$ **Do** $B[c] \leftarrow 0^m$
3.   **For** $j \in 1 \ldots m$ **Do** $B[p_j] \leftarrow B[p_j]\ |\ 0^{j-1} 1 0^{m-j}$
4. **Searching**
5. $pos \leftarrow 0$
6.   **While** $pos \leq n - m$ **Do**
7. $j \leftarrow m,\ last \leftarrow m$
8. $D \leftarrow 1^m$
9.   **While** $D \neq 0^m$ **Do**
10. $\cdot$ $D \leftarrow D\ \&\ B[t_{pos+j}]$
11. $j \leftarrow j - 1$
12.   **If** $D\ \&\ 10^{m-1} \neq 0^m$ **Then**
13.   **If** $j > 0$ **Then** $last \leftarrow j$
14.   **Else** report an occurrence at $pos + 1$
15.   **End of if**
16. $D \leftarrow D << 1$
17.   **End of while**
18. $pos \leftarrow pos + last$
19.   **End of while**

Fig. 2.16. Bit-parallel pseudo-code for **BNDM**.

the position of the window is stored in the variable *last*. Pseudo-code for the algorithm is given in Figure 2.16.

BNDM has the same worst-case complexity $O(mn)$ as **BDM**, and also the same optimal average complexity $O(n \log_{|\Sigma|} m/m)$.

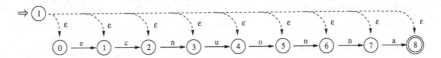

Fig. 2.17. Nondeterministic automaton recognizing all factors of the reverse string of "announce".

From an automaton point of view, the bit-parallel factor search is a simulation of a nondeterministic automaton that recognizes all suffixes of the reverse pattern. For example, if we search the pattern "announce", we simulate the automaton shown in Figure 2.17. It turns out that the minimal deterministic version of this automaton is the *suffix automaton* used in the classic **BDM**. The difference between **BNDM** and **BDM** is conceptually the same as that between **Shift-Or** and **KMP**. The former simulates a nondeterministic automaton using bit-parallelism, and the latter first obtains a representation of the deterministic automaton.

Example of BNDM using English We search for the string "announce" in the text "CPM_annual_conference_announce".

$$B = \begin{cases} \begin{array}{c|c} \text{a} & 1\,0\,0\,0\,0\,0\,0\,0 \\ \hline \text{c} & 0\,0\,0\,0\,0\,0\,1\,0 \\ \hline \text{e} & 0\,0\,0\,0\,0\,0\,0\,1 \\ \hline \text{n} & 0\,1\,1\,0\,0\,1\,0\,0 \\ \hline \text{o} & 0\,0\,0\,1\,0\,0\,0\,0 \\ \hline \text{u} & 0\,0\,0\,0\,1\,0\,0\,0 \\ \hline \text{*} & 0\,0\,0\,0\,0\,0\,0\,0 \end{array} \end{cases}$$

$D = 1\,1\,1\,1\,1\,1\,1\,1$

1. $\boxed{\text{CPM\_annu}}$ al_conference_announce

    $last \leftarrow 8$

    $$\begin{array}{rl} & 1\,1\,1\,1\,1\,1\,1\,1 \\ \text{Reading u} & 0\,0\,0\,0\,1\,0\,0\,0 \\ \hline D = & 0\,0\,0\,0\,1\,0\,0\,0 \end{array}$$

    $$\begin{array}{rl} & 0\,0\,0\,1\,0\,0\,0\,0 \\ \text{Reading n} & 0\,1\,1\,0\,0\,1\,0\,0 \\ \hline D = & 0\,0\,0\,0\,0\,0\,0\,0 \end{array}$$

2. CPM_annu $\boxed{\text{al\_confe}}$ rence_announce

    $last \leftarrow 8$

    $$\begin{array}{rl} & 1\,1\,1\,1\,1\,1\,1\,1 \\ \text{Reading e} & 0\,0\,0\,0\,0\,0\,0\,1 \\ \hline D = & 0\,0\,0\,0\,0\,0\,0\,1 \end{array}$$

    $$\begin{array}{rl} & 0\,0\,0\,0\,0\,0\,1\,0 \\ \text{Reading f} & 0\,0\,0\,0\,0\,0\,0\,0 \\ \hline D = & 0\,0\,0\,0\,0\,0\,0\,0 \end{array}$$

3. CPM_annual_confe $\boxed{\text{rence\_an}}$ nounce

    $last \leftarrow 8$

    $$\begin{array}{rl} & 1\,1\,1\,1\,1\,1\,1\,1 \\ \text{Reading n} & 0\,1\,1\,0\,0\,1\,0\,0 \\ \hline D = & 0\,1\,1\,0\,0\,1\,0\,0 \end{array}$$

    $$\begin{array}{rl} & 1\,1\,0\,0\,1\,0\,0\,0 \\ \text{Reading a} & 1\,0\,0\,0\,0\,0\,0\,0 \\ \hline D = & 1\,0\,0\,0\,0\,0\,0\,0 \end{array}$$

The position d_8 is active, but $j > 0$, so we set $last \leftarrow 6$.

4. CPM_annual_conference_ $\boxed{\text{announce}}$

    $last \leftarrow 8$

    $$\begin{array}{rl} & 1\,1\,1\,1\,1\,1\,1\,1 \\ \text{Reading e} & 0\,0\,0\,0\,0\,0\,0\,1 \\ \hline D = & 0\,0\,0\,0\,0\,0\,0\,1 \end{array}$$

    $$\begin{array}{rl} & 0\,0\,0\,0\,0\,0\,1\,0 \\ \text{Reading c} & 0\,0\,0\,0\,0\,0\,1\,0 \\ \hline D = & 0\,0\,0\,0\,0\,0\,1\,0 \end{array}$$

    $$\begin{array}{rl} & 0\,0\,0\,0\,0\,1\,0\,0 \\ \text{Reading n} & 0\,1\,1\,0\,0\,1\,0\,0 \\ \hline D = & 0\,0\,0\,0\,0\,1\,0\,0 \end{array}$$

    $$\begin{array}{rl} & 0\,0\,0\,0\,1\,0\,0\,0 \\ \text{Reading u} & 0\,0\,0\,0\,1\,0\,0\,0 \\ \hline D = & 0\,0\,0\,0\,1\,0\,0\,0 \end{array}$$

    $$\begin{array}{rl} & 0\,0\,0\,1\,0\,0\,0\,0 \\ \text{Reading o} & 0\,0\,0\,1\,0\,0\,0\,0 \\ \hline D = & 0\,0\,0\,1\,0\,0\,0\,0 \end{array}$$

    $$\begin{array}{rl} & 0\,0\,1\,0\,0\,0\,0\,0 \\ \text{Reading n} & 0\,1\,1\,0\,0\,1\,0\,0 \\ \hline D = & 0\,0\,1\,0\,0\,0\,0\,0 \end{array}$$

    $$\begin{array}{rl} & 0\,1\,0\,0\,0\,0\,0\,0 \\ \text{Reading n} & 0\,1\,1\,0\,0\,1\,0\,0 \\ \hline D = & 0\,1\,0\,0\,0\,0\,0\,0 \end{array}$$

    $$\begin{array}{rl} & 1\,0\,0\,0\,0\,0\,0\,0 \\ \text{Reading a} & 1\,0\,0\,0\,0\,0\,0\,0 \\ \hline D = & 1\,0\,0\,0\,0\,0\,0\,0 \end{array}$$

The position d_8 is active and $j = 0$, so we mark an occurrence.

Example of BNDM using DNA We search for the string ATATA in the sequence AGATACGATATATAC.

$$B \doteq \begin{cases} \begin{array}{|c|c|} \hline A & 1\,0\,1\,0\,1 \\ \hline T & 0\,1\,0\,1\,0 \\ \hline * & 0\,0\,0\,0\,0 \\ \hline \end{array} \end{cases}$$

$D = 1\,1\,1\,1\,1$

1. AGATA CGATATATAC

   $last \leftarrow 5$

	1 1 1 1 1
Reading A	1 0 1 0 1
$D =$	1 0 1 0 1

	0 1 0 1 0
Reading T	0 1 0 1 0
$D =$	0 1 0 1 0

	1 0 1 0 0
Reading A	1 0 1 0 1
$D =$	1 0 1 0 0

   The position d_5 is active, but $j > 0$, so we set $last \leftarrow 2$.

	0 1 0 0 0
Reading G	0 0 0 0 0
$D =$	0 0 0 0 0

2. AG ATACG ATATATAC

   $last \leftarrow 5$

	1 1 1 1 1
Reading G	0 0 0 0 0
$D =$	0 0 0 0 0

3. AGATACG ATATA TAC

   $last \leftarrow 5$

	1 1 1 1 1
Reading A	1 0 1 0 1
$D =$	1 0 1 0 1

	0 1 0 1 0
Reading T	0 1 0 1 0
$D =$	0 1 0 1 0

	1 0 1 0 0
Reading A	1 0 1 0 1
$D =$	1 0 1 0 0

The position d_5 is active, but $j > 0$, so we set $last \leftarrow 2$.

	0 1 0 0 0
Reading T	0 1 0 1 0
$D =$	0 1 0 0 0

	1 0 0 0 0
Reading A	1 0 1 0 1
$D =$	1 0 0 0 0

The position d_5 is active and $j = 0$, so we mark an occurrence.

4. AGATACGAT ATATA C

   $last \leftarrow 5$

	1 1 1 1 1
Reading A	1 0 1 0 1
$D =$	1 0 1 0 1

	0 1 0 1 0
Reading T	0 1 0 1 0
$D =$	0 1 0 1 0

	1 0 1 0 0
Reading A	1 0 1 0 1
$D =$	1 0 1 0 0

   The position d_5 is active, but $j > 0$, so we set $last \leftarrow 2$.

	0 1 0 0 0
Reading T	0 1 0 1 0
$D =$	0 1 0 0 0

	1 0 0 0 0
Reading A	1 0 1 0 1
$D =$	1 0 0 0 0

   The position d_5 is active and $j = 0$, so we mark a new occurrence. We then shift to $pos + last$ and $pos > n - m$, so the search stops.

2.4.3 Backward Oracle Matching algorithm

For patterns longer than w, the normal **BDM** algorithm would be necessary but the complexity of the construction of the suffix automaton makes it impractical. A solution has been proposed recently [ACR01]. It is based on the observation that, to shift the window in the general factor search approach (Figure 2.13), it is not necessary to know that u is a factor. It suffices to know that σu is not.

The *factor oracle* structure has this particularity. Built on a string p, it recognizes *more* than the set of factors of p, but it is easy to understand and implement and is compact, so that the efficiency lost by reading more letters in the backward search is recovered by doing fewer page faults.

To simplify notation, we denote by θ an object that is not defined. For instance, in an automaton, $\delta(q, \alpha) = \theta$ means that there is no outgoing transition from q labeled with α.

2.4.3.1 Factor oracle

The *factor oracle* built on a string $p = p_1 p_2 \ldots p_m$ is a deterministic acyclic automaton that has $m + 1$ states and m to $2m - 1$ transitions. We denote its transition function by δ.

The $m+1$ states correspond to the $m+1$ positions between the characters of p, including a first position 0 before the whole pattern. A state $0 < i \leq m$ corresponds to the prefix $p_1 \ldots p_i$.

The first m transitions spell out the pattern itself in a line; for $0 < i \leq m$, we build a transition from state $i - 1$ to i labeled p_i. In practice, these transitions and states can be stored implicitly with the pattern itself.

Then, we build what we call the "external transitions," of which there are at most $m - 1$. We associate to each state i another state $j < i$, called its "supply state" and denoted $j = S(i)$. This function is the "supply function." It is built together with the external transitions. $S(0)$ is set to θ.

The construction algorithm proceeds by inspecting each state from 1 to m. We assume that we have reached state $i-1$ and begun to inspect the i-th state. We go down the supply function from state $i - 1$. We use a variable k initialized to $S(i - 1)$ and we repeat the following steps.

ST_1 If $k = \theta$, then $S(i) \leftarrow 0$.

ST_2 If $k \neq \theta$ and there does not exist a transition from state k labeled by p_i, then build a transition from state k to state i by p_i, and return to step ST_1 with $k \leftarrow S(k)$.

ST_3 If $k \neq \theta$ and there exists a transition from k labeled by p_i leading to a state j, then set $S(i) \leftarrow j$ and stop processing state i.

This construction is simple. Moreover, it is clear that it can be done *on-line*, which means that we can add the letters p_i one after another and build the new state i and all the new transitions at this time. Pseudo-code for the *on-line* construction is given in Figure 2.18. The algorithm is linear in the size of the pattern.

Oracle_add_letter(Oracle($p = p_1 p_2 \ldots p_m$), σ)
1. Create a new state $m + 1$
2. $\delta(m, \sigma) \leftarrow m + 1$
3. $k \leftarrow S(m)$
4. **While** $k \neq \theta$ AND $\delta(k, \sigma) = \theta$ **Do**
5. $\delta(k, \sigma) \leftarrow m + 1$
6. $k \leftarrow S(k)$
7. **End of while**
8. **If** $k = \theta$ **Then** $s \leftarrow 0$
9. **Else** $s \leftarrow \delta(k, \sigma)$
10. $S(m + 1) \leftarrow s$
11. **Return** Oracle($p = p_1 p_2 \ldots p_m \sigma$)

Oracle-on-line($p = p_1 p_2 \ldots p_m$)
12. Create Oracle(ε) with:
13.   One single initial state 0
14. $S(0) \leftarrow \theta$
15. **For** $j \in 1 \ldots m$ **Do**
16.   Oracle($p = p_1 p_2 \ldots p_j$) $\leftarrow$ **Oracle_add_letter**(Oracle($p = p_1 p_2 \ldots p_{j-1}$), p_j)
17. **End of for**

Fig. 2.18. Construction of the factor oracle. The function **Oracle_add_letter** adds a letter σ to Oracle($p = p_1 p_2 \ldots p_m$) to get Oracle($p\sigma$). The *on-line* construction algorithm adds the letters p_i one by one to obtain finally Oracle($p = p_1 p_2 \ldots p_m$).

The factor oracle built on p recognizes all the factors of p. It really recognizes more, but not so many in practice, and it recognizes only one string of size m, the pattern itself.

To code it, the easiest way in practice is to use a $(m + 1) \times A$ table, where A is the alphabet size of the pattern. This representation has the advantage of giving $O(1)$ access time to the transitions, which speeds up the search algorithm. However, for very long patterns, an implementation in $O(m)$ space has to be considered.

2.4.3.2 Search with the factor oracle

The search algorithm with the factor oracle, called **Backward Oracle Matching (BOM)**, is the simple transcription of the factor search approach (Figure 2.13). We read backwards in the window the text characters in the factor oracle of the reverse pattern p^{rv}. If we fail on a letter σ after reading a string u, we know that σu is not a factor of p and we can safely shift the window after the letter σ. If the beginning of the window is reached, then, since the factor oracle recognizes only one string of size $|p|$, we mark a match and we shift the window by one character. Pseudo-code for **BOM** is given in Figure 2.19.

BOM$(p = p_1 p_2 \ldots p_m,\ T = t_1 t_2 \ldots t_n)$
1.   Preprocessing
2.   **Oracle-on-line**(p^{rv})
                 δ is its transition function
3.   Searching
4. $pos \leftarrow 0$
5.   **While** $pos \leq n - m$ **Do**
6. $Current \leftarrow$ initial state of Oracle(p^{rv})
7. $j \leftarrow m$
8.   **While** $j > 0$ AND $Current \neq \theta$ **Do**
9. $Current \leftarrow \delta(Current, t_{pos+j})$
10. $j \leftarrow j - 1$
11.   **End of while**
12.   **If** $Current \neq \theta$ **Then**
13.   mark an occurrence at $pos + 1$
14.   **End of if**
15. $pos \leftarrow pos + j + 1$
16.   **End of while**

Fig. 2.19. Pseudo-code of the **BOM** algorithm.

BOM is $O(mn)$ time in the worst case. From experimental results it is conjectured that it is optimal on average.

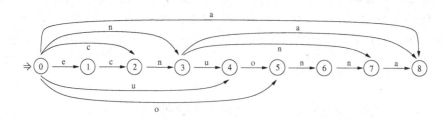

Fig. 2.20. Factor oracle for the reverse string of "announce".

Example using English We search for the string "announce" in the text "CPM_annual_conference_announce". The factor oracle of the reverse pattern of "announce" is given in Figure 2.20.

1. [CPM_annu] al_conference_announce

   Reading [CPM_ann u] in the factor oracle.

   Fail on the next character n.

2. CPM_ann [ual_conf] erence_announce

   Fail on the character f.

3. CPM_annual_conf [erence_a] nnounce

   Reading [erence_ a] in the factor oracle.

   Fail on the next character _.

4. CPM_annual_conference_ [announce]

   Reading [announc e] in the factor oracle.

Reading [announ c e] in the factor oracle.

Reading [annou n ce] in the factor oracle.

Reading [anno u nce] in the factor oracle.

Reading [ann o unce] in the factor oracle.

Reading [an n ounce] in the factor oracle.

Reading [a n nounce] in the factor oracle.

Reading [a nnounce] in the factor oracle.

We mark an occurrence.

Example using DNA We search for the string ATATA in the sequence AG-ATACGATATATAC. The factor oracle of the reverse pattern of ATATA is given in Figure 2.21.

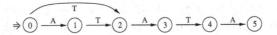

Fig. 2.21. Factor oracle for the reverse string of ATATA.

1. [AGATA] CGATATATAC

   Reading [AGAT A] in the factor oracle.

   Reading [AGA T A] in the factor oracle.

   Reading [AG A TA] in the factor oracle.

   Fail on the next character G.

2. AG [ATACG] ATATATAC

   Fail on the character G.

3. AGATACG [ATATA] TAC

   Reading [ATAT A] in the factor oracle.

   Reading [ATA T A] in the factor oracle.

   Reading [AT A TA] in the factor oracle.

   Reading [A T ATA] in the factor oracle.

   Reading [A TATA] in the factor oracle.

   We mark an occurrence.

4. AGATACGA │TATAT│ AC

   Reading [TATA│T│] in the factor
   oracle.

   Reading [TAT│A│T] in the factor
   oracle.

   Reading [TA│T│AT] in the factor
   oracle.

   Reading [T│A│TAT] in the factor
   oracle.

   Fail on the character T.

5. AGATACGAT │ATATA│ C

   Reading [ATAT│A│] in the factor
   oracle.

Reading [ATA│T│A] in the factor
oracle.

Reading [AT│A│TA] in the factor
oracle.

Reading [A│T│ATA] in the factor
oracle.

Reading [│A│TATA] in the factor
oracle.

We mark a new occurrence.

6. AGATACGATA │TATAC│
   Fail on the character C.

2.5 Experimental map

We present in this section a map of the efficiency of different string matching algorithms, showing zones where they are most efficient in practice. The experiments were performed on a $w = 32$ bits Ultra Sparc 1 running SunOs 5.6. Texts of 10 megabytes were randomly built, as were the patterns. The experiments were repeated until we obtained a relative error below 2% with 95% confidence. We tested optimized implementations of all the algorithms presented. However, only **Shift-Or**, **Horspool**, **BNDM**, and **BOM** have a zone in the map, since the others were too slow.

The map is shown in Figure 2.22. We show the length w of a register word to recall that it is the maximum size of string that **BNDM** can manage with a single word implementation.

Results on DNA sequences turn out to be the same as those for a random text of size 4. A more surprising fact is that results on English are about the same as those for a random text of size 16.

The map shows clearly that the **Horspool** algorithm becomes more and more difficult to beat as the alphabet grows. The **BNDM** algorithm is confined to a small zone for small alphabet sizes, but the map does not reflect its ability to handle extended strings. The **Shift-Or** wins only for small strings on very small alphabet sizes.

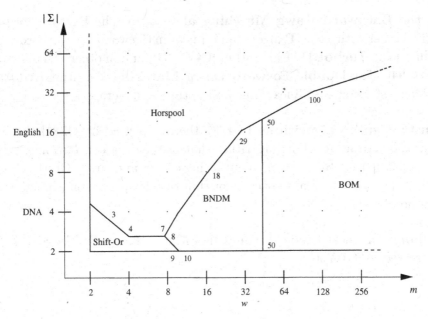

Fig. 2.22. Map of experimental efficiency for different string matching algorithms.

2.6 Other algorithms and references

Many other algorithms exist for searching a string in a text. We give in this section the most important references on string matching research.

On the Knuth-Morris-Pratt algorithm Many variants exist based on **MP** [MP70] and **KMP** [KMP77], the most important one being the **Simon** algorithm [Sim93]. Simon shows that the underlying automaton of **KMP** can be completed and stored in an efficient way. Some complete analyses on **KMP** can be found in [Rég89]. The **Simon** algorithm has been analyzed in [Han93].

On the Boyer-Moore algorithm As for **KMP**, many variants of **BM** [BM77] exist. The principal ones are the **Boyer-Moore-Galil** [Gal79] and the **Turbo-BM** [CGR92] algorithms. The **BM** algorithm has been analyzed in [BYGR90, BYR92, Col94]. The underlying automaton was analyzed in [BYG89a, Cho90, BYCG94, BBYDS96]. The **Horspool** algorithm has been analyzed in [MRS96].

On the Backward Dawg Matching algorithm The **BDM** algorithm used together with a **KMP** algorithm is linear in the worst case. An example of this is the **TurboBDM** algorithm [CCG$^+$94], and another is **TurboRF** [CCG$^+$94]. The **Double Forward Dawg Matching** algorithm [AR00] is the simplest worst-case linear time and optimal on average.

Constant space algorithms In 1981 there appeared in [GS81] the first linear time string matching algorithm that uses only a constant amount of additional space. Since then, many others have appeared [CP91, Cro92, CR95]. Finding a constant space algorithm that is optimal on average is an open problem.

Hashing The most famous hashing algorithm is **Karp-Rabin** [KR87]. It is analyzed in [GBY90].

3

Multiple string matching

3.1 Basic concepts

The single string matching problem may be extended in a natural way to search simultaneously for a set of strings $P = \{p^1, p^2, \ldots p^r\}$, where each p^i is a string $p^i = p_1^i p_2^i \ldots p_{m_i}^i$ over a finite character set Σ. Denote by $|P|$ the sum of the lengths of the strings in P, more formally $|P| = \sum_{i=1}^r |p^i| = \sum_{i=1}^r m_i$. Let ℓmin be the minimum length of a pattern in P and ℓmax the maximum. As before, the search is done in a text $T = t_1 t_2 \ldots t_n$.

Strings in P may be factors, prefixes, suffixes, or even the same as others. For example, if we search for the set $\{\texttt{ATATA}, \texttt{TATA}\}$ in a DNA sequence, each time we find an occurrence of $\texttt{ATATA}$ we also find an occurrence of the second string. Hence, the total number of occurrences can be $r \times n$. To make the multistring matching problem precise, we consider that we are interested in reporting all pairs (i, j) such that $t_{j-|p^i|+1} \ldots t_j$ is equal to p^i.

The simplest solution to this problem is to repeat r searches with one of the algorithms of Chapter 2. This leads to a total worst-case complexity of $O(|P|)$ for the preprocessing and $O(r \times n)$ for the search.

The worst-case search complexity can be reduced to $O(n + nocc)$, where $nocc$ is the total number of occurrences, by using some kind of *extension* of the search algorithms for a single pattern. The average complexity can also be improved, although it is difficult to think in terms of "average" complexity, since many parameters play a role in the running time of the algorithms. The most important parameters are the size of the alphabet, the number of patterns, the distribution of the lengths of the patterns (particularly the minimum size), and the memory available.

We again denote by θ an object that is not defined. For instance, when we write **While** $q \neq \theta$ **Do**, it means we iterate while q is defined.

Troughout this chapter, we will consider the example in Figure 3.1. We

41

will simultaneously search for the three strings "announce", "annual", and "annually".

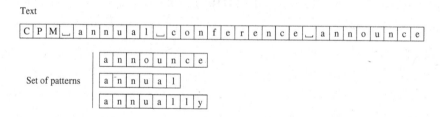

Fig. 3.1. Simultaneously searching three strings in our example text.

As with a single string, sets of natural language strings usually contain fewer repetitions than sets of DNA sequences. To show the tricky cases that could occur, we also show the behavior of our algorithms when searching for the set of strings ATATATA,TATAT,ACGATAT in the sequence AGATACGATATATAC.

The three approaches for searching a single string (Chapter 2) lead to several extensions for searching a set of strings. For each approach, there are usually many possible extensions, according to the way the set of patterns is managed and the way the shifts are obtained. The notion of a *search window* is not relevant for multiple string matching, which will become clear soon. We present in this chapter the empirically most efficient extensions, which are usually also the simplest.

Prefix searching (Figure 3.2) The search is done forward, reading the characters of the text one after another with an automaton built on the set P. For each position of the text, we compute through this automaton the longest suffix of the text read that is also a prefix of one of the strings of P. The most famous algorithm that uses this approach is **Aho-Corasick** [AC75].

Suffix searching (Figure 3.3) A position *pos* is slid along the text, from which we search backward for a suffix of any of the strings. As with a single pattern, we shift *pos* according to the next occurrence of the suffix read in P. This approach may avoid reading all the characters of the text.

Factor searching (Figure 3.4) A position *pos* is also slid along the text, from which we read backwards a factor of some prefix of size ℓmin of the strings in P. It also may avoid reading all the characters of the text.

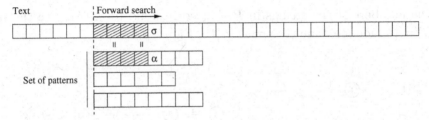

Fig. 3.2. First approach: We compute the longest prefix of a pattern in the set that is also a suffix of the text read. It requires reading all the characters of the text at least once.

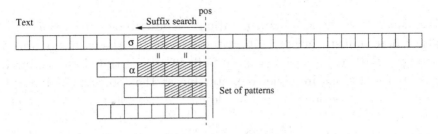

Fig. 3.3. Second approach: We search backwards for a suffix of one of the strings. It avoids, on average, reading all characters of the text.

Before describing these three approaches in depth, we introduce a basic data structure on a set of strings, called a *trie*. This structure is used by most of the classical multistring matching algorithms. The *trie* of the set $P = \{p^1, p^2, \ldots p^r\}$ is a rooted directed tree that represents the set P; that is, every path starting from the root is labeled by one of the strings p^i, and, conversely, every string $p^i \in P$ labels a path from the root. Below, unless specified, paths start at the root. Every state q corresponding to an entire string is marked as *terminal*, and a function $F(q)$ points to a list of

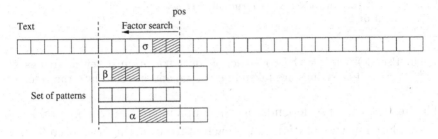

Fig. 3.4. Third approach: We search for a factor of any of the patterns in the current window.

all the numbers of the strings in P that correspond to q. We give the trie for $P = \{\texttt{announce},\texttt{annual},\texttt{annually}\}$ in Figure 3.5.

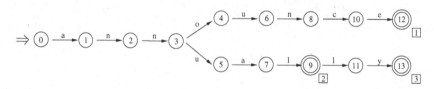

Fig. 3.5. Trie for $P = \{\texttt{announce}, \texttt{annual}, \texttt{annually}\}$. The function F of each terminal state is represented with squares. It indicates the identifier of the string in P.

We usually use the automata notation for describing a trie, since a trie is also a deterministic acyclic automaton recognizing the corresponding set of strings. The trie of a set P can be built in $O(|P|)$ time by inserting the strings p^i one by one into the tree, starting at the root, and building the corresponding transitions. Pseudo-code for the trie construction is given in Figure 3.6.

Trie$(P = \{p^1, p^2, \ldots, p^r\})$
1.   Create an initial non terminal state 0
2.   **For** $i \in 1 \ldots r$ **Do**
3. $Current \leftarrow$ initial state 0
4. $j \leftarrow 1$
5.   **While** $j \leq m_i$ AND $\delta(Current, p^i_j) \neq \theta$ **Do**
6. $Current \leftarrow \delta(Current, p^i_j)$
7. $j \leftarrow j + 1$
8.   **End of while**
9.   **While** $j \leq m_i$ **Do**
10.   Create a new non terminal state $State$
11. $\delta(Current, p^i_j) \leftarrow State$
12. $Current \leftarrow State$
13. $j \leftarrow j + 1$
14.   **End of while**
15.   **If** $Current$ is already terminal **Then** $F(Current) \leftarrow F(Current) \cup \{i\}$
16.   **Else** mark $Current$ as terminal, $F(Current) \leftarrow \{i\}$
17.   **End of for**

Fig. 3.6. Pseudo-code for the construction of a trie from a set of strings $P = \{p^1, p^2, \ldots, p^r\}$. The strings are taken one by one and inserted into the tree.

The size of the trie depends on the implementation of the transitions. The simplest implementation is for each state q of the trie to code $\delta(q, *)$ in a table of size $|\Sigma|$. Then the total size of the trie of a set P is worst-case $|\Sigma| \times |P|$. This representation is usually used when the sizes of the set of strings and of the alphabet are not too large. It has the advantage of passing through a transition in constant time $O(1)$ by performing an access to a table.

Since the total number of transitions is at most $|P|$, it is possible to code all the transitions in $O(|P|)$ space, independently of the size of the alphabet. However, the time to pass through a transition increases. If the transitions of each state are coded with a linked list, sorted or not, this time grows to $O(|\Sigma|)$ in the worst and average cases. It can be reduced to $O(\log|\Sigma|)$ by coding the transitions with balanced trees [CLR90], but this complicates the code.

We now describe in detail the three general approaches to search for a set of strings.

3.2 Prefix based approach

The extension of the prefix based approach leads to the **Multiple Shift-And** and **Aho-Corasick** algorithms. As with a single pattern (Section 2.2), we assume that we have read the text up to position i and that we know the length of the longest suffix of $t_1 \ldots t_i$ that is a prefix of a pattern $p^k \in P$. The algorithmic problem is to calculate this length after reading the next character of the text.

In the single pattern case, there were two ways of finding this length. One was based on managing a bit array with bit-parallelism. For multiple pattern matching, this technique is only practical for very small patterns, because the total length $|P|$ has to be smaller than a few computer words. Nevertheless, this possibility is widely used for extended string matching (Chapter 4) and approximate string matching (Chapter 6). We call this algorithm **Multiple Shift-And**.

The solution, when the length of the set is too large to fit in computer words, is to find a mechanism that computes the size of the longest suffix of the text read that is also a prefix of one of the strings of P, in amortized constant time per character. This is what the **Aho-Corasick** algorithm does, with a linear time $O(|P|)$ preprocessing phase.

3.2.1 Multiple Shift-And algorithm

The bit-parallelism approach is only valuable when the set $P = \{p^1, \ldots, p^r\}$ has a total length $|P|$ small enough to fit in a few computer words. For simplicity, we assume below that $|P|$ is smaller than w. The idea is to perform with bit-parallelism all the computations required by the **Shift-**

And algorithm (Section 2.2.2) for the r strings in the same computer word [BYG89b].

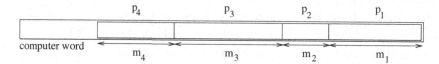

Fig. 3.7. **Multiple Shift-And** algorithm. The total size of the patterns has to fit in w.

We pack the strings together in the computer word, as in Figure 3.7. Then, for each new character of the text, we perform the computations for the strings of P like in the **Shift-And** algorithm. The initialization word DI is the concatenation of the initialization words for each string, that is,

$$DI \leftarrow 0^{m_r-1}1 \ldots 0^{m_2-1}10^{m_1-1}1$$

Similarly, the final test is

$$DF \leftarrow 10^{m_r-1} \ldots 10^{m_2-1}10^{m_1-1}$$

The main loop is the same as for the **Shift-And** algorithm. Pseudo-code is given in Figure 3.8.

The **Shift-Or** trick (Section 2.2.2) cannot be used here, since the shift "$<<$" only introduces a zero to the right, and we need a zero in each position that begins a new string of P in the computer word.

Example using English We search for the set of strings $P = \{$announce, annual, annually$\}$ in the text "annual_announce".

Table B

a	0 0 0 1 0 0 0 1 0 1 0 0 0 1 0 0 0 0 0 0 0 1
c	0 0 0 0 0 0 0 0 0 0 0 0 0 1 0 0 0 0 0 0
e	0 0 0 0 0 0 0 0 0 0 0 0 0 1 0 0 0 0 0 0
l	0 1 1 0 0 0 0 0 1 0 0 0 0 0 0 0 0 0 0 0 0
n	0 0 0 0 0 1 1 0 0 0 0 1 1 0 0 0 1 0 0 1 1 0
o	0 0 0 0 0 0 0 0 0 0 0 0 0 0 0 0 1 0 0 0
u	0 0 0 0 1 0 0 0 0 1 0 0 0 0 0 1 0 0 0 0
y	1 0 0 0 0 0 0 0 0 0 0 0 0 0 0 0 0 0 0 0 0
*	0 0 0 0 0 0 0 0 0 0 0 0 0 0 0 0 0 0 0 0 0

DI = 0 0 0 0 0 0 0 1 0 0 0 0 0 1 0 0 0 0 0 0 0 1
DF = 1 0 0 0 0 0 0 0 1 0 0 0 0 0 1 0 0 0 0 0 0 0
D = 0 0 0 0 0 0 0 0 0 0 0 0 0 0 0 0 0 0 0 0 0

1. Reading **a**

0 0 0 0 0 0 0 1 0 0 0 0 0 1 0 0 0 0 0 0 0 1
$B[a]$ 0 0 0 1 0 0 0 1 0 1 0 0 0 1 0 0 0 0 0 0 0 1
$D =$ 0 0 0 0 0 0 0 1 0 0 0 0 0 1 0 0 0 0 0 0 0 1

2. Reading **n**

0 0 0 0 0 0 1 1 0 0 0 0 1 1 0 0 0 0 0 0 1 1
$B[n]$ 0 0 0 0 0 1 1 0 0 0 0 1 1 0 0 0 1 0 0 1 1 0
$D =$ 0 0 0 0 0 0 1 0 0 0 0 0 1 0 0 0 0 0 0 0 1 0

3. Reading **n**

0 0 0 0 0 1 0 1 0 0 0 1 0 1 0 0 0 0 0 1 0 1
$B[n]$ 0 0 0 0 0 1 1 0 0 0 0 1 1 0 0 0 1 0 0 1 1 0
$D =$ 0 0 0 0 0 1 0 0 0 0 0 1 0 0 0 0 0 0 0 1 0 0

Multiple Shift-And$(P = \{p^1, p^2, \ldots, p^r\}, T = t_1 t_2 \ldots t_n)$
1.   Preprocessing
2.   For $c \in \Sigma$ Do $B[c] \leftarrow 0^{|P|}$
3. $\ell \leftarrow 0$
4.   For $k \in 1 \ldots r$ Do
5.   For $j \in 1 \ldots m_k$ Do $B[p_j^k] \leftarrow B[p_j^k] \mid 0^{|P|-\ell-j} 10^{\ell+j-1}$
6. $\ell \leftarrow \ell + m_k$
7.   End of for
8. $DI \leftarrow 0^{m_r-1} 1 \ldots 0^{m_2-1} 1 0^{m_1-1} 1$
9. $DF \leftarrow 1 0^{m_r-1} \ldots 1 0^{m_2-1} 1 0^{m_1-1}$
10. Searching
11. $D \leftarrow 0^{|P|}$
12.   For $pos \in 1 \ldots n$ Do
13. $D \leftarrow ((D << 1) \mid DI) \ \& \ B[t_{pos}]$
14.   If $D \ \& \ DF \neq 0^{|P|}$ Then
15.   Check which patterns match
16.   Report the corresponding occurrences ending in pos
17.   End of if
18.   End of for

Fig. 3.8. **Multiple Shift-And** algorithm. The total length of the patterns $|P|$ has to be less than w. We let $m_k = |p^k|$.

4. Reading u

```
     0 0 0 0 1 0 0 1 0 0 1 0 0 1 0 0 0 0 1 0 0 1
B[u] 0 0 0 0 1 0 0 0 0 0 1 0 0 0 0 0 0 1 0 0 0 0
D =  0 0 0 0 1 0 0 0 0 0 1 0 0 0 0 0 0 0 0 0 0 0
```

5. Reading a

```
     0 0 0 1 0 0 0 1 0 1 0 0 0 1 0 0 0 0 0 0 0 1
B[a] 0 0 0 1 0 0 0 1 0 1 0 0 0 1 0 0 0 0 0 0 0 1
D =  0 0 0 1 0 0 0 1 0 1 0 0 0 1 0 0 0 0 0 0 0 1
```

6. Reading l

```
     0 0 1 0 0 0 1 1 1 0 0 0 1 1 0 0 0 0 0 0 1 1
B[l] 0 1 1 0 0 0 0 0 1 0 0 0 0 0 0 0 0 0 0 0 0 0
D =  0 0 1 0 0 0 0 0 1 0 0 0 0 0 0 0 0 0 0 0 0 0
```

$D \ \& \ DF \neq 0^{|P|}$, we check the patterns that match, and we mark an occurrence of **annual**.

7. Reading _

```
     0 1 0 0 0 0 0 1 0 0 0 0 0 1 0 0 0 0 0 0 0 1
B[_] 0 0 0 0 0 0 0 0 0 0 0 0 0 0 0 0 0 0 0 0 0 0
D =  0 0 0 0 0 0 0 0 0 0 0 0 0 0 0 0 0 0 0 0 0 0
```

8. Reading a

```
     0 0 0 0 0 0 0 1 0 0 0 0 0 1 0 0 0 0 0 0 0 1
B[a] 0 0 1 0 0 0 1 0 1 0 0 0 1 0 0 0 0 0 0 0 0 1
D =  0 0 0 0 0 0 0 1 0 0 0 0 0 1 0 0 0 0 0 0 0 1
```

9. Reading n

```
     0 0 0 0 0 0 1 1 0 0 0 0 1 1 0 0 0 0 0 0 1 1
B[n] 0 0 0 0 0 1 1 0 0 0 0 1 1 0 0 0 1 0 0 1 1 0
D =  0 0 0 0 0 0 1 0 0 0 0 0 1 0 0 0 0 0 0 0 1 0
```

10. Reading n

```
     0 0 0 0 0 1 0 1 0 0 0 1 0 1 0 0 0 0 0 1 0 1
B[n] 0 0 0 0 0 1 1 0 0 0 0 1 1 0 0 0 1 0 0 1 1 0
D =  0 0 0 0 0 1 0 0 0 0 0 1 0 0 0 0 0 0 0 1 0 0
```

11. Reading o

```
     0 0 0 0 1 0 0 1 0 0 1 0 0 1 0 0 0 0 1 0 0 1
B[o] 0 0 0 0 0 0 0 0 0 0 0 0 0 0 0 0 0 0 1 0 0 0
D =  0 0 0 0 0 0 0 0 0 0 0 0 0 0 0 0 0 0 1 0 0 0
```

12. Reading u

```
     0 0 0 0 0 0 1 0 0 0 0 0 1 0 0 0 1 0 0 0 1
B[u] 0 0 0 0 1 0 0 0 0 0 1 0 0 0 0 0 0 1 0 0 0 0
D =  0 0 0 0 0 0 0 0 0 0 0 0 0 0 0 0 0 1 0 0 0 0
```

13. Reading **n**

$$
\begin{array}{ll}
 & 0\,0\,0\,0\,0\,0\,0\,1\,0\,0\,0\,0\,0\,1\,0\,0\,1\,0\,0\,0\,0\,1 \\
B[\mathbf{n}] & 0\,0\,0\,0\,0\,1\,1\,0\,0\,0\,0\,1\,1\,0\,0\,0\,1\,0\,0\,1\,1\,0 \\
\hline
D = & 0\,0\,0\,0\,0\,0\,0\,0\,0\,0\,0\,0\,0\,0\,0\,0\,1\,0\,0\,0\,0\,0
\end{array}
$$

14. Reading **c**

$$
\begin{array}{ll}
 & 0\,0\,0\,0\,0\,0\,0\,1\,0\,0\,0\,0\,0\,1\,0\,1\,0\,0\,0\,0\,0\,1 \\
B[\mathbf{c}] & 0\,0\,0\,0\,0\,0\,0\,0\,0\,0\,0\,0\,0\,0\,0\,1\,0\,0\,0\,0\,0\,0 \\
\hline
D = & 0\,0\,0\,0\,0\,0\,0\,0\,0\,0\,0\,0\,0\,0\,0\,1\,0\,0\,0\,0\,0\,0
\end{array}
$$

15. Reading **e**

$$
\begin{array}{ll}
 & 0\,0\,0\,0\,0\,0\,0\,1\,0\,0\,0\,0\,0\,1\,1\,0\,0\,0\,0\,0\,0\,1 \\
B[\mathbf{c}] & 0\,0\,0\,0\,0\,0\,0\,0\,0\,0\,0\,0\,0\,0\,1\,0\,0\,0\,0\,0\,0\,0 \\
\hline
D = & 0\,0\,0\,0\,0\,0\,0\,0\,0\,0\,0\,0\,0\,0\,1\,0\,0\,0\,0\,0\,0\,0
\end{array}
$$

$D \ \& \ DF \neq 0^{|P|}$, we check the patterns that match, and we mark an occurrence of **announce**.

Example using DNA

We search for the set of strings $P = \{\text{ATATATA}, \text{TATAT}, \text{ACGATAT}\}$ in the text **AGATACGATATATAC**.

Table B

A	0 1 0 1 0 0 1 0 1 0 1 0 1 0 1 0 1 0 1
C	0 0 0 0 0 1 0 0 0 0 0 0 0 0 0 0 0 0 0
G	0 0 0 0 1 0 0 0 0 0 0 0 0 0 0 0 0 0 0
T	1 0 1 0 0 0 0 1 0 1 0 1 0 1 0 1 0 1 0
*	0 0 0 0 0 0 0 0 0 0 0 0 0 0 0 0 0 0 0

$$
\begin{array}{ll}
DI = & 0\,0\,0\,0\,0\,0\,1\,0\,0\,0\,0\,1\,0\,0\,0\,0\,0\,0\,1 \\
DF = & 1\,0\,0\,0\,0\,0\,0\,1\,0\,0\,0\,0\,1\,0\,0\,0\,0\,0\,0 \\
D \ = & 0\,0\,0\,0\,0\,0\,0\,0\,0\,0\,0\,0\,0\,0\,0\,0\,0\,0\,0
\end{array}
$$

1. Reading **A**

$$
\begin{array}{ll}
 & 0\,0\,0\,0\,0\,0\,1\,0\,0\,0\,0\,1\,0\,0\,0\,0\,0\,0\,1 \\
B[\mathbf{A}] & 0\,1\,0\,1\,0\,0\,1\,0\,1\,0\,1\,0\,1\,0\,1\,0\,1\,0\,1 \\
\hline
D = & 0\,0\,0\,0\,0\,0\,1\,0\,0\,0\,0\,0\,0\,0\,0\,0\,0\,0\,1
\end{array}
$$

2. Reading **G**

$$
\begin{array}{ll}
 & 0\,0\,0\,0\,0\,1\,1\,0\,0\,0\,0\,1\,0\,0\,0\,0\,0\,1\,1 \\
B[\mathbf{G}] & 0\,0\,0\,0\,1\,0\,0\,0\,0\,0\,0\,0\,0\,0\,0\,0\,0\,0\,0 \\
\hline
D = & 0\,0\,0\,0\,0\,0\,0\,0\,0\,0\,0\,0\,0\,0\,0\,0\,0\,0\,0
\end{array}
$$

3. Reading **A**

$$
\begin{array}{ll}
 & 0\,0\,0\,0\,0\,0\,1\,0\,0\,0\,0\,1\,0\,0\,0\,0\,0\,0\,1 \\
B[\mathbf{A}] & 0\,1\,0\,1\,0\,0\,1\,0\,1\,0\,1\,0\,1\,0\,1\,0\,1\,0\,1 \\
\hline
D = & 0\,0\,0\,0\,0\,0\,1\,0\,0\,0\,0\,0\,0\,0\,0\,0\,0\,0\,1
\end{array}
$$

4. Reading **T**

$$
\begin{array}{ll}
 & 0\,0\,0\,0\,0\,1\,1\,0\,0\,0\,0\,1\,0\,0\,0\,0\,0\,1\,1 \\
B[\mathbf{T}] & 1\,0\,1\,0\,0\,0\,0\,1\,0\,1\,0\,1\,0\,1\,0\,1\,0\,1\,0 \\
\hline
D = & 0\,0\,0\,0\,0\,0\,0\,0\,0\,0\,1\,0\,0\,0\,0\,0\,1\,0
\end{array}
$$

5. Reading **A**

$$
\begin{array}{ll}
 & 0\,0\,0\,0\,0\,0\,1\,0\,0\,0\,1\,1\,0\,0\,0\,0\,1\,0\,1 \\
B[\mathbf{A}] & 0\,1\,0\,1\,0\,0\,1\,0\,1\,0\,1\,0\,1\,0\,1\,0\,1\,0\,1 \\
\hline
D = & 0\,0\,0\,0\,0\,0\,1\,0\,0\,0\,1\,0\,0\,0\,0\,0\,1\,0\,1
\end{array}
$$

6. Reading **C**

$$
\begin{array}{ll}
 & 0\,0\,0\,0\,0\,1\,1\,0\,0\,1\,0\,1\,0\,0\,0\,1\,0\,1\,1 \\
B[\mathbf{C}] & 0\,0\,0\,0\,0\,1\,0\,0\,0\,0\,0\,0\,0\,0\,0\,0\,0\,0\,0 \\
\hline
D = & 0\,0\,0\,0\,0\,1\,0\,0\,0\,0\,0\,0\,0\,0\,0\,0\,0\,0\,0
\end{array}
$$

7. Reading **G**

$$
\begin{array}{ll}
 & 0\,0\,0\,0\,1\,0\,1\,0\,0\,0\,0\,1\,0\,0\,0\,0\,0\,0\,1 \\
B[\mathbf{G}] & 0\,0\,0\,0\,1\,0\,0\,0\,0\,0\,0\,0\,0\,0\,0\,0\,0\,0\,0 \\
\hline
D = & 0\,0\,0\,0\,1\,0\,0\,0\,0\,0\,0\,0\,0\,0\,0\,0\,0\,0\,0
\end{array}
$$

8. Reading **A**

$$
\begin{array}{ll}
 & 0\,0\,0\,1\,0\,0\,1\,0\,0\,0\,0\,1\,0\,0\,0\,0\,0\,0\,1 \\
B[\mathbf{A}] & 0\,1\,0\,1\,0\,0\,1\,0\,1\,0\,1\,0\,1\,0\,1\,0\,1\,0\,1 \\
\hline
D = & 0\,0\,0\,1\,0\,0\,1\,0\,0\,0\,0\,0\,0\,0\,0\,0\,0\,0\,1
\end{array}
$$

9. Reading **T**

$$
\begin{array}{ll}
 & 0\,0\,1\,0\,0\,1\,1\,0\,0\,0\,0\,1\,0\,0\,0\,0\,0\,1\,1 \\
B[\mathbf{T}] & 1\,0\,1\,0\,0\,0\,0\,1\,0\,1\,0\,1\,0\,1\,0\,1\,0\,1\,0 \\
\hline
D = & 0\,0\,1\,0\,0\,0\,0\,0\,0\,0\,1\,0\,0\,0\,0\,0\,1\,0
\end{array}
$$

10. Reading **A**

$$
\begin{array}{ll}
 & 0\,1\,0\,0\,0\,0\,1\,0\,0\,0\,1\,1\,0\,0\,0\,0\,1\,0\,1 \\
B[\mathbf{A}] & 0\,1\,0\,1\,0\,0\,1\,0\,1\,0\,1\,0\,1\,0\,1\,0\,1\,0\,1 \\
\hline
D = & 0\,1\,0\,0\,0\,0\,1\,0\,0\,0\,1\,0\,0\,0\,0\,0\,1\,0\,1
\end{array}
$$

11. Reading **T**

$$
\begin{array}{ll}
 & 1\,0\,0\,0\,0\,1\,1\,0\,0\,1\,0\,1\,0\,0\,0\,1\,0\,1\,1 \\
B[\mathbf{T}] & 1\,0\,1\,0\,0\,0\,0\,1\,0\,1\,0\,1\,0\,1\,0\,1\,0\,1\,0 \\
\hline
D = & 1\,0\,0\,0\,0\,0\,0\,0\,1\,0\,1\,0\,0\,0\,1\,0\,1\,0
\end{array}
$$

$D \ \& \ DF \neq 0^{|P|}$, we check the patterns that match, and we mark an occurrence of **ACGATAT**.

12. Reading A

$$
\begin{array}{ll}
 & 0\,0\,0\,0\,0\,0\,1\,0\,1\,0\,1\,1\,0\,0\,1\,0\,1\,0\,1 \\
B[\mathtt{A}] & 0\,1\,0\,1\,0\,0\,1\,0\,1\,0\,1\,0\,1\,0\,1\,0\,1\,0\,1 \\
\hline
D = & 0\,0\,0\,0\,0\,0\,1\,0\,1\,0\,1\,0\,0\,0\,1\,0\,1\,0\,1
\end{array}
$$

13. Reading T

$$
\begin{array}{ll}
 & 0\,0\,0\,0\,0\,1\,1\,1\,0\,1\,0\,1\,0\,1\,0\,1\,0\,1\,1 \\
B[\mathtt{T}] & 1\,0\,1\,0\,0\,0\,1\,0\,1\,0\,1\,0\,1\,0\,1\,0\,1\,0 \\
\hline
D = & 0\,0\,0\,0\,0\,0\,0\,1\,0\,1\,0\,1\,0\,1\,0\,1\,0\,1\,0
\end{array}
$$

D & $DF \neq 0^{|P|}$, we check the patterns that match, and we mark an occurrence of **TATAT**.

14. Reading A

$$
\begin{array}{ll}
 & 0\,0\,0\,0\,0\,0\,1\,0\,1\,0\,1\,1\,1\,0\,1\,0\,1\,0\,1 \\
B[\mathtt{A}] & 0\,1\,0\,1\,0\,0\,1\,0\,1\,0\,1\,0\,1\,0\,1\,0\,1\,0\,1 \\
\hline
D = & 0\,0\,0\,0\,0\,0\,1\,0\,1\,0\,1\,0\,1\,0\,1\,0\,1\,0\,1
\end{array}
$$

D & $DF \neq 0^{|P|}$, we check the patterns that match, and we mark an occurrence of ATATATA.

15. Reading C

$$
\begin{array}{ll}
 & 0\,0\,0\,0\,0\,1\,1\,1\,0\,1\,0\,1\,0\,1\,0\,1\,0\,1\,1 \\
B[\mathtt{C}] & 0\,0\,0\,0\,1\,0\,0\,0\,0\,0\,0\,0\,0\,0\,0\,0\,0\,0 \\
\hline
D = & 0\,0\,0\,0\,0\,0\,0\,0\,0\,0\,0\,0\,0\,0\,0\,0\,0\,0
\end{array}
$$

3.2.2 Basic Aho-Corasick algorithm

The algorithm of Aho and Corasick [AC75] is an extension of the **Knuth-Morris-Pratt** algorithm (Section 2.2.1) for a set of patterns.

The algorithm uses a special automaton, called the *Aho-Corasick automaton*, built on P. It is the trie of P augmented with a "supply function" S_{AC}.

Formally, we denote by q a state of the trie of P, and by $L(q)$ the label of the path from the initial state to q. Then $S_{AC}(q)$ is defined, except for the initial state, as the state reached when the automaton reads the longest suffix of $L(q)$ that is also a prefix of some $p^i \in P$. This is a kind of extension of a *border* (Section 2.2.1) to a set of strings. The supply state of the initial state is set to θ. A *supply link* goes from each state q to $S_{AC}(q)$, and a *supply path* is a chain of supply links.

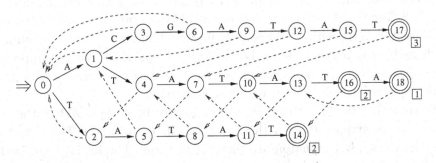

Fig. 3.9. Aho-Corasick automaton for the set {ATATATA, TATAT, ACGATAT}. The dashed links represent the state-to-state supply function S_{AC}. Double-circled states are terminal.

The Aho-Corasick automaton for the set {ATATATA, TATAT, ACGATAT} is shown in Figure 3.9. On this automaton, for instance, $L(15) = $ ACGATA, its longest suffix that is also a prefix of one of the patterns is ATA, which leads to state 7, and hence $S_{AC}(15) = 7$. The terminal states are those of the trie that correspond to an entire pattern, and also all states whose supply paths go down through another terminal state on their way to the root. In Figure 3.9, for instance, state 16 is terminal because $S_{AC}(16)$ is terminal.

We assume that a prefix $t_1 t_2 \ldots t_i$ of the text has already been read, and that the longest suffix of $t_1 \ldots t_i$ that is also a prefix of one of the patterns leads to a state *Current* in the Aho-Corasick automaton. We denote this longest suffix $v = L(Current)$. We want to read t_{i+1} and compute for $t_1 \ldots t_i t_{i+1}$ the new longest suffix u. There are two cases.

1. If there exists an outgoing transition from *Current* to another state f in the trie labeled by t_{i+1}, then the new *Current* state becomes f, and $u = L(f) = u t_{i+1}$ is the new longest prefix of one of the patterns that is a suffix of $t_1 \ldots t_{i+1}$.

2. If not (i.e., , we fail reading t_{i+1} in the tree), we go down the supply path of q until either

   (a) we find a state on the path followed by t_{i+1}. In this case, the current state becomes the arrival state f by the transition t_{i+1}, and $u = L(f)$.

   (b) we reach θ, which means that the longest suffix u we search for is the empty string ε, and we move to the initial state.

Pseudo-code for the search algorithm is given in Figure 3.10. The complexity of the search phase is simple to evaluate, if we observe that we cannot go down more supply links than text characters we read. The number of supply links crossed through is then bounded by n, and the number of transitions used (real transitions plus supply links) is bounded by $2n$. The number of character comparisons depends on how the transitions of the automaton are implemented. The complexity is $O(n + nocc)$ if they are coded with a table, and $O(n \log |\Sigma| + nocc)$ with balanced trees.

To construct the Aho-Corasick automaton we begin by building the trie of the set of strings P with the algorithm in Figure 3.6. The states of the Aho-Corasick automaton are those of the trie. The initial state is the same and the terminal states of the trie are also terminal. We build the supply function S_{AC} on this trie in transversal order, which is the order we numbered the states in Figure 3.9.

We assume that we have computed the supply function of all the states before state *Current* in transversal order. We consider the parent *Parent* of *Current* in the trie, leading to *Current* by σ, that is, $Current = \delta_{AC}(Parent, \sigma)$. The supply state $S_{AC}(Parent)$ has already been computed. We search

---

Aho-Corasick($P = \{p^1, p^2, \ldots, p^r\}$, $T = t_1 t_2 \ldots t_n$)
1.   Preprocessing
2. $AC \leftarrow$ **Build_AC**(P)
3.   Searching
4. $Current \leftarrow$ Initial state of the automaton AC
5.   **For** $pos \in 1 \ldots n$ **Do**
6.   **While** $\delta_{AC}(Current, t_{pos}) = \theta$ AND $S_{AC}(Current) \neq \theta$ **Do**
7. $Current \leftarrow S_{AC}(Current)$
8.   **End of while**
9.   **If** $\delta_{AC}(Current, t_{pos}) \neq \theta$ **Then**
10. $Current \leftarrow \delta_{AC}(Current, t_{pos})$
11.   **Else** $Current \leftarrow$ initial state of AC
12.   **End of if**
13.   **If** $Current$ is terminal **Then**
14.   Mark all the occurrences ($F(Current), pos$)
15.   **End of if**
16.   **End of for**

Fig. 3.10. **Aho-Corasick** algorithm to search for a set $P = \{p^1, p^2, \ldots, p^r\}$ of strings. It uses the Aho-Corasick automaton to compute at each text character t_{pos} the longest prefix of any pattern p^k that is also a suffix of the text read $t_1 \ldots t_{pos}$.

for the state where u ends, u being the longest suffix of $v = L(Current)$ that labels a path in the trie. The string v has the form $v'\sigma$. If there exists such a nonempty string u, since it is a suffix of v, it must be of the form $u = u'\sigma$. In that case, u' is a suffix of v' that is the label of a path in the trie.

If $S_{AC}(Parent)$ has an outgoing transition by σ to a state h, then $w = L(S_{AC}(Parent))$ is the longest suffix of v' that is the label of a path, and $w\sigma$ is also a label of a path in the trie. Consequently, it is the longest suffix u of $v = v'\sigma$ that we are searching for, and $S_{AC}(Current)$ has to be set to h.

If $S_{AC}(Parent)$ does not have an outgoing transition by σ, we consider $S_{AC}(S_{AC}(Parent))$ and so on. We repeat the operation, until either we find a state on the supply path that has an outgoing transition by σ, or we find θ, which means that u is the empty string ε and $S_{AC}(Current)$ has to be set to the initial state.

The mechanism is similar to the **Aho-Corasick** search algorithm itself. Its pseudo-code is given in Figure 3.11. Complexity is evaluated with the observation we made for the whole algorithm: We do not go down more supply links than the total number of real transitions, which is bounded by $O(|P|)$. So the number of total transitions used (real transitions plus supply links) is bounded by $2 \times |P|$. Like for the search phase, the complexity in terms of comparisons of characters depends on how the transitions of the automaton are implemented. It is $O(|P|)$ if they are coded with a table, and $O(|P| \log |\Sigma|)$ with balanced trees.

Build_AC$(P = \{p^1, p^2, \ldots, p^r\})$
1. $AC\_trie \leftarrow$ **Trie**(P)
       δ_{AC} is its transition function
2. $Initial\_state \leftarrow$ root of AC_trie
3. $S_{AC}(Initial\_state) \leftarrow \theta$
4.   **For** $Current$ in transversal order **Do**
5. $Parent \leftarrow$ parent of $Current$ in AC_trie
6. $\sigma \leftarrow$ label of the transition from $Parent$ to $Current$
7. $Down \leftarrow S_{AC}(Parent)$
8.   **While** $Down \neq \theta$ AND $\delta_{AC}(Down, \sigma) = \theta$ **Do**
9. $Down \leftarrow S_{AC}(Down)$
10.   **End of while**
11.   **If** $Down \neq \theta$ **Then**
12. $S_{AC}(Current) \leftarrow \delta_{AC}(Down, \sigma)$
13.   **If** $S_{AC}(Current)$ is terminal **Then**
14.   Mark $Current$ as terminal
15. $F(Current) \leftarrow F(Current) \cup F(S_{AC}(Current))$
16.   **End of if**
17.   **Else** $S_{AC}(Current) \leftarrow Initial\_state$
18.   **End of if**
19.   **End of for**

Fig. 3.11. Construction of the Aho-Corasick automaton. The state $Current$ goes in transversal order through the trie AC_trie built on P. The state $Down$ goes down the supply links from the parent of $Current$, looking for an outgoing transition labeled with the same character as between $Current$ and its parent. $F(Current)$ is initialized as empty when $Current$ is first marked as terminal.

Example using English We search for the set of strings $P = \{$announce, annual, annually$\}$ in the text "annual_announce". The Aho-Corasick automaton built on P is shown in Figure 3.12.

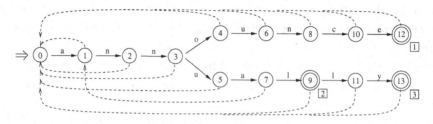

Fig. 3.12. Aho-Corasick automaton of our example set $P = \{$announce, annual, annually$\}$. Double-circled states are terminal.

Current ← 0.

1. Reading a
   Current ← $1 = \delta(0, a)$

2. Reading n
   Current ← $2 = \delta(1, n)$

3. Reading n
   Current ← $3 = \delta(2, n)$

4. Reading u
   Current ← $5 = \delta(3, u)$

5. Reading a
   Current ← $7 = \delta(5, a)$

6. Reading l
   Current ← $9 = \delta(7, a)$.
   The state 9 is terminal; we mark an occurrence of $F(9) \to$ **annual**.

7. Reading _
   $\delta(9, \_) = \theta$. We jump to $0 = S_{AC}(9)$.
   $\delta(0, \_) = \theta$, we jump to $\theta = S_{AC}(0)$.
   We continue the search from the initial state 0, *Current* ← 0.

8. Reading a
   Current ← $1 = \delta(0, a)$

9. Reading n
   Current ← $2 = \delta(1, n)$

10. Reading n
    Current ← $3 = \delta(2, n)$

11. Reading o
    Current ← $4 = \delta(3, o)$

12. Reading u
    Current ← $6 = \delta(4, u)$

13. Reading n
    Current ← $8 = \delta(6, n)$

14. Reading c
    Current ← $10 = \delta(8, c)$

15. Reading e
    Current ← $12 = \delta(10, e)$.
    The state 12 is terminal; we mark an occurrence of $F(12) \to$ **announce**.

Example using DNA We search for the set of strings $P = \{$ATATATA, TATAT, ACGATAT$\}$ in the text AGATACGATATATAC. We again use the Aho-Corasick automaton built on P already shown in Figure 3.9.

Current ← 0.

1. Reading A
   Current ← $1 = \delta(0, A)$

2. Reading G
   $\delta(1, G) = \theta$. We jump to $0 = S_{AC}(1)$.
   $\delta(0, G) = \theta$; we jump to $\theta = S_{AC}(0)$.
   We continue the search from the initial state 0, *Current* ← 0.

3. Reading A
   Current ← $1 = \delta(0, A)$

4. Reading T
   Current ← $4 = \delta(1, T)$

5. Reading A
   Current ← $7 = \delta(4, A)$

6. Reading C
   $\delta(7, C) = \theta$. We jump to $5 = S_{AC}(7)$.
   $\delta(5, C) = \theta$; we jump to $1 = S_{AC}(7)$.
   $\delta(1, C) = 3$, *Current* ← 3.

7. Reading G
   Current ← $6 = \delta(3, G)$

8. Reading A
   Current ← $9 = \delta(6, A)$

9. Reading T
   $Current \leftarrow 12 = \delta(9, T)$

10. Reading A
    $Current \leftarrow 15 = \delta(12, A)$

11. Reading T
    $Current \leftarrow 17 = \delta(12, T)$. The state 17 is terminal; we mark an occurrence of $F(17) \rightarrow$ ACGATAT.

12. Reading A
    $\delta(17, A) = \theta$. We jump to $10 = S_{AC}(17)$. $\delta(10, A) = 13$, $Current \leftarrow 13$.

13. Reading T
    $Current \leftarrow 16 = \delta(13, T)$. The state 16 is terminal; we mark an occurrence of $F(16) \rightarrow$ TATAT.

14. Reading A
    $Current \leftarrow 18 = \delta(16, A)$. The state 18 is terminal; we mark an occurrence of $F(18) \rightarrow$ ATATATA.

15. Reading C
    $\delta(18, C) = \theta$. We jump to $13 = S_{AC}(18)$. $\delta(13, C) = \theta$; we jump to $11 = S_{AC}(13)$. $\delta(11, C) = \theta$; we jump to $7 = S_{AC}(11)$. $\delta(7, C) = \theta$; we jump to $1 = S_{AC}(7)$. $\delta(1, C) = 3$, $Current \leftarrow 3$.

3.2.3 Advanced Aho-Corasick algorithm

The above algorithm permits a powerful variant. The idea is to precompute all the transitions simulated by the supply function. We then obtain a complete automaton (all the states have an outgoing transition by every character of the alphabet) that we name the *extended Aho-Corasick automaton*.

This completion can be computed using the supply function. We first complete the outgoing transitions of the initial state with a loop, which means $\delta(0, \sigma) \leftarrow 0$ for each new letter σ. Now, let *Current* be a state of the automaton taken in transversal order. We compute the missing outgoing transitions of *Current* by using the formula $\delta(Current, \sigma) = \delta(S_{AC}(Current), \sigma)$ for each new letter σ.

The drawback to this automaton is the large amount of memory space it requires. It is $O(|P| \times |\Sigma|)$ independently of the way the transitions are implemented. This construction is useful for relatively small sets and alphabets. A trade-off that is often used is to compute the new transitions on *the fly* if there is memory left. This was done in the first version of the well-known Unix application *Grep*.

3.3 Suffix based approach

The experimental results of Chapter 2 show that the suffix based approach is usually faster than the prefix based one. So it is natural to try to extend the suffix based approach to sets of patterns. The first attempt was that of Commentz-Walter in 1979 [CW79]. It is a direct extension of the **Boyer-Moore** algorithm. The **Horspool** algorithm has also been extended, but it is much less powerful for multiple string matching than for single patterns. A stronger extension is the **Wu-Manber** algorithm, which is practical, simple, and efficient.

3.3.1 Commentz-Walter idea

The **Commentz-Walter** [CW79] algorithm is a "natural" extension of the **Boyer-Moore** algorithm (Section 2.3.1). This algorithm is never faster in practice than **Aho-Corasick** or other algorithms presented below. However, it is historically important because it was the first expected sublinear multistring matching algorithm, and it was implemented in the second version of the Unix application *Grep*. Currently, this algorithm does not have a real case of application, and we just present the idea it is based on.

The **Commentz-Walter** algorithm represents $P = \{p^1, \ldots, p^r\}$ using a trie of the reverse patterns $P^{rv} = \{(p^1)^{rv}, \ldots, (p^r)^{rv}\}$ inside which the text is read. A position *pos* is slid along the text, beginning at position ℓmin so as not to skip a possible occurrence. For each such new position, we read backwards the longest suffix u of $t_1 \ldots t_{pos}$ that is also a suffix of one of the patterns. If we find an occurrence, we mark it. Then, we shift the position of the search to the right, using the three functions d_1, d_2, d_3 of the **Boyer-Moore** algorithm extended to a set of strings. The first two functions are computed for each state of the trie, and to shift we consider them at the last state q we crossed when reading the longest suffix u.

- $d_1(q)$ is the minimal shift such that $u = L(q)$ matches a factor of some $p^j \in P$.
- $d_2(q)$ is the minimal shift such that a suffix of $u = L(q)$ matches a prefix of some $p^j \in P$.

The last function $d_3[\alpha, k]$ is computed for each character α of the alphabet for positions $0 \leq k < \ell max$. It is the minimal shift such that α read at position $pos - k$ matches another character of some $p^j \in P$.

For a visual idea of what these three functions do, the reader may refer to Figures 2.8, 2.9, and 2.10 of Chapter 2, where the three corresponding functions of the **Boyer-Moore** algorithm are shown.

We combine these three functions to compute a shift. Suppose that we read backwards k characters of the text from a position *pos* and this led to state q. The shift $s[q, pos, k]$ is then computed with the following formula:

$$s[q, pos, k] = \min \left\{ \begin{array}{l} \max(d_1[q], d_3[t_{pos-k}, k]) \\ d_2[q] \end{array} \right.$$

The formula is the direct extension of the computation of the window shifts in the **Boyer-Moore** algorithm. As $d_2 \leq \ell min$, the longest shift is bounded by ℓmin, which is a necessary condition to avoid skipping an occurrence when shifting the position pos.

The **Commentz-Walter** algorithm is worst-case time $O(n \times \ell max)$ but sublinear on average if the number of patterns is not too large. The computation of the three functions d_1, d_2, and d_3 can be done in $O(|P|)$ time.

3.3.2 Set Horspool algorithm

The **Horspool** algorithm, similarly to **Boyer-Moore**, is directly extensible to a set of patterns. The new algorithm, which we call **Set Horspool**, can also be considered as a simplification of **Commentz-Walter**.

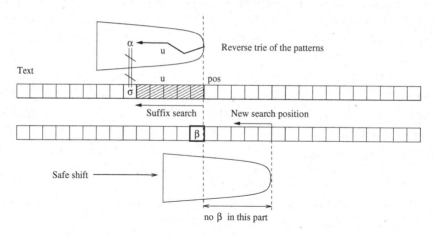

Fig. 3.13. **Horspool** algorithm for a set of patterns. The set is shifted according to the last character of the search window.

The general scheme is shown in Figure 3.13. We start reading the text backwards from a position pos initialized to ℓmin to avoid skipping any occurrence. We read these characters in the trie built on the reverse patterns. If we reach a terminal state, we mark an occurrence. When we fail reading the text, we shift the position pos using the first character read (β in the figure). We shift until β is aligned with another β in the trie. If such a β does not exist, we simply shift by ℓmin characters.

The **Set Horspool** algorithm is $O(n \times \ell max)$ time in the worst case. In

Set Horspool $(P = \{p^1, p^2, \ldots, p^r\},\ T = t_1 t_2 \ldots t_n)$
1.   Preprocessing
2. $HO \leftarrow \mathbf{Trie}(P^{rv} = \{(p^1)^{rv}, \ldots, (p^r)^{rv}\})$
           δ_{HO} is its transition function
3.   **For** $c \in \Sigma$ **Do** $d[c] \leftarrow \ell min$
4.   **For** $j \in 1 \ldots r$ **Do**
5.   **For** $k \in 1 \ldots m_j - 1$ **Do** $d[p_k^j] \leftarrow \min(d[p_k^j],\ m_j - k)$
6.   **End of for**
7.   Searching
8. $pos \leftarrow \ell min$
9.   **While** $pos \le n$ **Do**
10. $j \leftarrow 0,\ Current \leftarrow$ initial state of HO
11.   **While** $pos - j > 0$ AND $\delta_{HO}(t_{pos-j}, Current) \ne \theta$ **Do**
12.   **If** $Current$ is terminal **Then**
13.   Mark all the occurrences $(F(Current), pos)$
14.   **End of if**
15. $Current \leftarrow \delta_{HO}(t_{pos-j}, Current)$
16. $j \leftarrow j + 1$
17.   **End of while**
18. $pos \leftarrow pos + d[t_{pos}]$
19.   **End of while**

Fig. 3.14. Horspool algorithm for a set of patterns. The shift is obtained with the first character t_{pos} read.

general, it is only efficient for a very small number of patterns on a relatively large alphabet.

Example using English We search for the set $P = \{\texttt{announce, annual, annually}\}$ in the text "`CPM_annual_conference_announce`". The trie of the reverse patterns is shown in Figure 3.15

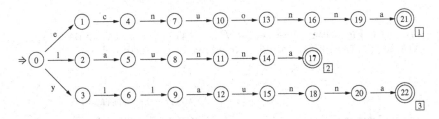

Fig. 3.15. Trie for the reverse set of $P = \{\texttt{announce, annual, annually}\}$, $P^{rv} = \{\texttt{ecnuonna, launna, yllaunna}\}$. Double-circled states are terminal.

$\ell min = 6,$

$$d = \begin{cases} \begin{array}{|c|c|c|c|c|c|c|c|c|} \hline \texttt{a} & \texttt{c} & \texttt{e} & \texttt{l} & \texttt{n} & \texttt{o} & \texttt{u} & \texttt{y} & \texttt{*} \\ \hline 1 & 1 & 6 & 1 & 2 & 4 & 2 & 6 & 6 \\ \hline \end{array} \end{cases}$$

1. CPM_a $\boxed{\texttt{n}}$ nual_conference_announce

   $\texttt{n} \notin \{\texttt{e}, \texttt{l}, \texttt{y}\},\ d[\texttt{n}] = 2$

2. CPM_ann $\boxed{\texttt{u}}$ al_conference_announce

   $\texttt{u} \notin \{\texttt{e}, \texttt{l}, \texttt{y}\},\ d[\texttt{u}] = 2$

3. CPM_annua $\boxed{\texttt{l}}$ _conference_announce

   We read in the trie l, a, u, n, n, a. We reach the terminal state 17 and mark an occurrence of $F(17) \rightarrow$ annual.

   We re-use the first character read, $d[\texttt{l}] = 1$.

4. CPM_annual $\boxed{\texttt{\_}}$ conference_announce

   $\texttt{\_} \notin \{\texttt{e}, \texttt{l}, \texttt{y}\},\ d[\texttt{\_}] = 6$

5. CPM_annual_confe $\boxed{\texttt{r}}$ ence_announce

   $\texttt{r} \notin \{\texttt{e}, \texttt{l}, \texttt{y}\},\ d[\texttt{r}] = 6$

6. CPM_annual_conference_ $\boxed{\texttt{a}}$ nnounce

   $\texttt{a} \notin \{\texttt{e}, \texttt{l}, \texttt{y}\},\ d[\texttt{a}] = 1$

7. CPM_annual_conference_a $\boxed{\texttt{n}}$ nounce

   $\texttt{n} \notin \{\texttt{e}, \texttt{l}, \texttt{y}\},\ d[\texttt{n}] = 2$

8. CPM_annual_conference_ann $\boxed{\texttt{o}}$ unce

   $\texttt{o} \notin \{\texttt{e}, \texttt{l}, \texttt{y}\},\ d[\texttt{o}] = 4$

9. CPM_annual_conference_announc $\boxed{\texttt{e}}$

   We read in the trie e, c, n, u, o, n, n, a. We reach the terminal state 21 and mark an occurrence of $F(21) \rightarrow$ announce.

Example using DNA We search for the set of strings $P = \{\texttt{ATATATA},$ $\texttt{TATAT}, \texttt{ACGATAT}\}$ in the text $\texttt{AGATACGATATATAC}$. The trie of the reverse patterns is shown in Figure 3.16

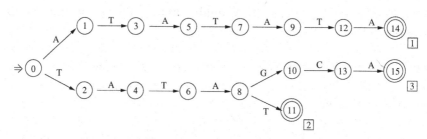

Fig. 3.16. Trie for the reverse set of $P = \{\texttt{ATATATA}, \texttt{TATAT}, \texttt{ACGATAT}\}$, $P^{rv} = \{\texttt{ATATATA}, \texttt{TATAT}, \texttt{TATAGCA}\}$. Double-circled states are terminal.

$\ell min = 5,$

$$\delta = \begin{cases} \begin{array}{|c|c|c|c|c|} \hline \texttt{A} & \texttt{C} & \texttt{G} & \texttt{T} & \texttt{*} \\ \hline 1 & 5 & 4 & 1 & 5 \\ \hline \end{array} \end{cases}$$

1. AGAT $\boxed{\texttt{A}}$ CGATATATAC

   We read in the trie A, T, A, and we fail on the next G. We re-use the last character of the window, $d[\texttt{A}] = 1$.

2. AGATA $\boxed{\texttt{C}}$ GATATATAC

   $\texttt{C} \notin \{\texttt{A}, \texttt{T}\},\ d[\texttt{C}] = 5.$

3. AGATACGATA $\boxed{\texttt{T}}$ ATAC

   We read in the trie T, A, T, A, G, C, A. We reach the terminal state 15 and mark an occurrence of $F(15) \rightarrow$ ACGATAT.

   We re-use the last character of the window, $d[\texttt{T}] = 1$.

4. AGATACGATAT $\boxed{\text{A}}$ TAC

   We read in the trie A, T, A, T, A, and we fail on the next G.

   We re-use the first character read, $d[\text{A}] = 1$.

5. AGATACGATATA $\boxed{\text{T}}$ AC

   We read in the trie T, A, T, A, T. We reach the terminal state 11 and mark an occurrence of $F(11) \to$ TATAT.

   We re-use the first character read, $d[\text{T}] = 1$.

6. AGATACGATATAT $\boxed{\text{A}}$ C

   We read in the trie A, T, A, T, A, T, A. We reach the terminal state 14 and mark an occurrence of $F(14) \to$ ATATATA.

   We re-use the first character read, $d[\text{A}] = 1$.

7. AGATACGATATATA $\boxed{\text{C}}$

   C $\notin \{$A, T$\}$, $d[\text{C}] = 5$. Then $pos > n$ and we stop the search.

3.3.3 Wu-Manber algorithm

The poor performance of the extension of **Horspool** to search a set of patterns is a direct consequence of the fact that the lengths of the shifts are usually decreasing, due to the high probability of finding each character of the alphabet in one of the strings.

The algorithm of Wu and Manber [WM94] bypasses this obstacle by reading blocks of characters, which reduces the probability that each block appears in one of the patterns. We consider blocks of length B. The difficulty is that there could be $|\Sigma|^B$ different blocks, requiring too much memory if B becomes large.

Wu and Manber overcome this problem by hashing all the possible blocks using a function h_1 into a limited size table $SHIFT$. Two blocks B_1 and B_2 can be associated with the same position in $SHIFT$. If we consider that for each new position we are reading a block Bl instead of the last character of the **Horspool** algorithm, then the shift given by Bl, $SHIFT(h_1(Bl))$, must be safe. To guarantee this, we save in $SHIFT(j)$ the minimum of the shifts of the blocks Bl such that $j = h_1(Bl)$. More precisely, the table $SHIFT$ is built in the following way:

- If a block Bl does not appear in any string of P, we can safely shift $\ell min - B + 1$ characters to the right. Hence we initialize the table by placing $\ell min - B + 1$ everywhere.
- If Bl appears in one of the strings of P, we find its rightmost occurrence ending in j in a string p^i, and set the value of $SHIFT(h_1(Bl))$ to $m_i - j$. To compute all the values of the table $SHIFT$, we consider separately each $p^i = p_1^i \ldots p_{m_i}^i$. For each block $B = p_{j-B+1}^i \ldots p_j^i$, we find its corresponding cell $h_1(B)$ in $SHIFT$, and we place in $SHIFT(h_1(B))$ the minimum between the previous value and $m_i - j$.

Wu-Manber($P = \{p^1, p^2, \ldots, p^r\}$, $T = t_1 t_2 \ldots t_n$)
1.   Preprocessing
2.   Computation of B
3.   Construction of the hash tables $SHIFT$ and $HASH$
4.   Searching
5. $pos \leftarrow \ell min$
6.   **While** $pos \leq n$ **Do**
7. $i \leftarrow h_1(t_{pos-B+1} \ldots t_{pos})$
8.   **If** $SHIFT[i] = 0$ **Then**
9. $list \leftarrow HASH[\, h_2(t_{pos-B+1} \ldots t_{pos})\,]$
10.   Verify all the patterns in $list$ one by one against the text
11. $pos \leftarrow pos+1$
12.   **Else** $pos \leftarrow pos + SHIFT[i]$
13.   **End of if**
14.   **End of while**

Fig. 3.17. **Wu-Manber** algorithm for searching a set of strings.

The size B varies with ℓmin, with the number of patterns, and with the size of the alphabet. Wu and Manber show that the value $B = \log_{|\Sigma|}(2 \times \ell min \times r)$ yields the best experimental results. The size of the table $SHIFT$ can also vary with the memory space available.

We can shift the search position along the text as long as the value of the shift is strictly positive. When the shift is zero, the text to the left of the search position may be one of the pattern strings. In this case Wu and Manber use a new hash table $HASH$. Each position $HASH(j)$ contains a list of all the strings whose last block is hashed to j by a second hash function h_2. This table permits us to select from P a subset of strings whose last block maps the block Bl read in the text.

For the search, similarly to the **Set Horspool** algorithm, we slide a position pos along the text, reading backwards a block Bl of B characters. The position pos is initialized to ℓmin. If $j = SHIFT(h_1(Bl)) > 0$, then we shift the window to $pos + j$ and continue the search. Otherwise, $SHIFT(h_1(Bl)) = 0$ and we select a set of strings using $HASH$ that we compare to the text. Pseudo-code is given in Figure 3.17.

The original description of the algorithm [WM94] is quite fuzzy. Nothing is given in the article that permits you to calculate the best size of the tables $SHIFT$ and $HASH$. Likewise, the hash functions are not specified. All these parameters affect the complexity. In practice, well parametrized, this algorithm is very fast. It is implemented in *Agrep* (Section 7.1.2).

We now present our two running examples. The **Wu-Manber** algorithm uses many hash functions and tables that are difficult to represent. We have chosen some that do not correspond to a real example, but permit us to show the interesting cases. We let $B = 2$ in the following tables.

Example using English We search for the set $P = \{\texttt{announce}, \texttt{annual},$ $\texttt{annually}\}$ in the text "CPM_annual_conference_announce".

$$SHIFT[Bl] = \left\{ \begin{array}{|c||c|c|c|c|c|c|c|c|c|c|} \hline \text{string} & \text{ll} & \text{no ou} & \text{an} & \text{un nc} & \text{ua al} & \text{ly} & \text{nn nu} & \text{ce} & * \\ \hline \text{shift} & 1 & 3 & 4 & 1 & 0 & 0 & 2 & 0 & 5 \\ \hline \end{array} \right.$$

$$HASH[Bl] = \left\{ \begin{array}{|c||c|c|c|} \hline \text{string} & \text{ce ly} & \text{ua al} & * \\ \hline \text{string number in } P & 3,1 & 2 & \emptyset \\ \hline \end{array} \right.$$

1. CPM_ $\boxed{\texttt{an}}$ nual_conference_announce
   $SHIFT[\text{an}] = 4$.

2. CPM_annu $\boxed{\texttt{al}}$ _conference_announce
   $SHIFT[\text{al}] = 0$. $L = HASH[\text{al}] = \{2\}$.

   We compare p^2 against the text and mark its occurrence. We then shift the search position by 1.

3. CPM_annua $\boxed{\texttt{l\_}}$ conference_announce
   $SHIFT[\text{l\_}] = 5$.

4. CPM_annual_con $\boxed{\texttt{fe}}$ rence_announce
   $SHIFT[\text{fe}] = 5$.

5. CPM_annual_conferen $\boxed{\texttt{ce}}$ _announce
   $SHIFT[\text{ce}] = 0$. $L = HASH[\text{ce}] = \{3,1\}$.

   We compare p^1 and p^3 against the text. No string matches. We shift the search position by 1.

6. CPM_annual_conferenc $\boxed{\texttt{e\_}}$ announce
   $SHIFT[\text{e\_}] = 5$.

7. CPM_annual_conference_ann $\boxed{\texttt{ou}}$ nce
   $SHIFT[\text{ou}] = 3$.

8. CPM_annual_conference_announ $\boxed{\texttt{ce}}$
   $SHIFT[\text{ce}] = 0$. $L = HASH[\text{ce}] = \{3,1\}$.

   We compare p^1 and p^3 against the text. The test succeeds for the string p^1. Hence, we mark its occurrence.

Example using DNA We search the set of strings $P = \{\texttt{ATATATA}, \texttt{TATAT},$ $\texttt{ACGATAT}\}$ in the text $\texttt{AGATACGATATATAC}$.

$$SHIFT[Bl] = \left\{ \begin{array}{|c||c|c|c|c|c|} \hline \text{string} & \text{GA TA} & \text{AT} & \text{CG GA} & \text{AC} & * \\ \hline \text{shift} & 0 & 0 & 3 & 4 & 4 \\ \hline \end{array} \right.$$

$$HASH[Bl] = \left\{ \begin{array}{|c||c|c|c|} \hline \text{string} & \text{TA} & \text{AT} & * \\ \hline \text{string number in } P & 1 & 2,3 & \emptyset \\ \hline \end{array} \right.$$

1. AGA $\boxed{\text{TA}}$ CGATATATAC
   $SHIFT[\text{TA}] = 0.\ L = HASH[\text{TA}] = \{1\}.$

   We compare p^1 against the text. The test fails. We shift the search position by 1.

2. AGAT $\boxed{\text{AC}}$ GATATATAC
   $SHIFT[\text{AC}] = 4.$

3. AGATACGA $\boxed{\text{TA}}$ TATAC
   $SHIFT[\text{TA}] = 0.\ L = HASH[\text{TA}] = \{1\}.$

   We compare p^1 against the text. The test fails. We shift the search position by 1.

4. AGATACGAT $\boxed{\text{AT}}$ ATAC
   $SHIFT[\text{AT}] = 0.\ L = HASH[\text{AT}] = \{2, 3\}.$

   We compare p^2 and p^3 against the text. The string p^3 matches. We mark its occurrence. We shift the search position by 1.

5. AGATACGATA $\boxed{\text{TA}}$ TAC
   $SHIFT[\text{TA}] = 0.\ L = HASH[\text{TA}] = \{1\}.$

   We compare p^1 against the text. The test fails. We shift the search position by 1.

6. AGATACGATAT $\boxed{\text{AT}}$ AC
   $SHIFT[\text{AT}] = 0.\ L = HASH[\text{AT}] = \{2, 3\}.$

   We compare p^2 and p^3 against the text. The string p^2 matches. We mark its occurrence. We shift the search position by 1.

7. AGATACGATATA $\boxed{\text{TA}}$ C
   $SHIFT[\text{TA}] = 0.\ L = HASH[\text{TA}] = \{1\}.$

   We compare p^1 against the text. The string p^1 matches. We mark its occurrence. We shift the search position by 1.

8. AGATACGATATAT $\boxed{\text{AC}}$
   $SHIFT[\text{AC}] = 4.$

3.4 Factor based approach

The general factor based approach can be extended directly to a set of strings. We search backwards for the longest suffix u of the text that is also a factor of one of the strings in P. If we fail on a letter σ, then σu is not a factor in any of the strings; thus no string of P can overlap σu.

There are, however, two technical difficulties to overcome. The first problem is to shift the set of patterns safely to avoid skipping an occurrence; the second difficulty is to recognize the factors of a set of strings.

The first two factor based algorithms were the **Dawg-Match** [CCG+93, CCG+99] and the **MultiBDM** [CR94, Raf97]. They were developed with the aim of obtaining fast algorithms on average with good worst-case complexity. Indeed, they are all worst-case linear in the size of the text. But they are inherently complicated, and in practice their performance is poor.

As we aim to present the simplest and most efficient algorithms, we will not describe these two.

The two algorithms left that use the factor based approach are **Set Backward Dawg Matching (SBDM)** and **Set Backward Oracle Matching (SBOM)** [AR99]. They extend **BDM** and **BOM**, respectively (Chapter 2). We present the **SBDM** idea, on which **SBOM** is based.

Bit-parallelism is only valuable for a small set of strings. However, similarly to the **Multiple Shift-And** (Section 3.2.1), it permits efficient extended string matching (Chapter 4) and also approximate matching (Chapter 6). We present it first.

3.4.1 Multiple BNDM algorithm

The use of bit-parallelism to search a set of strings $P = \{p^1, \ldots, p^r\}$ is efficient for sets such that $r \times \ell min$ fits in a few computer words [NR00]. For simplicity we assume below that $r \times \ell min \leq w$.

To perform longer shifts, we keep only the prefixes of size ℓmin of the patterns. If we match a prefix, we directly verify the entire string against the text.

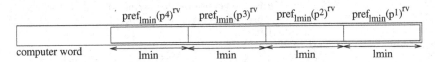

Fig. 3.18. **Multiple BNDM** algorithm. The total $r \times \ell min$ has to fit in w. The notation $pref_{\ell min}(p^i)$ denotes the prefix of size ℓmin of p^i.

The prefixes are packed together as in Figure 3.18 and the search is similar to **BNDM** (Section 2.4.2), with the search performed for all the prefixes at the same time. The only difference is that we need to clear some bits after a shift. The mask CL in Figure 3.19 does that. It prevents the bits used to search for p^i from interfering with those used for p^{i+1}. The variable *last* is still used, but in this case it represents the position where a prefix of one of the strings begins. Pseudo-code of the whole algorithm is shown in Figure 3.19.

Example using English We search the text "CPM_annual_conference_announce" for the set of strings $P = \{$announce, annual, annually$\}$.

Multiple BNDM $(p = p_1 p_2 \ldots p_m,\ T = t_1 t_2 \ldots t_n)$

1.   Preprocessing
2.   **For** $c \in \Sigma$ **Do** $B[c] \leftarrow 0^{|P|}$
3. $\ell \leftarrow 0$
4.   **For** $k \in 1 \ldots r$ **Do**
5. $\ell \leftarrow \ell + \ell min$
6.   **For** $j \in 1 \ldots \ell min$ **Do** $B[p_j^k] \leftarrow B[p_j^k] \mid 0^{|P|-\ell+j-1}10^{\ell-j}$
7.   **End of for**
8. $CL \leftarrow (1^{\ell min-1}0)^r$
9. $DF \leftarrow (10^{\ell min-1})^r$
10.   Searching
11. $pos \leftarrow 0$
12.   **While** $pos \leq n - m$ **Do**
13. $j \leftarrow \ell min,\ last \leftarrow \ell min$
14. $D = 1^{|P|}$
15.   **While** $D \neq 0^{|P|}$ **Do**
16. $D \leftarrow D\ \&\ B[t_{pos+j}]$
17. $j \leftarrow j - 1$
18.   **If** $D\ \&\ DF \neq 0^{|P|}$ **Then**
19.   **If** $j > 0$ **Then** $last \leftarrow j$
20.   **Else**   /* at least one prefix matches */
21.   Check which prefixes of length ℓmin match
                            p^i needs to be checked if
                                $D\ \&\ 0^{|P|-\ell min \times i}10^{\ell min-1}0^{\ell min \times (i-1)}\ \neq\ 0^{|P|}$
22.   Verify the corresponding string(s) against the text
23.   Report the occurrence(s) at $pos + 1$
24.   **End of if**
25.   **End of if**
26. $D \leftarrow (D << 1)\ \&\ CL$ /* Shifting and cleaning */
27.   **End of while**
28. $pos \leftarrow pos + last$
29.   **End of while**

Fig. 3.19. Bit-parallel code for the **Multiple BNDM** algorithm.

$$B = \left\{ \begin{array}{l|l} \texttt{a} & 1\ 0\ 0\ 0\ 1\ 0\ 1\ 0\ 0\ 0\ 1\ 0\ 1\ 0\ 0\ 0\ 0\ 0 \\ \texttt{l} & 0\ 0\ 0\ 0\ 1\ 0\ 0\ 0\ 0\ 0\ 1\ 0\ 0\ 0\ 0\ 0\ 0 \\ \texttt{n} & 0\ 1\ 1\ 0\ 0\ 0\ 0\ 1\ 1\ 0\ 0\ 0\ 0\ 1\ 1\ 0\ 0\ 1 \\ \texttt{o} & 0\ 0\ 0\ 0\ 0\ 0\ 0\ 0\ 0\ 0\ 0\ 0\ 0\ 0\ 1\ 0\ 0 \\ \texttt{u} & 0\ 0\ 0\ 1\ 0\ 0\ 0\ 0\ 0\ 1\ 0\ 0\ 0\ 0\ 0\ 0\ 1\ 0 \\ \texttt{*} & 0\ 0\ 0\ 0\ 0\ 0\ 0\ 0\ 0\ 0\ 0\ 0\ 0\ 0\ 0\ 0\ 0\ 0 \end{array} \right.$$

$$\begin{array}{ll} DF & = & 1\ 0\ 0\ 0\ 0\ 1\ 0\ 0\ 0\ 0\ 0\ 1\ 0\ 0\ 0\ 0\ 0 \\ CL & = & 1\ 1\ 1\ 1\ 1\ 0\ 1\ 1\ 1\ 1\ 1\ 0\ 1\ 1\ 1\ 1\ 1\ 0 \end{array}$$

$$\begin{array}{rl} & 1\ 1\ 1\ 1\ 1\ 1\ 1\ 1\ 1\ 1\ 1\ 1\ 1\ 1\ 1\ 1\ 1\ 1 \\ B[\texttt{n}] & 0\ 1\ 1\ 0\ 0\ 0\ 0\ 1\ 1\ 0\ 0\ 0\ 0\ 1\ 1\ 0\ 0\ 1 \\ \hline D = & 0\ 1\ 1\ 0\ 0\ 0\ 0\ 1\ 1\ 0\ 0\ 0\ 0\ 1\ 1\ 0\ 0\ 1 \end{array}$$

$$\begin{array}{rl} & 1\ 1\ 0\ 0\ 0\ 0\ 1\ 1\ 0\ 0\ 0\ 0\ 1\ 1\ 0\ 0\ 1\ 0 \\ B[\texttt{a}] & 1\ 0\ 0\ 0\ 1\ 0\ 1\ 0\ 0\ 0\ 1\ 0\ 1\ 0\ 0\ 0\ 0\ 0 \\ \hline D = & 1\ 0\ 0\ 0\ 0\ 0\ 1\ 0\ 0\ 0\ 0\ 0\ 1\ 0\ 0\ 0\ 0\ 0 \end{array}$$

$D\ \&\ DF \neq 0^{|P|}$ and $j > 0$, then
$last \leftarrow 4$

$$\begin{array}{rl} & 0\ 0\ 0\ 0\ 0\ 0\ 0\ 0\ 0\ 0\ 0\ 0\ 0\ 0\ 0\ 0\ 0\ 0 \\ B[\_] & 0\ 0\ 0\ 0\ 0\ 0\ 0\ 0\ 0\ 0\ 0\ 0\ 0\ 0\ 0\ 0\ 0\ 0 \\ \hline D = & 0\ 0\ 0\ 0\ 0\ 0\ 0\ 0\ 0\ 0\ 0\ 0\ 0\ 0\ 0\ 0\ 0\ 0 \end{array}$$

1. $\boxed{\texttt{CPM\_an}}$ nual_conference_announce
    $last \leftarrow 6.$
    $D \leftarrow 1\ 1\ 1\ 1\ 1\ 1\ 1\ 1\ 1\ 1\ 1\ 1\ 1\ 1\ 1\ 1\ 1\ 1$

2. CPM_ | annual | _conference_announce
   last ← 6.
   $D ←$ 1 1 1 1 1 1 1 1 1 1 1 1 1 1 1 1 1 1 1 1

```
              1 1 1 1 1 1 1 1 1 1 1 1 1 1 1 1 1 1 1 1
B[1]   0 0 0 0 0 1 0 0 0 0 0 1 0 0 0 0 0 0
D =    0 0 0 0 0 1 0 0 0 0 0 1 0 0 0 0 0 0

       0 0 0 0 1 0 0 0 0 0 1 0 0 0 0 0 0 0
B[a]   1 0 0 0 1 0 1 0 0 0 1 0 1 0 0 0 0 0
D =    0 0 0 0 1 0 0 0 0 0 1 0 0 0 0 0 0 0

       0 0 0 1 0 0 0 0 0 1 0 0 0 0 0 0 0 0
B[u]   0 0 0 1 0 0 0 0 0 1 0 0 0 0 0 0 1 0
D =    0 0 0 1 0 0 0 0 0 1 0 0 0 0 0 0 0 0

       0 0 1 0 0 0 0 0 1 0 0 0 0 0 0 0 0 0
B[n]   0 1 1 0 0 0 0 1 1 0 0 0 0 1 1 0 0 1
D =    0 0 1 0 0 0 0 0 1 0 0 0 0 0 0 0 0 0

       0 1 0 0 0 0 0 1 0 0 0 0 0 0 0 0 0 0
B[n]   0 1 1 0 0 0 0 1 1 0 0 0 0 1 1 0 0 1
D =    0 1 0 0 0 0 0 1 0 0 0 0 0 0 0 0 0 0

       1 0 0 0 0 0 1 0 0 0 0 0 0 0 0 0 0 0
B[a]   1 0 0 0 1 0 1 0 0 0 1 0 1 0 0 0 0 0
D =    1 0 0 0 0 0 1 0 0 0 0 0 0 0 0 0 0 0
```

D & $DF ≠ 0^{|P|}$ and $j = 0$, so we check the patterns "annual" and "annually" against the text and mark the occurrence of "annual".

3. CPM_annual | _confe | rence_announce
   last ← 6.
   $D ←$ 1 1 1 1 1 1 1 1 1 1 1 1 1 1 1 1 1 1 1 1

```
              1 1 1 1 1 1 1 1 1 1 1 1 1 1 1 1 1 1 1 1
B[e]   0 0 0 0 0 0 0 0 0 0 0 0 0 0 0 0 0 0
D =    0 0 0 0 0 0 0 0 0 0 0 0 0 0 0 0 0 0
```

4. CPM_annual_confe | rence_ | announce
   last ← 6.
   $D ←$ 1 1 1 1 1 1 1 1 1 1 1 1 1 1 1 1 1 1 1 1

```
              1 1 1 1 1 1 1 1 1 1 1 1 1 1 1 1 1 1 1 1
B[_]   0 0 0 0 0 0 0 0 0 0 0 0 0 0 0 0 0 0
D =    0 0 0 0 0 0 0 0 0 0 0 0 0 0 0 0 0 0
```

5. CPM_annual_conference_ | announ | ce
   last ← 6.
   $D ←$ 1 1 1 1 1 1 1 1 1 1 1 1 1 1 1 1 1 1 1 1

```
              1 1 1 1 1 1 1 1 1 1 1 1 1 1 1 1 1 1 1 1
B[n]   0 1 1 0 0 0 0 1 1 0 0 0 0 1 1 0 0 1
D =    0 1 1 0 0 0 0 1 1 0 0 0 0 1 1 0 0 1

       1 1 0 0 0 0 1 1 0 0 0 0 1 1 0 0 1 0
B[u]   0 0 0 1 0 0 0 0 0 1 0 0 0 0 0 0 1 0
D =    0 0 0 0 0 0 0 0 0 0 0 0 0 0 0 0 1 0

       0 0 0 0 0 0 0 0 0 0 0 0 0 0 0 1 0 0
B[o]   0 0 0 0 0 0 0 0 0 0 0 0 0 0 0 1 0 0
D =    0 0 0 0 0 0 0 0 0 0 0 0 0 0 0 1 0 0

       0 0 0 0 0 0 0 0 0 0 0 0 0 0 1 0 0 0
B[n]   0 1 1 0 0 0 0 1 1 0 0 0 0 1 1 0 0 1
D =    0 0 0 0 0 0 0 0 0 0 0 0 0 0 1 0 0 0

       0 0 0 0 0 0 0 0 0 0 0 0 0 1 0 0 0 0
B[n]   0 1 1 0 0 0 0 1 1 0 0 0 0 1 1 0 0 1
D =    0 0 0 0 0 0 0 0 0 0 0 0 0 1 0 0 0 0

       0 0 0 0 0 0 0 0 0 0 0 0 1 0 0 0 0 0
B[a]   1 0 0 0 1 0 1 0 0 0 1 0 1 0 0 0 0 0
D =    0 0 0 0 0 0 0 0 0 0 0 0 1 0 0 0 0 0
```

D & $DF ≠ 0^{|P|}$ and $j = 0$, so we check the string "announce" against the text and mark its occurrence.

The next shift of the search window gives $pos > n − \ell min$ and the search stops.

Example using DNA We search for the set of strings $P = \{$ATATATA, TATAT, ACGATAT$\}$ in the text AGATACGATATATAC.

```
        A  1 0 1 0 1 0 1 0 1 0 1 0 0 1 0
        C  0 0 0 0 0 0 0 0 0 0 0 1 0 0 0
B =     G  0 0 0 0 0 0 0 0 0 0 0 0 1 0 0
        T  0 1 0 1 0 1 0 1 0 1 0 0 0 0 1
        *  0 0 0 0 0 0 0 0 0 0 0 0 0 0 0
```

DF = 1 0 0 0 0 1 0 0 0 0 1 0 0 0 0
CL = 1 1 1 1 0 1 1 1 1 0 1 1 1 1 0

1. $\boxed{\text{AGATA}}$ CGATATATAC
   $last \leftarrow 5.$
   $D \leftarrow 1\,1\,1\,1\,1\,1\,1\,1\,1\,1\,1\,1\,1\,1\,1$

   $$
   \begin{array}{ll}
    & 1\,1\,1\,1\,1\,1\,1\,1\,1\,1\,1\,1\,1\,1\,1 \\
   B[\text{A}] & 1\,0\,1\,0\,1\,0\,1\,0\,1\,0\,1\,0\,0\,1\,0 \\
   \hline
   D = & 1\,0\,1\,0\,1\,0\,1\,0\,1\,0\,1\,0\,0\,1\,0
   \end{array}
   $$

   D & $DF \neq 0^{|P|}$ and $j > 0$, then
   $last \leftarrow 4$

   $$
   \begin{array}{ll}
    & 0\,1\,0\,1\,0\,1\,0\,1\,0\,0\,0\,0\,1\,0\,0 \\
   B[\text{T}] & 0\,1\,0\,1\,0\,1\,0\,1\,0\,1\,0\,0\,0\,0\,1 \\
   \hline
   D = & 0\,1\,0\,1\,0\,1\,0\,1\,0\,0\,0\,0\,0\,0\,0
   \end{array}
   $$

   D & $DF \neq 0^{|P|}$ and $j > 0$, then
   $last \leftarrow 3$

   $$
   \begin{array}{ll}
    & 1\,0\,1\,0\,0\,0\,1\,0\,0\,0\,0\,0\,0\,0\,0 \\
   B[\text{A}] & 1\,0\,1\,0\,1\,0\,1\,0\,1\,0\,1\,0\,0\,1\,0 \\
   \hline
   D = & 1\,0\,1\,0\,0\,0\,1\,0\,0\,0\,0\,0\,0\,0\,0
   \end{array}
   $$

   D & $DF \neq 0^{|P|}$ and $j > 0$, then
   $last \leftarrow 2$

   $$
   \begin{array}{ll}
    & 0\,1\,0\,0\,0\,1\,0\,0\,0\,0\,0\,0\,0\,0\,0 \\
   B[\text{G}] & 0\,0\,0\,0\,0\,0\,0\,0\,0\,0\,0\,1\,0\,0 \\
   \hline
   D = & 0\,0\,0\,0\,0\,0\,0\,0\,0\,0\,0\,0\,0\,0\,0
   \end{array}
   $$

2. AG $\boxed{\text{ATACG}}$ ATATATAC
   $last \leftarrow 5.$
   $D \leftarrow 1\,1\,1\,1\,1\,1\,1\,1\,1\,1\,1\,1\,1\,1\,1$

   $$
   \begin{array}{ll}
    & 1\,1\,1\,1\,1\,1\,1\,1\,1\,1\,1\,1\,1\,1\,1 \\
   B[\text{G}] & 0\,0\,0\,0\,0\,0\,0\,0\,0\,0\,0\,1\,0\,0 \\
   \hline
   D = & 0\,0\,0\,0\,0\,0\,0\,0\,0\,0\,0\,1\,0\,0
   \end{array}
   $$

   $$
   \begin{array}{ll}
    & 0\,0\,0\,0\,0\,0\,0\,0\,0\,0\,1\,0\,0\,0 \\
   B[\text{C}] & 0\,0\,0\,0\,0\,0\,0\,0\,0\,0\,1\,0\,0\,0 \\
   \hline
   D = & 0\,0\,0\,0\,0\,0\,0\,0\,0\,0\,1\,0\,0\,0
   \end{array}
   $$

   $$
   \begin{array}{ll}
    & 0\,0\,0\,0\,0\,0\,0\,0\,0\,1\,0\,0\,0\,0 \\
   B[\text{A}] & 1\,0\,1\,0\,1\,0\,1\,0\,1\,0\,1\,0\,0\,1\,0 \\
   \hline
   D = & 0\,0\,0\,0\,0\,0\,0\,0\,0\,1\,0\,0\,0\,0
   \end{array}
   $$

   D & $DF \neq 0^{|P|}$ and $j > 0$, then
   $last \leftarrow 2$

   $$
   \begin{array}{ll}
    & 0\,0\,0\,0\,0\,0\,0\,0\,0\,0\,0\,0\,0\,0\,0 \\
   B[\text{T}] & 0\,1\,0\,1\,0\,1\,0\,1\,0\,1\,0\,0\,0\,0\,1 \\
   \hline
   D = & 0\,0\,0\,0\,0\,0\,0\,0\,0\,0\,0\,0\,0\,0\,0
   \end{array}
   $$

3. AGAT $\boxed{\text{ACGAT}}$ ATATAC
   $last \leftarrow 5.$
   $D \leftarrow 1\,1\,1\,1\,1\,1\,1\,1\,1\,1\,1\,1\,1\,1\,1$

   $$
   \begin{array}{ll}
    & 1\,1\,1\,1\,1\,1\,1\,1\,1\,1\,1\,1\,1\,1\,1 \\
   B[\text{T}] & 0\,1\,0\,1\,0\,1\,0\,1\,0\,1\,0\,0\,0\,0\,1 \\
   \hline
   D = & 0\,1\,0\,1\,0\,1\,0\,1\,0\,1\,0\,0\,0\,0\,1
   \end{array}
   $$

   D & $DF \neq 0^{|P|}$ and $j > 0$, then
   $last \leftarrow 4$

   $$
   \begin{array}{ll}
    & 1\,0\,1\,0\,0\,0\,1\,0\,1\,0\,0\,0\,0\,1\,0 \\
   B[\text{A}] & 1\,0\,1\,0\,1\,0\,1\,0\,1\,0\,1\,0\,0\,1\,0 \\
   \hline
   D = & 1\,0\,1\,0\,0\,0\,1\,0\,1\,0\,0\,0\,0\,1\,0
   \end{array}
   $$

   D & $DF \neq 0^{|P|}$ and $j > 0$, then
   $last \leftarrow 3$

   $$
   \begin{array}{ll}
    & 0\,1\,0\,0\,0\,1\,0\,1\,0\,0\,0\,0\,1\,0\,0 \\
   B[\text{G}] & 0\,0\,0\,0\,0\,0\,0\,0\,0\,0\,0\,1\,0\,0 \\
   \hline
   D = & 0\,0\,0\,0\,0\,0\,0\,0\,0\,0\,0\,1\,0\,0
   \end{array}
   $$

   $$
   \begin{array}{ll}
    & 0\,0\,0\,0\,0\,0\,0\,0\,0\,0\,1\,0\,0\,0 \\
   B[\text{C}] & 0\,0\,0\,0\,0\,0\,0\,0\,0\,0\,1\,0\,0\,0 \\
   \hline
   D = & 0\,0\,0\,0\,0\,0\,0\,0\,0\,0\,1\,0\,0\,0
   \end{array}
   $$

   $$
   \begin{array}{ll}
    & 0\,0\,0\,0\,0\,0\,0\,0\,0\,1\,0\,0\,0\,0 \\
   B[\text{A}] & 1\,0\,1\,0\,1\,0\,1\,0\,1\,0\,1\,0\,0\,1\,0 \\
   \hline
   D = & 0\,0\,0\,0\,0\,0\,0\,0\,0\,1\,0\,0\,0\,0
   \end{array}
   $$

   D & $DF \neq 0^{|P|}$ and $j = 0$, so we check
   the pattern ACGATAT against the text
   and mark its occurrence.

4. AGATACG $\boxed{\text{ATATA}}$ TAC
   $last \leftarrow 5.$
   $D \leftarrow 1\,1\,1\,1\,1\,1\,1\,1\,1\,1\,1\,1\,1\,1\,1$

   $$
   \begin{array}{ll}
    & 1\,1\,1\,1\,1\,1\,1\,1\,1\,1\,1\,1\,1\,1\,1 \\
   B[\text{A}] & 1\,0\,1\,0\,1\,0\,1\,0\,1\,0\,1\,0\,0\,1\,0 \\
   \hline
   D = & 1\,0\,1\,0\,1\,0\,1\,0\,1\,0\,1\,0\,0\,1\,0
   \end{array}
   $$

   D & $DF \neq 0^{|P|}$ and $j > 0$, then
   $last \leftarrow 4$

   $$
   \begin{array}{ll}
    & 0\,1\,0\,1\,0\,1\,0\,1\,0\,0\,0\,0\,1\,0\,0 \\
   B[\text{T}] & 0\,1\,0\,1\,0\,1\,0\,1\,0\,1\,0\,0\,0\,0\,1 \\
   \hline
   D = & 0\,1\,0\,1\,0\,1\,0\,1\,0\,0\,0\,0\,0\,0\,0
   \end{array}
   $$

   D & $DF \neq 0^{|P|}$ and $j > 0$, then
   $last \leftarrow 3$

   $$
   \begin{array}{ll}
    & 1\,0\,1\,0\,0\,0\,1\,0\,0\,0\,0\,0\,0\,0\,0 \\
   B[\text{A}] & 1\,0\,1\,0\,1\,0\,1\,0\,1\,0\,1\,0\,0\,1\,0 \\
   \hline
   D = & 1\,0\,1\,0\,0\,0\,1\,0\,0\,0\,0\,0\,0\,0\,0
   \end{array}
   $$

   D & $DF \neq 0^{|P|}$ and $j > 0$, then

$last \leftarrow 2$

$$
\begin{array}{ll}
 & 0\,1\,0\,0\,0\,1\,0\,0\,0\,0\,0\,0\,0\,0 \\
B[\mathrm{T}] & 0\,1\,0\,1\,0\,1\,0\,1\,0\,1\,0\,0\,0\,0\,1 \\
\hline
D = & 0\,1\,0\,0\,0\,1\,0\,0\,0\,0\,0\,0\,0\,0
\end{array}
$$

D & $DF \neq 0^{|P|}$ and $j > 0$, then $last \leftarrow 1$

$$
\begin{array}{ll}
 & 1\,0\,0\,0\,0\,0\,0\,0\,0\,0\,0\,0\,0\,0 \\
B[\mathrm{A}] & 1\,0\,1\,0\,1\,0\,1\,0\,1\,0\,1\,0\,0\,1\,0 \\
\hline
D = & 1\,0\,0\,0\,0\,0\,0\,0\,0\,0\,0\,0\,0\,0
\end{array}
$$

D & $DF \neq 0^{|P|}$ and $j = 0$, so we check the string **ATATATA** against the text and mark its occurrence.

5. **AGATACGA** | **TATAT** | **AC**

$last \leftarrow 5$.
$D \leftarrow 1\,1\,1\,1\,1\,1\,1\,1\,1\,1\,1\,1\,1\,1$

$$
\begin{array}{ll}
 & 1\,1\,1\,1\,1\,1\,1\,1\,1\,1\,1\,1\,1\,1 \\
B[\mathrm{T}] & 0\,1\,0\,1\,0\,1\,0\,1\,0\,1\,0\,0\,0\,0\,1 \\
\hline
D = & 0\,1\,0\,1\,0\,1\,0\,1\,0\,1\,0\,0\,0\,0\,1
\end{array}
$$

D & $DF \neq 0^{|P|}$ and $j > 0$, then $last \leftarrow 4$

$$
\begin{array}{ll}
 & 1\,0\,1\,0\,0\,0\,1\,0\,1\,0\,0\,0\,0\,1\,0 \\
B[\mathrm{A}] & 1\,0\,1\,0\,1\,0\,1\,0\,1\,0\,1\,0\,0\,1\,0 \\
\hline
D = & 1\,0\,1\,0\,0\,0\,1\,0\,1\,0\,0\,0\,0\,1\,0
\end{array}
$$

D & $DF \neq 0^{|P|}$ and $j > 0$, then $last \leftarrow 3$

$$
\begin{array}{ll}
 & 0\,1\,0\,0\,0\,1\,0\,1\,0\,0\,0\,0\,1\,0\,0 \\
B[\mathrm{T}] & 0\,1\,0\,1\,0\,1\,0\,1\,0\,1\,0\,0\,0\,0\,1 \\
\hline
D = & 0\,1\,0\,0\,0\,1\,0\,1\,0\,0\,0\,0\,0\,0\,0
\end{array}
$$

D & $DF \neq 0^{|P|}$ and $j > 0$, then $last \leftarrow 2$

$$
\begin{array}{ll}
 & 1\,0\,0\,0\,0\,0\,1\,0\,0\,0\,0\,0\,0\,0 \\
B[\mathrm{A}] & 1\,0\,1\,0\,1\,0\,1\,0\,1\,0\,1\,0\,0\,1\,0 \\
\hline
D = & 1\,0\,0\,0\,0\,0\,1\,0\,0\,0\,0\,0\,0\,0
\end{array}
$$

D & $DF \neq 0^{|P|}$ and $j > 0$, then $last \leftarrow 1$

$$
\begin{array}{ll}
 & 0\,0\,0\,0\,0\,1\,0\,0\,0\,0\,0\,0\,0\,0 \\
B[\mathrm{T}] & 0\,1\,0\,1\,0\,1\,0\,1\,0\,1\,0\,0\,0\,0\,1 \\
\hline
D = & 0\,0\,0\,0\,0\,1\,0\,0\,0\,0\,0\,0\,0\,0
\end{array}
$$

D & $DF \neq 0^{|P|}$ and $j = 0$, so we check the string **TATAT** against the text and mark its occurrence.

6. **AGATACGAT** | **ATATA** | **C**

$last \leftarrow 5$.
$D \leftarrow 1\,1\,1\,1\,1\,1\,1\,1\,1\,1\,1\,1\,1\,1$

$$
\begin{array}{ll}
 & 1\,1\,1\,1\,1\,1\,1\,1\,1\,1\,1\,1\,1\,1 \\
B[\mathrm{A}] & 1\,0\,1\,0\,1\,0\,1\,0\,1\,0\,1\,0\,0\,1\,0 \\
\hline
D = & 1\,0\,1\,0\,1\,0\,1\,0\,1\,0\,1\,0\,0\,1\,0
\end{array}
$$

D & $DF \neq 0^{|P|}$ and $j > 0$, then $last \leftarrow 4$

$$
\begin{array}{ll}
 & 0\,1\,0\,1\,0\,1\,0\,1\,0\,0\,0\,0\,1\,0\,0 \\
B[\mathrm{T}] & 0\,1\,0\,1\,0\,1\,0\,1\,0\,1\,0\,0\,0\,0\,1 \\
\hline
D = & 0\,1\,0\,1\,0\,1\,0\,1\,0\,0\,0\,0\,0\,0\,0
\end{array}
$$

D & $DF \neq 0^{|P|}$ and $j > 0$, then $last \leftarrow 3$

$$
\begin{array}{ll}
 & 1\,0\,1\,0\,0\,0\,1\,0\,0\,0\,0\,0\,0\,0 \\
B[\mathrm{A}] & 1\,0\,1\,0\,1\,0\,1\,0\,1\,0\,1\,0\,0\,1\,0 \\
\hline
D = & 1\,0\,1\,0\,0\,0\,1\,0\,0\,0\,0\,0\,0\,0
\end{array}
$$

D & $DF \neq 0^{|P|}$ and $j > 0$, then $last \leftarrow 2$

$$
\begin{array}{ll}
 & 0\,1\,0\,0\,0\,1\,0\,0\,0\,0\,0\,0\,0\,0 \\
B[\mathrm{T}] & 0\,1\,0\,1\,0\,1\,0\,1\,0\,1\,0\,0\,0\,0\,1 \\
\hline
D = & 0\,1\,0\,0\,0\,1\,0\,0\,0\,0\,0\,0\,0\,0
\end{array}
$$

D & $DF \neq 0^{|P|}$ and $j > 0$, then $last \leftarrow 1$

$$
\begin{array}{ll}
 & 1\,0\,0\,0\,0\,0\,0\,0\,0\,0\,0\,0\,0\,0 \\
B[\mathrm{A}] & 1\,0\,1\,0\,1\,0\,1\,0\,1\,0\,1\,0\,0\,1\,0 \\
\hline
D = & 1\,0\,0\,0\,0\,0\,0\,0\,0\,0\,0\,0\,0\,0
\end{array}
$$

D & $DF \neq 0^{|P|}$ and $j = 0$, so we check the string **ATATATA** against the text, but we fail to recognize an occurrence.

7. **AGATACGATA** | **TATAC**

$last \leftarrow 5$.
$D \leftarrow 1\,1\,1\,1\,1\,1\,1\,1\,1\,1\,1\,1\,1\,1$

$$
\begin{array}{ll}
 & 1\,1\,1\,1\,1\,1\,1\,1\,1\,1\,1\,1\,1\,1 \\
B[\mathrm{C}] & 0\,0\,0\,0\,0\,0\,0\,0\,0\,0\,0\,1\,0\,0\,0 \\
\hline
D = & 0\,0\,0\,0\,0\,0\,0\,0\,0\,0\,0\,1\,0\,0\,0
\end{array}
$$

$$
\begin{array}{ll}
 & 0\,0\,0\,0\,0\,0\,0\,0\,0\,1\,0\,0\,0\,0 \\
B[\mathrm{A}] & 1\,0\,1\,0\,1\,0\,1\,0\,1\,0\,1\,0\,0\,1\,0 \\
\hline
D = & 0\,0\,0\,0\,0\,0\,0\,0\,0\,1\,0\,0\,0\,0
\end{array}
$$

D & $DF \neq 0^{|P|}$ and $j > 0$, then $last \leftarrow 3$

$$
\begin{array}{ll}
 & 0\,0\,0\,0\,0\,0\,0\,0\,0\,0\,0\,0\,0\,0 \\
B[\mathrm{T}] & 0\,1\,0\,1\,0\,1\,0\,1\,0\,1\,0\,0\,0\,0\,1 \\
\hline
D = & 0\,0\,0\,0\,0\,0\,0\,0\,0\,0\,0\,0\,0\,0
\end{array}
$$

3.4.2 Set Backward Dawg Matching idea

The **SBDM** algorithm uses a suffix automaton to recognize backwards the factors in a window of size ℓmin that is shifted along the text.

3.4.2.1 Suffix automaton for a set of strings

The suffix automaton for a set of strings [BBE$^+$87] is an automaton that recognizes the suffixes of the set of strings P it is built on. Let γ be the number of states of the trie built on P ($\gamma \leq |P| + 1$). Then the number of states of the suffix automaton is at least γ and at most 2γ. It is also $O(\gamma)$ in its number of transitions.

The construction algorithm is an extension of the construction for a single string (Section 2.4.1), but this time the resulting automaton is not necessarily minimal. The construction is linear in the size of P, but it is complex and slow.

3.4.2.2 Search algorithm

The suffix automaton is built in $O(r \times \ell min)$ time on $P^{rv}_{\ell min}$, the set of reverse prefixes of length ℓmin of the strings in P [BBE$^+$87]. The search is done through a window of size ℓmin, which we slide along the text. In this window, we read backwards the longest suffix that is also a factor of one of the prefixes of length ℓmin of the strings in P. Two cases may occur.

(i) We fail to recognize a factor, that is, we reach a letter σ that does not correspond to a transition in the suffix automaton of $P^{rv}_{\ell min}$. No other prefix of a string can overlap the part of the window read. We therefore shift the window so that its new starting position corresponds to the position next to σ.

(ii) We reach the beginning of the window in a state q of the suffix automaton. This means that we recognized a prefix $L(q)$ of a string in $F(q)$ (Section 3.1). We then verify a possible occurrence by comparing each string in $F(q)$ against the text. We finally move the search window by 1 and start the search again.

The worst-case complexity of **SBDM** is $O(n \times |P|)$, which is very high. However, for reasonable numbers of strings on a not too small alphabet, this algorithm is sublinear on average. The practical limit of this algorithm is the construction of the suffix automaton. For large sets of strings, it is too slow to be amortized by the time saved on the search phase. Moreover, the memory the suffix automaton requires quickly becomes too large as the set increases. We do not describe this algorithm in depth, nor give a pseudocode, because **SBOM** uses the same approach but overcomes the bottleneck of the suffix automaton with a lighter and simpler data structure. **SBOM** is faster than **SBDM** in all cases.

Note that the algorithm can be improved using the variable *last*, as was done for **BDM** (Section 2.4.1).

3.4.3 Set Backward Oracle Matching algorithm

The **Set Backward Oracle Matching algorithm** (**SBOM**) [AR99] uses a factor oracle of the set of strings. The factor oracle of P recognizes at least all the factors of the strings in P. The search algorithm is similar to **SDBM**. We slide a window of size ℓmin along the text, reading backward a suffix of the window in the factor oracle. If we fail on a letter σ, we can safely shift the window past σ. If not, we reach the beginning of the window and verify a subset of P against the text.

3.4.3.1 Factor oracle of a set of strings

The factor oracle construction on a set of strings resembles the Aho-Corasick automaton construction. The only difference appears when going down the supply path looking for an outgoing transition labeled by σ. In the Aho-Corasick automaton construction, if this transition does not exist, we just jump to the next state on the supply path (Section 3.2.2). In the factor oracle construction, we create in addition a transition labeled by σ from each state on the supply path to the state where the original transition leads.

More precisely, we begin by building the trie of the set of strings P with the algorithm given in Figure 3.6. The states of the factor oracle are those of the trie as well as the initial state I and the terminal states. Hence, the factor oracle has at most $|P| + 1$ states, including the initial one.

To build the "external transitions," which are at most $|P|$, we associate to each state q a "supply state," computed simultaneously with the new transitions in transversal order. The supply state of the initial state is set to θ.

To explain the construction, we assume that we have already computed the supply function of all the states before state *Current* in transversal order. We consider the parent *Parent* of *Current* in the trie, leading to *Current* by σ, that is, $Current = \delta_{OR}(Parent, \sigma)$. The supply state $S_{OR}(Parent)$ has already been computed, and we go down the supply function from state $S_{OR}(Parent)$. We use a variable *Down* initialized to $S_{OR}(Parent)$ and we repeat the following steps.

ST_1 If $Down = \theta$, then $S_{OR}(Current) \leftarrow I$.

ST_2 If $Down \neq \theta$ and there does not exist a transition from $Down$ labeled by σ, then build a transition from state $Down$ to state $Current$ by σ and return to step ST_1 with $Down \leftarrow S_{OR}(Down)$.

ST_3 If $Down \neq \theta$ and there exists a transition from $Down$ labeled by σ leading to a state Im, then set $S_{OR}(Current) \leftarrow Im$ and stop processing state $Current$.

The resulting factor automaton recognizes at least all factors of P [AR99]. The construction algorithm is worst-case time $O(|P|)$. Its pseudo-code is given in Figure 3.20.

Build_Oracle_Multiple($P = \{p^1, p^2, \ldots, p^r\}$)
1. $OR\_trie \leftarrow$ **Trie**(P)
            δ_{OR} is its transition function
2.   Mark the states that correspond to an entire string p^i as terminal
3. $I \leftarrow$ root of OR_trie
4. $S_{OR}(I) \leftarrow \theta$
5.   **For** $Current$ in transversal order **Do**
6. $Parent \leftarrow$ parent in OR_trie of $Current$
7. $\sigma \leftarrow$ label of the transition from $Parent$ to $Current$
8. $Down \leftarrow S_{OR}(Parent)$
9.   **While** $Down \neq \theta$ AND $\delta_{OR}(Down, \sigma) = \theta$ **Do**
10. $\delta_{OR}(Down, \sigma) \leftarrow Current$
11. $Down \leftarrow S_{OR}(Down)$
12.   **End of while**
13.   **If** $Down \neq \theta$ **Then**
14. $S_{OR}(Current) \leftarrow \delta_{OR}(Down, \sigma)$
15.   **Else** $S_{OR}(Current) \leftarrow I$
16.   **End of if**
17.   **End of for**

Fig. 3.20. Construction of the factor oracle for a set $P = \{p^1, p^2, \ldots, p^r\}$. The state $Current$ goes through the trie OR_trie built on P in transversal order. The state $Down$ goes down the supply links from the parent of $Current$ looking for an outgoing transition labeled with the same character as between $Current$ and its parent, creating it if it does not exist.

3.4.3.2 Search with the factor oracle

The factor oracle is built in $O(r \times \ell min)$ time on the reverse prefixes of length ℓmin of the strings in P. The search is done through a window of size ℓmin, which we slide along the text. In this window, we read backwards the longest suffix that labels a path from the initial state. Two cases may occur.

(i) We fail to recognize a factor, that is, we reach a letter σ that does not correspond to a transition in the factor oracle of $P^{rv}_{\ell min}$. No other prefix of a string can overlap the part of the window read. We therefore shift the window so that its new starting position corresponds to the position next to σ.

(ii) We reach the beginning of the window in a state q of the factor oracle. When using a suffix automaton in **SBDM**, we can be sure at this step that we recognized a prefix of one of the strings. However, the factor oracle accepts paths of size ℓmin ending in terminal states that do not correspond to any prefix. Hence, we have to verify first that we read the prefix $L(q)^{rv}$ and only if this is the case we verify a possible occurrence by comparing each string in $F(q)$ against the text. We finally move the search window by 1 and start the search again.

SBOM$(P = \{p^1, p^2, \ldots, p^r\}, T = t_1 t_2 \ldots t_n)$

1.   **Preprocessing**
2. $\ell min \leftarrow$ minimal length of strings in $p^i \in P$
3. $Or \leftarrow$ **Build_Oracle_Multiple**$(\{pref_{\ell min}(p^1)^{rv}, pref_{\ell min}(p^2)^{rv}$
            $\ldots, pref_{\ell min}(p^r)^{rv}\})$
          δ_{Or} is its transition function
4.   **For** q state of Or **Do** $F(q) \leftarrow \emptyset$
5.   **For** $i \in 1 \ldots r$ **Do**
6. $F(q) \leftarrow F(q) \cup \{i\}$, where q is the state reached by $pref_{\ell min}(p^i)^{rv}$
7.   **End of for**
8.   **Searching**
9. $pos \leftarrow 0$
10.   **While** $pos \leq n - \ell min$ **Do**
11. $Current \leftarrow$ initial state of Or
12. $j \leftarrow \ell min$
13.   **While** $j \geq 1$ AND $Current \neq \theta$ **Do**
14. $Current \leftarrow \delta_{Or}(Current, t_{pos+j})$
15. $j \leftarrow j - 1$
16.   **End of while**
17.   **If** $Current \neq \theta$ AND $j = 0$ AND $T_{pos+1 \ldots pos+\ell min} = L(Current)^{rv}$ **Then**
18.   Verify all the patterns in $F(Current)$ one by one against the text
19. $j \leftarrow 1$
20.   **End of if**
21. $pos \leftarrow pos + j$
22.   **End of while**

Fig. 3.21. Pseudo-code for the **SBOM** algorithm. The notation $pref_{\ell min}(p^i)$ denotes the prefix of size ℓmin of the string p^i.

Pseudo-code for **SBOM** is given Figure 3.21. Its worst-case complexity is $O(n \times |P|)$, the same as **SBDM**. However, this algorithm is sublinear on average. The construction of the factor oracle is fast and requires little memory, which permits using this algorithm to search large sets of strings on relatively small texts.

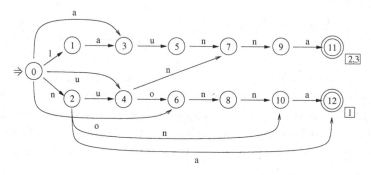

Fig. 3.22. Factor oracle for the reverse set of $P_{\ell min} = \{\text{announ}, \text{annual}\}$. Double-circled states are terminal.

Example using English We search the text "CPM_annual_conference_announce" for the set of strings $P = \{\text{announce}, \text{annual}, \text{annually}\}$. The factor oracle of the reverse set of $P_{\ell min} = \{\text{announ}, \text{annual}\}$ is shown in Figure 3.22.

1. ┌─────────┐
   │ CPM_an │ nual_conference_announce
   └─────────┘
   We read n, a in the factor oracle. We fail on the next _. We then shift the window after "_".

2. CPM_ ┌────────┐
        │ annual │ _conference_announce
        └────────┘
   We read l, a, u, n, n, a in the factor oracle. We reach the beginning of the window in state 11. We compare the strings $F(11) \rightarrow$ annual, annually. We mark an occurrence of "annual". We then shift the window by 1.

3. CPM_a ┌────────┐
         │ nnual_ │ conference_announce
         └────────┘
   We fail reading "_" in the oracle. We shift the window after "_".

4. CPM_annual_ ┌────────┐
               │ confer │ ence_announce
               └────────┘
   We fail reading r in the oracle. We shift the window after r.

5. CPM_annual_confer ┌────────┐
                     │ ence_a │ nnounce
                     └────────┘
   We read a in the oracle, but we fail on the next letter "_". We shift the window after "_".

6. CPM_annual_conference_ ┌────────┐
                          │ announ │ ce
                          └────────┘
   We read n, u, o, n, n, a in the factor oracle. We reach the beginning of the window in state 12. We compare the strings $F(12) \rightarrow$ announce. We mark an occurrence of "announce". We then shift the window by 1.

7. CPM_annual_conferencea_ ┌────────┐
                           │ nnounc │ e
                           └────────┘
   We fail reading c in the oracle. We shift the window after c. Then $pos > n - \ell min$ and the search stops.

Example using DNA We search for the set of strings $P = \{$ATATATA, TATAT, ACGATAT$\}$ in the text AGATACGATATATAC. The factor oracle for the reverse set of $P^{\ell min} = \{$ATATA, TATAT, ACGAT$\}$ is shown in Figure 3.23.

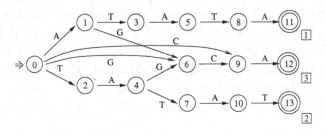

Fig. 3.23. Factor oracle for the reverse set of $P_{\ell min} = \{$ATATA, TATAT, ACGAT$\}$. Double-circled states are terminal.

1. $\boxed{\text{AGATA}}$ CGATATATAC

We read A, T, A in the factor oracle, and we fail on the next G. We then shift the window after G.

2. AG $\boxed{\text{ATACG}}$ ATATATAC

We read G, C, A in the factor oracle, and we fail on the next T. We then shift the window after T.

3. AGAT $\boxed{\text{ACGAT}}$ ATATAC

We read T, A, G, C, A in the factor oracle. We reach the beginning of the window in state 12. We compare the strings $F(12) \to$ ACGATAT. We mark an occurrence and shift the window by 1.

4. AGATA $\boxed{\text{CGATA}}$ TATAC

We read A, T, A in the factor oracle, and we fail on the next G. We then shift the window after G.

5. AGATACG $\boxed{\text{ATATA}}$ TAC

We read A, T, A, T, A in the factor oracle. We reach the beginning of the window in state 11. We compare the string $F(11) \to$ ATATATA. We mark an occurrence and shift the window by 1.

6. AGATACGA $\boxed{\text{TATAT}}$ AC

We read T, A, T, A, T in the factor oracle. We reach the beginning of the window in state 13. We compare the string $F(13) \to$ TATAT. We mark an occurrence and shift the window by 1.

7. AGATACGAT $\boxed{\text{ATATA}}$ C

We read A, T, A, T, A in the factor oracle. We reach the beginning of the window in state 11. We compare the string $F(11) \to$ ATATATA and fail. We shift the window by 1.

8. AGATACGATA $\boxed{\text{TATAC}}$

We read C, A in the factor oracle and fail on the next T. We shift the window and the search stops since $pos > n - \ell min$.

3.5 Experimental maps

We present in this section some maps of efficiency for the different multiple string matching algorithms, showing for all of them the zone in which they are most efficient in practice. The text of 10 megabytes is randomly built, as are the patterns. The experiments were performed on a $w = 32$ bits Ultra Sparc 1 running SunOs 5.6. The sets contain 5, 10, 100, and 1000 strings of the same length, varying from 5 to 100 in steps of 5. We tested all the algorithms presented. The **Wu-Manber** algorithm used in these experiments is the implementation found in *Agrep*. Its performance may vary, depending on the hash functions and the sizes of the tables used.

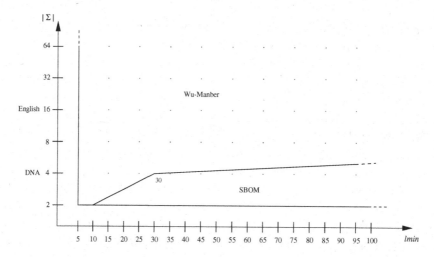

Fig. 3.24. Map of the most efficient algorithms when searching for 5 strings.

The maps are shown in Figures 3.24 to 3.27. The most efficient algorithms are just **Wu-Manber**, the advanced **Aho-Corasick**, and **SBOM**. As the set grows in size, **SBOM** becomes more and more attractive. The advanced **Aho-Corasick** also improves in comparison with the others for short strings, since it reads the text only once.

3.6 Other algorithms and references

Dynamic multiple string matching The algorithms presented in this chapter preprocess a fixed set of strings (a dictionary) in order to perform the search. However, if we need to modify the dictionary by adding or removing a string, we need to preprocess the new dictionary from scratch. The problem of searching for a set of strings in a text and allowing efficient modifications of the set is called *dynamic string matching*. It has been solved

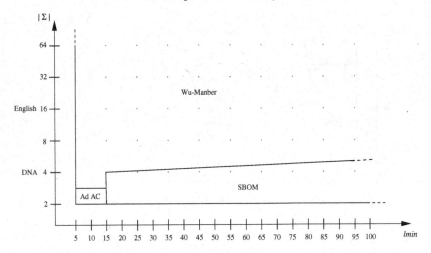

Fig. 3.25. Map of the most efficient algorithms when searching for 10 strings.

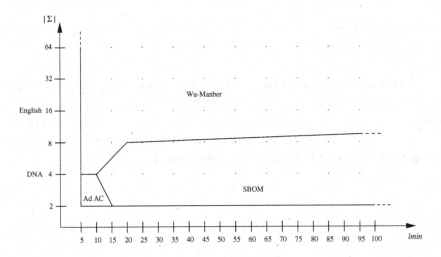

Fig. 3.26. Map of the most efficient algorithms when searching for 100 strings.

recently [SV96] with optimal worst-case complexities: (i) preprocessing of the set of strings in $O(|P|)$ time; (ii) adding or removing a string p in $O(|p|)$ time; and (iii) finding all occurrences of P in the text in $O(n + nocc)$ time, where $nocc$ is the number of occurrences of P in the text.

An application of dynamic string matching is in the matching of a set of strings with variable length "don't cares" [KR95].

On the Commentz-Walter algorithm Several variations of the **Commentz-Walter** algorithm have been designed to limit its worst-case com-

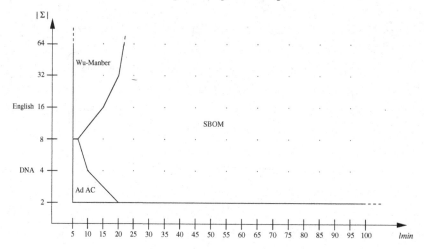

Fig. 3.27. Map of the most efficient algorithms when searching for 1000 strings.

plexity [Sri86] by using additional memory. These algorithms are, however, not efficient in practice.

On matching a set of strings on unbounded alphabets The problem of matching a set of strings of the same length m on an unbounded alphabet has been investigated [Bre95]. The resulting algorithm runs in $O((\log(|P|)/m + 1) \times n)$ comparisons after an $O(|P| \times m \times \log |A|)$ preprocessing time, where A is the alphabet on which the set P is built.

4

Extended string matching

4.1 Basic concepts

Up to now we have considered search patterns that are sequences of characters. However, in many cases one may be interested in a more sophisticated form of searching. The most complex patterns that we consider in this book are regular expressions, which are covered in Chapter 5. However, regular expression searching is costly in processing time and complex to program, so one should resort to it only if necessary. In many cases one needs far less flexibility, and the search problem can be solved more efficiently with much simpler algorithms.

We have designed this chapter on "extended strings" as a middle point between simple strings and regular expressions. We provide simple search algorithms for a number of enhancements over the basic string search, which can be solved more easily than general regular expressions. We focus on those used in text searching and computational biology applications.

We consider four extensions to the string search problem: classes of characters, bounded length gaps, optional characters, and repeatable characters. The first one allows specifying sets of characters at any pattern or text position. The second permits searching patterns containing bounded length gaps, which is of interest for protein searching (e.g., PROSITE patterns [Gus97, HBFB99]). The third allows certain characters to appear optionally in a pattern occurrence, and the last permits a given character to appear multiple times in an occurrence, which includes wild cards. We finally consider some limited multipattern search capabilities.

Different occurrences of a pattern may have different lengths, and there may be several occurrences starting or ending at the same text position. Among the several choices for reporting these occurrences, we choose to report all the initial or all the final occurrence positions, depending on what is more natural for each algorithm.

In this chapter we make heavy use of bit-parallel algorithms. With some extra work, other algorithms can be adapted to handle some extended patterns as well, but bit-parallel algorithms provide the maximum flexibility and in general the best performance. We show that **Shift-And** can be adapted by changing the mechanism to simulate a new nondeterministic automaton. **BNDM** can be adapted as well, although we will be faced with the problem that the pattern occurrences need not have the same length as the pattern, so it will be necessary to verify, each time we arrive at the beginning of a window, whether we have a real match or not.

All the techniques in this chapter can be plugged into the algorithms in Chapter 6 for approximate searching. Some can also be combined with regular expression searching (Chapter 5).

4.2 Classes of characters

4.2.1 Classes in the pattern

Our simplest extension of string matching permits each pattern position to match a *set* of characters rather than a single character. The pattern is a sequence over $\wp(\Sigma)$, that is, $p = p_1 p_2 \ldots p_m$, where $p_j \subseteq \Sigma$. We say that $p' \in \Sigma^*$ is an occurrence of p whenever $p'_j \in p_j$ for all $j \in 1 \ldots m$. A simple string is a particular case of this type of pattern.

It is usual to denote sets of characters by enumerating their components in square brackets, or by using ranges of characters when a total linear order is clear. For example, "[Aa]nnual" matches "Annual" and "annual", while "[0-9][0-9]/[0-9][0-9]/199[0-9]" matches dates in the 1990s. We will use this notation throughout the chapter, as well as the symbol Σ to denote a pattern position matching the whole alphabet.

Two simple extensions that can be expressed using classes of characters are (1) "don't care" symbols, which match any text character, corresponding to the class Σ; (2) case-insensitive searching, which corresponds to replacing each pattern character by a class formed from its uppercase and its lowercase version; for example, "[Aa][Nn][Nn][Uu][Aa][Ll]" matches the string "annual" in case-insensitive form.

Assume that we have a bit-parallel algorithm, such as **Shift-And** or **BNDM** (Chapter 2). The only connection between the pattern and the text is made at preprocessing time by building a table B, which for each character c gives the bit mask of the pattern positions matching c. Now assume that p is a sequence of classes of characters. The bit-parallel algorithms can be used directly provided we change the preprocessing. We replace line 3 of **Shift-And** (Figure 2.6) by

For $j \in 1 \dots m$ **Do**
    For $c \in p_j$ **Do** $B[c] \leftarrow B[c] \mid 0^{m-j}10^{j-1}$
End of for

or, alternatively, line 3 of **BNDM** (Figure 2.16) by

For $j \in 1 \dots m$ **Do**
    For $c \in p_j$ **Do** $B[c] \leftarrow B[c] \mid 0^{j-1}10^{m-j}$
End of for

Shift-Or needs to reverse the bits and change "|" to "&". Figure 4.1 shows an example of the resulting mask B for the **Shift-And**.

c	$B[c]$	c	$B[c]$
0	1 0 0 0 0 0 0 0 0 0 0 0 0 0	9	1 1 1 0 0 0 0 0 0 0 0 0 0 0
1	1 0 0 1 0 0 0 0 0 0 0 0 0 0	A	0 0 0 0 0 0 0 0 0 0 0 0 0 1
2	1 0 0 0 0 0 0 0 0 0 0 0 0 0	a	0 0 0 0 0 0 0 0 0 1 0 0 1
3	1 0 0 0 0 0 0 0 0 0 0 0 0 0	f	0 0 0 0 0 1 0 0 0 0 0 0 0 0
4	1 0 0 0 0 0 0 0 0 0 0 0 0 0	l	0 0 0 0 0 0 0 0 0 1 0 0 0 0
5	1 0 0 0 0 0 0 0 0 0 0 0 0 0	n	0 0 0 0 0 0 0 0 0 0 0 1 1 0
6	1 0 0 0 0 0 0 0 0 0 0 0 0 0	o	0 0 0 0 0 0 1 0 0 0 0 0 0 0
7	1 0 0 0 0 0 0 0 0 0 0 0 0 0	s	0 0 0 0 0 0 0 0 1 0 0 0 0 0
8	1 0 0 0 0 0 0 0 0 0 0 0 0 0	_	0 0 0 0 1 0 0 1 0 0 0 0 0 0

Fig. 4.1. The resulting mask B for the pattern "`[Aa]nnals_of_199[0-9]`".

Non-bit-parallel algorithms can be extended to handle classes of characters too, but none of them provide the same combination of simplicity and performance robustness. Let us examine first the **Horspool** algorithm (Section 2.3.2). We need to change, in Figure 2.12, line 3 in the preprocessing and line 8 in the search. However, the performance of **Horspool** degrades rapidly, especially if there is a large class near the end of the pattern. This is because the shifts for all the characters contained in the large class will be short. Thus its performance is extremely sensitive to the number, size, and position of the classes.

Now consider **BDM** (Section 2.4.1). No efficient algorithm is known to extend the deterministic suffix automaton to handle classes of characters [NR00]. The same is true for the **BOM** algorithm of Section 2.4.3.

From the classical algorithms, the extension that performs best is the classical **Boyer-Moore** algorithm (Section 2.3.1). However, it is complex to implement and does not perform as well as **BNDM** [NR00].

Performance of **Shift-And/Shift-Or** is unaffected by the use of classes of characters. However, it is inferior to that of **BNDM** in most cases. But **BNDM** is affected because it is more likely to find occurrences of pattern factors in the window. A rough analysis is as follows: If S is the average size of a class, then the result is the same as if we had an alphabet of size $|\Sigma|/S$, and hence the average complexity of **BNDM** becomes $O(n \log_{|\Sigma|/S}(m)/m)$.

Just as **BNDM** is better than **Horspool** with smaller alphabets, it is more resistant than **Horspool** to the size and number of classes in the pattern. When the classes become too numerous or too large, it may be better to switch to **Shift-Or**, which is slightly faster than **Shift-And**. However, in the extensions that we consider next **Shift-Or** is not faster, and **Shift-And** is preferable because it is more intuitive.

4.2.2 Classes in the text

In computational biology applications there may be uncertainty on some text characters; that is, one knows that a given text position holds some character in a given set, but cannot tell which one. This situation is modeled by allowing classes of characters in the text. It is normally represented by using new character codes that are known to represent given sets of "normal" character codes.

Formally, the text is a sequence over $\wp(\Sigma)$, that is, $T = t_1 t_2 \ldots t_n$, where $t_i \subseteq \Sigma$. The pattern is said to occur at text position $t_{i+1} \ldots t_{i+m}$ if $p_j \cap t_{i+j} \neq \emptyset$ for all $j \in 1 \ldots m$.

Bit-parallelism gives a simple way to deal with this. Let us say that character code c represents the set $\{c_1, c_2, \ldots, c_k\}$. Then, *after* building the mask B of the normal characters in the preprocessing of either **Shift-And** or **BNDM**, we add for each such c

$B[c] \leftarrow 0^m$
For $i \in 1 \ldots k$ **Do** $B[c] \leftarrow B[c] \mid B[c_i]$

which makes c match every pattern position that matches some c_i.

This can be extended to permit special characters that are sets of other special characters, as long as they are processed in the correct order. More-

over, it can be combined with classes of characters in the pattern, which are
dealt with when the table B of the normal characters is built.

On small alphabets, such as that of DNA sequences, an interesting choice
is to extend the character set to $\Sigma' = \{0 \ldots 2^{|\Sigma|} - 1\}$ and represent the set
using bit-parallelism. The new alphabet is formed by bit masks of length
$|\Sigma|$, where the i-th bit indicates the presence in the set of the i-th character.
For example, if the alphabet is $\{A, G, C, T\}$, then single characters will be
represented by $A = 0001$, $G = 0010$, $C = 0100$, and $T = 1000$, and classes
will be represented by, for example, $\{A, C\} = 0101$.

Under this representation we need to build a different table B' that ranges
over the integers $\{0 \ldots 2^{|\Sigma|} - 1\}$. Assume for simplicity that $\Sigma = \{0 \ldots |\Sigma| - 1\}$. The construction of B', given B, is as follows:

> $B'[0] \leftarrow 0^m$
> **For** $c \in 0 \ldots |\Sigma| - 1$ **Do**
>   **For** $j \in 0 \ldots 2^c - 1$ **Do** $B'[2^c + j] \leftarrow B[c] \mid B'[j]$
> **End of for**

It takes $O(2^{|\Sigma|})$ time. With DNA, for example, the table B' has just 16
entries. The search process is unaltered: We simply use B' instead of B.

4.3 Bounded length gaps

An important case of protein searching is that of PROSITE patterns [Gus97,
HBFB99]. A PROSITE pattern contains classes of characters and bounded
length gaps, which match any string whose length is between given bounds.
In the notation of PROSITE, pattern characters or classes are separated
by hyphens and $x(a, b)$ denotes a gap of length between a and b. Also,
$x(a) = x(a, a)$ and $x = x(1)$, which is equivalent to the class Σ. For example,
the pattern $a - b - c - x(1, 3) - d - e$ matches `"abcfde"` and `"abcfddde"`,
but not `"abcffffde"`. Although we focus on the concrete case of PROSITE
patterns in this chapter, the algorithms can handle other types of pattern
with bounded length gaps.

Figure 4.2 shows an NFA for the pattern $a - b - c - x(1, 3) - d - e$. Between
the characters `"c"` and `"d"` we have inserted three transitions that can be
followed by any character, which corresponds to the maximum length of
the gap. Two ε-transitions leave the state where `"abc"` has been recognized
and skip one and two subsequent edges, respectively. This skips one to three
text characters before finding the `"de"` at the end of the pattern. The initial
self-loop allows the match to begin at any text position.

Let m be the number of symbols in the pattern, each symbol being a class

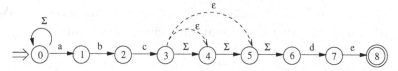

Fig. 4.2. A nondeterministic automaton for the pattern $a - b - c - x(1,3) - d - e$. Dashed arrows represent ε-transitions, which can be followed without consuming any input.

of characters or a gap specification of the form $x(a,b)$. Also let ℓmin and ℓmax be the minimum and maximum lengths of a pattern occurrence. Both can be obtained from the pattern in $O(m)$ time by adding 1 for each class of characters and adding a for the minimum and b for the maximum for each gap specification $x(a,b)$. Finally, let L be the number of states of the corresponding NFA, not including the first state. It is not hard to see that $L = \ell max$. In our example, $m = 6$, $\ell min = 6$, and $\ell max = L = 8$.

We now describe two bit-parallel algorithms presented in [NR01b] which are able to find patterns quickly patterns with gaps (PROSITE in particular). They extend **Shift-And** and **BNDM**.

4.3.1 Extending Shift-And

We augment the representation of **Shift-And** by adding the ε-transitions. We call "gap-initial" states those states i from which an ε-transition leaves. For each gap-initial state i corresponding to a gap $x(a,b)$, we define its "gap-final" state to be $(i + b - a + 1)$, that is, the one *following* the last state reached by an ε-transition leaving i. In Figure 4.2, we have one gap-initial state (3) and one gap-final state (6).

We create a bit mask I that has 1 in the gap-initial states and another mask F that has 1 in the gap-final states. In Figure 4.2, the corresponding I and F masks are 00000100 and 00100000, respectively. After performing the normal **Shift-And** step, we simulate all the ε-moves with the operation

$$D \;\leftarrow\; D \;|\; ((F - (D \;\&\; I)) \;\&\; \sim F)$$

The rationale is as follows. $D \;\&\; I$ isolates the *active* gap-initial states. Subtracting this from F has two possible outcomes for each gap-initial state i. First, if i is active, the result will have 1 in all the states from i to $(i+b-a)$, successfully propagating the active state i to the desired target states. Second, if i is inactive, the outcome will have 1 only in state $(i + b - a + 1)$. This undesired 1 is removed by operating on the result with "$\& \sim F$". Once the propagation has been done, we OR the result with the already active states in D. Note that the propagations of different gaps do not interfere with one another, since all the subtractions have a local effect.

Gaps-Shift-And $(p = p_1 p_2 \ldots p_m,\ T = t_1 t_2 \ldots t_n)$

1. Preprocessing
2. $L \leftarrow$ maximum length of an occurrence
3.   **For** $c \in \Sigma$ **Do** $B[c] \leftarrow 0^L$
4. $I \leftarrow 0^L$, $F \leftarrow 0^L$
5. $i \leftarrow 0$
6.   **For** $j \in 1 \ldots m$ **Do**
7.   **If** p_j is of the form $x(a,b)$ **Then**
8. $I \leftarrow I \mid 0^{L-i}10^{i-1}$
9. $F \leftarrow F \mid 0^{L-(i+b-a)-1}10^{i+b-a}$
10.   **For** $c \in \Sigma$ **Do** $B[c] \leftarrow B[c] \mid 0^{L-i-b}1^b0^i$
11. $i \leftarrow i + b$
12.   **Else** /* p_j is a class of characters */
13.   **For** $c \in p_j$ **Do** $B[c] \leftarrow B[c] \mid 0^{L-i-1}10^i$
14. $i \leftarrow i + 1$
15.   **End of if**
16.   **End of for**
17. Searching
18. $D \leftarrow 0^L$
19.   **For** $pos \in 1 \ldots n$ **Do**
20. $D \leftarrow ((D << 1) \mid 0^{L-1}1)\ \&\ B[t_{pos}]$
21. $D \leftarrow D \mid ((F - (D\ \&\ I))\ \&\ \sim F)$
22.   **If** $D\ \&\ 10^{L-1} \neq 0^L$ **Then** report an occurrence ending at pos
23.   **End of for**

Fig. 4.3. The extension of **Shift-And** to handle PROSITE expressions.

Figure 4.3 shows the complete algorithm. For simplicity we assume that there are no gaps at the beginning or at the end of the pattern and that consecutive gaps have been merged into one. The preprocessing takes $O(m|\Sigma|)$ time, while the scanning needs $O(n)$ time. If $\ell max > w$, however, we need several machine words for the simulation, and it then takes $O(n\lceil \ell max/w \rceil)$ time.

Example of Gaps-Shift-And We search for the pattern $a-b-c-x(1,3)-d-e$ in the text `"abcabcffdee"`.

$$B = \begin{cases} \begin{array}{|c|c|} \hline a & 00111001 \\ \hline b & 00111010 \\ \hline c & 00111100 \\ \hline d & 01111000 \\ \hline e & 10111000 \\ \hline * & 00111000 \\ \hline \end{array} \end{cases}$$

$I = 00000100$
$F = 00100000$
$D = 00000000$

1. Reading **a** 0 0 1 1 1 0 0 1
   $D =$ 0 0 0 0 0 0 0 1

   We now apply the propagation formula on D. The result is $((F - (D \& I)) \& \sim F) = ((00100000 - 00000000) \& 11011111) = 00000000$, and hence D does not change. We do not mention again the propagation formula unless it has an effect on D.

2. Reading **b** 0 0 1 1 1 0 1 0
   $D =$ 0 0 0 0 0 0 1 0

3. Reading **c** 0 0 1 1 1 1 0 0
   $D =$ 0 0 0 0 0 1 0 0

   At this point the ε-transitions take effect: $((F - (D \& I)) \& \sim F)$ yields $((00100000 - 00000100) \& 11011111) = 00011100$, where states 4 and 5 have been activated. The new D value is

   $D =$ 0 0 0 1 1 1 0 0.

4. Reading **a** 0 0 1 1 1 0 0 1
   $D =$ 0 0 1 1 1 0 0 1

5. Reading **b** 0 0 1 1 1 0 1 0
   $D =$ 0 0 1 1 0 0 1 0

6. Reading **c** 0 0 1 1 1 1 0 0
   $D =$ 0 0 1 0 0 1 0 0

   The propagation formula takes effect again and produces

   $D =$ 0 0 1 1 1 1 0 0.

7. Reading **f** 0 0 1 1 1 0 0 0
   $D =$ 0 0 1 1 1 0 0 0

8. Reading **f** 0 0 1 1 1 0 0 0
   $D =$ 0 0 1 1 0 0 0 0

9. Reading **d** 0 1 1 1 1 0 0 0
   $D =$ 0 1 1 0 0 0 0 0

10. Reading **e** 1 0 1 1 1 0 0 0
    $D =$ 1 0 0 0 0 0 0 0

    The last bit of D is set, so we mark an occurrence. The gap has matched the text "ff".

11. Reading **e** 1 0 1 1 1 0 0 0
    $D =$ 0 0 0 0 0 0 0 0

4.3.2 Extending BNDM

We now try to extend **BNDM** (Section 2.4.2) to handle patterns with gaps. To recognize all the reverse factors of the pattern, we use the same automaton of Figure 4.2 on the reversed pattern, but without the initial self-loop, and we consider that all the states are active at the beginning. Figure 4.4 shows the automaton for the pattern $a - b - c - x(1,3) - d - e$. A string read by this automaton is a factor of the pattern as long as there exists at least one active state. Note that now the arrows depart from the state next to "d", but the effect is the same as before.

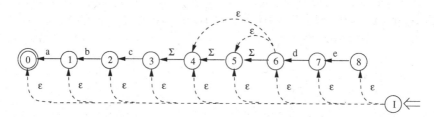

Fig. 4.4. A nondeterministic automaton to recognize all the reversed factors of the PROSITE pattern $a - b - c - x(1,3) - d - e$.

The bit-parallel simulation of this automaton is similar to that of the forward automaton. The only modifications are (*a*) we build it on the reversed pattern; (*b*) the bit mask D that registers the state of the search has to be initialized with $D = 1^L$ to represent the initial ε-transitions; and (*c*) we do not OR D with $0^{L-1}1$ when we shift it, since there is no longer an initial loop.

The backward matching algorithm shifts a window of size ℓmin along the text. Inside each window, the algorithm traverses the text backwards trying to recognize a factor of the pattern. Each time the automaton reaches its final state we have recognized a pattern prefix and we store the window position in the variable *last*.

If the backward search inside the window fails before reaching the beginning of the window, then the search window is shifted to the beginning of the longest prefix recognized, as in **BNDM**.

If the beginning of the window is reached with the automaton still holding active states, then some factor of length ℓmin of the pattern has been recognized in the window. Unlike exact string matching, where all occurrences have the length of the pattern, reaching the beginning of the window here does not automatically imply that we have recognized the whole pattern. We need to verify a possible occurrence, which can be as long as ℓmax, starting at the beginning of the window.

To carry out this verification, we read the characters again from the beginning of the window with the forward automaton of Figure 4.2, but without the initial self-loop. This makes the automaton *recognize* rather than *search for* the pattern. To simulate that automaton without the initial self-loop, we simply do

$$D \leftarrow (D << 1) \ \& \ B[t_{pos}]$$
$$D \leftarrow D \ | \ ((F - (D \ \& \ I)) \ \& \ \sim F)$$

This forward verification ends when either (1) the automaton reaches its final state, in which case we have found the pattern; or (2) the automaton runs out of active states, in which case there is no pattern occurrence starting at the window. Since there is no initial loop, the forward verification surely finishes after reading at most ℓmax text characters. We then shift the search window to the position of the last pattern prefix recognized and resume the search.

Figure 4.5 shows the complete algorithm. Its worst-case complexity is $O(n \times \ell max)$, which is poor in theory. In particular, let us consider the

---

Gaps-BNDM $(p = p_1 p_2 \dots p_m,\ T = t_1 t_2 \dots t_n)$

1.   Preprocessing
2. $L \leftarrow$ maximum length of an occurrence
3. $\ell min \leftarrow$ minimum length of an occurrence
4.   **For** $c \in \Sigma$ **Do** $B[c] \leftarrow 0^L$
5. $I \leftarrow 0^L$, $F \leftarrow 0^L$
6. $i \leftarrow 0$
7.   **For** $j \in 1 \dots m$ **Do**
8.   **If** p_j is of the form $x(a, b)$ **Then**
9. $I \leftarrow I \mid 0^{i+b} 10^{L-(i+b)-1}$
10. $F \leftarrow F \mid 0^{i+a-1} 10^{L-(i+a)}$
11.   **For** $c \in \Sigma$ **Do** $B[c] \leftarrow B[c] \mid 0^i 1^b 0^{L-i-b}$
12. $i \leftarrow i + b$
13.   **Else** /* p_j is a class of characters */
14.   **For** $c \in p_j$ **Do** $B[c] \leftarrow B[c] \mid 0^i 10^{L-i-1}$
15. $i \leftarrow i + 1$
16.   **End of if**
17.   **End of for**
18. Searching
19. $pos \leftarrow 0$
20.   **While** $pos \leq n - \ell min$ **Do**
21. $j \leftarrow \ell min$, $last \leftarrow \ell min$
22. $D \leftarrow 1^L$
23.   **While** $D \neq 0^L$ AND $j > 0$ **Do**
24. $D \leftarrow D\ \&\ B[t_{pos+j}]$
25. $D \leftarrow D \mid ((F - (D\ \&\ I))\ \&\ \sim F)$
26. $j \leftarrow j - 1$
27.   **If** $D\ \&\ 10^{L-1} \neq 0^L$ **Then** /* prefix recognized */
28.   **If** $j > 0$ **Then** $last \leftarrow j$
29.   **Else** check a possible occurrence starting at pos
30.   **End of if**
31. $D \leftarrow D << 1$
32.   **End of while**
33. $pos \leftarrow pos + last$
34.   **End of while**

Fig. 4.5. The extension of **BNDM** to handle PROSITE expressions.

maximum gap length G in the pattern. If $G \geq \ell min$, then *every* text window of length ℓmin *is* a factor of the pattern; so we will always traverse the whole window during the backward scan, for a minimum complexity of $O(n)$. Consequently, this approach should not be used when $G \geq \ell min$. It has been shown experimentally in [NR01b] that **Gaps-BNDM** is better than **Gaps-Shift-And** whenever $G + 1 < \ell min/2$.

Example of Gaps-BNDM We search for the pattern $a - b - c - x(1,3) - d - e$ in the text `"abcabcffdee"`.

$$B = \begin{cases} \begin{array}{c|c} \text{a} & 1\,0\,0\,1\,1\,1\,0\,0 \\ \text{b} & 0\,1\,0\,1\,1\,1\,0\,0 \\ \text{c} & 0\,0\,1\,1\,1\,1\,0\,0 \\ \text{d} & 0\,0\,0\,1\,1\,1\,1\,0 \\ \text{e} & 0\,0\,0\,1\,1\,1\,0\,1 \\ * & 0\,0\,0\,1\,1\,1\,0\,0 \end{array} \end{cases}$$

$I = 0\,0\,0\,0\,0\,1\,0\,0$
$F = 0\,0\,1\,0\,0\,0\,0\,0$

$\ell min = 6, \; \ell max = 8$

1. $\boxed{\text{abcabc}}$ ffdee

   $last \leftarrow 6$

   Reading c $\quad 0\,0\,1\,1\,1\,1\,0\,0$
   $\overline{\quad D = \quad 0\,0\,1\,1\,1\,1\,0\,0 \quad}$

   The propagation mechanism does not introduce any new active states in D.

   Reading b $\quad 0\,1\,0\,1\,1\,1\,0\,0$
   $\overline{\quad D = \quad 0\,1\,0\,1\,1\,0\,0\,0 \quad}$

   Reading a $\quad 1\,0\,0\,1\,1\,1\,0\,0$
   $\overline{\quad D = \quad 1\,0\,0\,1\,0\,0\,0\,0 \quad}$

   The last bit of D is activated and $j > 0$, so we set $last \leftarrow 3$.

   Reading c $\quad 0\,0\,1\,1\,1\,1\,0\,0$
   $\overline{\quad D = \quad 0\,0\,1\,0\,0\,0\,0\,0 \quad}$

   Reading b $\quad 0\,1\,0\,1\,1\,1\,0\,0$
   $\overline{\quad D = \quad 0\,1\,0\,0\,0\,0\,0\,0 \quad}$

   Reading a $\quad 1\,0\,0\,1\,1\,1\,0\,0$
   $\overline{\quad D = \quad 1\,0\,0\,0\,0\,0\,0\,0 \quad}$

   The last bit of D is active and $j = 0$, so we start a forward verification against the text `"abcabcff"`. The forward automaton finally dies without finding the pattern and we proceed to the next window, shifting by $last = 3$.

2. abc $\boxed{\text{abcffd}}$ ee

   $last \leftarrow 6$

   Reading d $\quad 0\,0\,0\,1\,1\,1\,1\,0$
   $\overline{\quad D = \quad 0\,0\,0\,1\,1\,1\,1\,0 \quad}$

   The propagation mechanism is activated, but it produces no effects.

   Reading f $\quad 0\,0\,0\,1\,1\,1\,0\,0$
   $\overline{\quad D = \quad 0\,0\,0\,1\,1\,1\,0\,0 \quad}$

   The propagation mechanism is activated, but again it produces no effects.

   Reading f $\quad 0\,0\,0\,1\,1\,1\,0\,0$
   $\overline{\quad D = \quad 0\,0\,0\,1\,1\,0\,0\,0 \quad}$

   Reading c $\quad 0\,0\,1\,1\,1\,1\,0\,0$
   $\overline{\quad D = \quad 0\,0\,1\,1\,0\,0\,0\,0 \quad}$

   Reading b $\quad 0\,1\,0\,1\,1\,1\,0\,0$
   $\overline{\quad D = \quad 0\,1\,0\,0\,0\,0\,0\,0 \quad}$

   Reading c $\quad 1\,0\,0\,1\,1\,1\,0\,0$
   $\overline{\quad D = \quad 1\,0\,0\,0\,0\,0\,0\,0 \quad}$

   The last bit of D is set and $j = 0$, so we perform a forward verification against the text `"abcffdee"`, which produces a match. Therefore, the current text position (4) is reported as the beginning of an occurrence.
   The window is shifted by $last = 6$ and we finish the search.

4.4 Optional characters

We now allow the possibility that some pattern positions may or may not appear in the text. We call these "optional characters" (or classes) and denote them by putting a question mark after the optional position. Consider the pattern `"abc?d?efg?h"`, which matches, for example, `"abefh"` and `"abdefgh"`. A nondeterministic automaton accepting this pattern is shown in Figure 4.6.

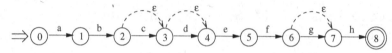

Fig. 4.6. A nondeterministic automaton accepting the pattern "abc?d?efg?h".

As the figure shows, multiple consecutive optional characters could exist. The simplest solution, for when that does not happen, is to set up a bit mask O with 1's in the optional positions (in our example, $O = 01001100$) and let the 1's in previous states of D propagate to them. Hence, after the normal update to D in, say, the **Shift-And** algorithm (i.e., after line 7 in Figure 2.6), we perform

$$D \;\leftarrow\; D \mid ((D << 1) \,\&\, O)$$

This solution works if we have read "abcdef" (then $D = 00100000$) and the next text character is "h", since the above operation would convert D into 01100000 before operating it against $B[\mathbf{h}] = 10000000$. However, it does not work if the text is "abefgh", where both consecutive optional characters have been omitted.

A general solution needs to propagate each active state in D so as to flood with 1's all the states ahead of it that correspond to optional characters. In our example, when D is 00000010 we would like it to become 00001110 after the flooding.

This is achieved in [Nav01b] with a mechanism resembling that of Section 4.3. Three masks, A, I, and F, mark the boundaries of *blocks* of consecutive optional characters. Each block starts at the position *before* the first optional character in the sequence and finishes at the position of the last optional character. For example, in Figure 4.6 the first block starts at position 2 and ends at position 4. The i-th bit of A is set if position i in p is optional, that of I is set if i is the position *preceding* the first optional character of a block, and that of F is set if i is the position of the last optional character of a block. In our example, $A = 01001100$, $I = 00100010$, and $F = 01001000$. After performing the normal transition on D, we do the following

$$Df \;\leftarrow\; D \mid F$$
$$D \;\leftarrow\; D \mid (A \,\&\, ((\sim (Df - I)) \wedge Df))$$

The first line sets the positions finishing blocks in D to 1. In the second line we add some active states to D. Since the states to add are AND-ed with A, let us consider what happens inside a specific block. We want the first 1 counting from the right to flood all the block bits to its left. We subtract I from Df, which is equivalent to subtracting 1 at each block. This subtraction cannot propagate outside the block because there is a 1 coming from "| F" in Df at the highest bit of the block. The effect of the subtraction is that all the bits until the first 1 (counting from the right) are reversed (e.g., $1000000 - 1 = 0111111$) and the rest are unchanged. In general, $b_x b_{x-1} \ldots b_{x-y} 10^z - 1 = b_x b_{x-1} \ldots b_{x-y} 01^z$. When this is reversed by the "$\sim$" operation we get $\sim b_x \sim b_{x-1} \ldots \sim b_{x-y} 10^z$. Finally, when this is XOR-ed with the same $Df = b_x b_{x-1} \ldots b_{x-y} 10^z$ we get $1^{x-y+1} 0^{z+1}$.

This gives the effect we wanted: The first 1 flooded all the bits to the left. The 1 itself has been converted to 0, but it is restored when the result is OR-ed with the original D. This works even if the last active state in the optional block is the leftmost bit of the block. Note that it is necessary to AND with A at the end to avoid propagating the XOR outside the block. We will see a combined example at the end of Section 4.5.

Note that optional characters cannot be expressed as gaps, since they can appear consecutively and they do not necessarily match with arbitrary characters. On the other hand, bounded length gaps *can* be expressed using optional characters; for example, $a - b - c - x(1, 3) - d - e$ is equivalent to "abc$\Sigma\Sigma$?Σ?de". However, the formula for the case of bounded length gaps is simpler and hence faster.

4.5 Wild cards and repeatable characters

"*Wild card*" is a term used to refer to a pattern position that matches an arbitrarily long text string, and it is usually denoted with a star. For example, "ann*al" matches the texts "annal", "annual", and "annals of biological". We are *not* using this notation because we prefer a more general one.

A wild card is a particular class of a more general feature called a "repeatable character." A repeatable character is a pattern position that can appear zero or more times in the text. We denote it with the character or class of characters followed by an asterisk; for example, AC*TCA matches ATCA, as well as ACCTCA and ACCCCCCTCA. Another example is "[a-zA-Z_] [a-zA-Z_0-9]*", which matches valid variable names in most programming languages. Under this definition, a wild card is expressed as "Σ*". The algorithms for repeatable characters are not slower nor harder to program than those for simple wild cards. Following regular expression notations, we also denote $c+ = cc*$.

Figure 4.7 shows a possible automaton for the pattern "abc+def*gh".

However, it is difficult to extend to the case where consecutive characters with stars appear, for example, "abc+def*g*h".

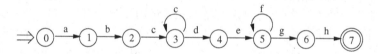

Fig. 4.7. A nondeterministic automaton accepting the pattern "abc+def*gh". The mechanism cannot be extended to consecutive stars.

A general solution that permits consecutive stars is based on the identity $c* = c+?$. We simulate directly the "+" and express the "*" operator in terms of "+" and "?". Figure 4.8 shows the automaton we use for "abc+def*gh". Hence, to deal with "*" we need to deal with repeatable and optional characters.

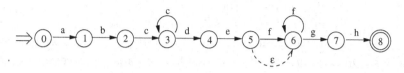

Fig. 4.8. A nondeterministic automaton accepting the pattern "abc+def*gh". It can deal with consecutive stars.

Let m be the pattern length, counting both normal characters and the three special symbols. The minimum length of an occurrence, ℓmin, is computed in $O(m)$ time as the number of normal characters in the pattern excluding those affected by "?" and "*" operators. On the other hand, the maximum length of an occurrence is unbounded when there are repeatable characters. Finally, let L be the number of states in the NFA (excluding the first one) computed as the number of normal characters in p.

For bit-parallel simulation of the operator "+" we need a table $S[c]$ that for each character c tells which pattern positions can remain active when we read the character c. In Figure 4.8, $S[\mathtt{c}] = 00000100$ and $S[\mathtt{f}] = 00100000$. A complete simulation step permitting optional and repeatable characters after reading text character t_{pos} is as follows:

$$
\begin{aligned}
D &\leftarrow ((D << 1) \mid 0^{L-1}1) \,\&\, B[t_{pos}]) \mid (D \,\&\, S[t_{pos}]) \\
Df &\leftarrow D \mid F \\
D &\leftarrow D \mid (A \,\&\, ((\sim (Df - I)) \wedge Df))
\end{aligned}
$$

The complete code is quite similar to that of patterns with gaps detailed in Section 4.3, the only change being in the simulation of a single step of the NFA. We present extended versions of **Shift-And** and of **BNDM**.

Some experimental results are presented in [Nav01b] regarding the use of optional and repeatable characters. It is shown that **Extended-BNDM** works better in most cases than **Extended-Shift-And**. The latter choice should be considered only when $\ell min \leq 3$ or when there are large repeatable classes of characters.

4.5.1 Extended Shift-And

Figure 4.9 shows pseudo-code for the **Shift-And** extension. It includes the necessary preprocessing of the pattern to deal with the symbols "+", "*", and "?". The code assumes that there are no optional or repeatable characters at the beginning or at the end of the pattern. It is not hard to augment the code to handle classes of characters.

Consider the **Extended-Shift-And** algorithm preprocessing. The preprocessing has two parts. Lines 2–17 build the mask A and the tables S and B, where S stores information about repeatable characters and A stores information about optional characters. The operator "*" is treated exactly like "+" followed by "?". Lines 18–29 build the I and F masks from A, by the simple mechanism of detecting in line 21 whether the current active bit of A belongs to a new block or not, and, if not, "moving" the bit of F that signals its end. The preprocessing takes $O(m + |\Sigma|)$ time and the search $O(n\lceil L/w \rceil)$ time.

The search code is simple compared to the preprocessing. It applies the formula to deal with optional and repeatable characters.

Example of Extended-Shift-And We search for the ending position of occurrences of the pattern "ab?c*de+f" in the text "acccdfabdeeef". We have $m = 9$ and $L = 6$. For each character we show the effect of the three lines of the processing done on D and Df.

c	B	S
a	0 0 0 0 0 1	0 0 0 0 0 0
b	0 0 0 0 1 0	0 0 0 0 0 0
c	0 0 0 1 0 0	0 0 0 1 0 0
d	0 0 1 0 0 0	0 0 0 0 0 0
e	0 1 0 0 0 0	0 1 0 0 0 0
f	1 0 0 0 0 0	0 0 0 0 0 0
*	0 0 0 0 0 0	0 0 0 0 0 0

$$A = 0\,0\,0\,1\,1\,0$$
$$I = 0\,0\,0\,0\,0\,1$$
$$F = 0\,0\,0\,1\,0\,0$$
$$D = 0\,0\,0\,0\,0\,0$$

Extended-Shift-And $(p = p_1 p_2 \ldots p_m, \ T = t_1 t_2 \ldots t_n)$

1.   Preprocessing
2. $L \leftarrow$ number of normal characters in p
3. $A \leftarrow 0^L$ /* build B, S and A */
4.   **For** $c \in \Sigma$ **Do** $B[c] \leftarrow 0^L$, $S[c] \leftarrow 0^L$
5. $i \leftarrow -1$
6.   **For** $j \in 1 \ldots m$ **Do**
7.   **If** $p_j = $ "+" **Then** $S[lastc] \leftarrow S[lastc] \mid 0^{L-i-1}10^i$
8.   **Else If** $p_j = $ "?" **Then** $A \leftarrow A \mid 0^{L-i-1}10^i$
9.   **Else If** $p_j = $ "*" **Then**
10. $S[lastc] \leftarrow S[lastc] \mid 0^{L-i-1}10^i$
11. $A \leftarrow A \mid 0^{L-i-1}10^i$
12.   **Else** /* p_j is a character */
13. $lastc \leftarrow p_j$
14. $i \leftarrow i+1$
15. $B[lastc] \leftarrow B[lastc] \mid 0^{L-i-1}10^i$
16.   **End of if**
17.   **End of for**
18. $I \leftarrow 0^L$, $F \leftarrow 0^L$ /* build I and F */
19.   **For** $i \in 0 \ldots L-1$ **Do**
20.   **If** $A \ \& \ 0^{L-i-1}10^i \neq 0^L$ **Then**
21.   **If** $F \ \& \ 0^{L-i}10^{i-1} = 0^L$ **Then**
22. $I \leftarrow I \mid 0^{L-i}10^{i-1}$
23. $F \leftarrow F \mid 0^{L-i-1}10^i$
24.   **Else**
25. $F \leftarrow F \ \& \ 1^{L-i}01^{i-1}$
26. $F \leftarrow F \mid 0^{L-i-1}10^i$
27.   **End of if**
28.   **End of if**
29.   **End of for**
30.   Searching
31. $D \leftarrow 0^L$
32.   **For** $pos \in 1 \ldots n$ **Do**
33. $D \leftarrow ((D << 1) \mid 0^{L-1}1) \ \& \ B[t_{pos}]) \mid (D \ \& \ S[t_{pos}])$
34. $Df \leftarrow D \mid F$
35. $D \leftarrow D \mid (A \ \& \ ((\sim (Df - I)) \wedge Df))$
36.   **If** $D \ \& \ 10^{L-1} \neq 0^L$ **Then** report an occurrence ending at pos
37.   **End of for**

Fig. 4.9. The extension of **Shift-And** to handle patterns with optional and repeatable characters.

1.	Reading a	B	0 0 0 0 0 1
		S	0 0 0 0 0 0
		D	0 0 0 0 0 1
		Df	0 0 0 1 0 1
		D	0 0 0 1 1 1

The propagation over the two optional characters "b?c*" took effect.

2.	Reading c	B	0 0 0 1 0 0
		S	0 0 0 1 0 0
		D	0 0 0 1 0 0
		Df	0 0 0 1 0 0
		D	0 0 0 1 0 0

This time there were no special propagation effects.

3. Reading c B 0 0 0 1 0 0
                 S 0 0 0 1 0 0
                 _____
                 D 0 0 0 1 0 0
                 Df 0 0 0 1 0 0
                 D 0 0 0 1 0 0

The S table permitted the third bit of D to stay active.

4. Reading c B 0 0 0 1 0 0
                 S 0 0 0 1 0 0
                 _____
                 D 0 0 0 1 0 0
                 Df 0 0 0 1 0 0
                 D 0 0 0 1 0 0

5. Reading d B 0 0 1 0 0 0
                 S 0 0 0 0 0 0
                 _____
                 D 0 0 1 0 0 0
                 Df 0 0 1 1 0 0
                 D 0 0 1 0 0 0

6. Reading f B 1 0 0 0 0 0
                 S 0 0 0 0 0 0
                 _____
                 D 0 0 0 0 0 0
                 Df 0 0 0 1 0 0
                 D 0 0 0 0 0 0

7. Reading a B 0 0 0 0 0 1
                 S 0 0 0 0 0 0
                 _____
                 D 0 0 0 0 0 1
                 Df 0 0 0 1 0 1
                 D 0 0 0 1 1 1

The propagation over the two optional characters "b?c*" took effect again.

8. Reading b B 0 0 0 0 1 0
                 S 0 0 0 0 0 0
                 _____
                 D 0 0 0 0 1 0
                 Df 0 0 0 1 1 0
                 D 0 0 0 1 1 0

The propagation over the optional character "c*" took effect.

9. Reading d B 0 0 1 0 0 0
                 S 0 0 0 0 0 0
                 _____
                 D 0 0 1 0 0 0
                 Df 0 0 1 1 0 0
                 D 0 0 1 0 0 0

No propagation effects this time. The previous propagation has allowed us to ignore a nonexistent "c" in the text.

10. Reading e B 0 1 0 0 0 0
                 S 0 1 0 0 0 0
                 _____
                 D 0 1 0 0 0 0
                 Df 0 1 0 1 0 0
                 D 0 1 0 0 0 0

11. Reading e B 0 1 0 0 0 0
                 S 0 1 0 0 0 0
                 _____
                 D 0 1 0 0 0 0
                 Df 0 1 0 1 0 0
                 D 0 1 0 0 0 0

The S table permits the automaton to stay alive while it keeps reading "e".

12. Reading e B 0 1 0 0 0 0
                 S 0 1 0 0 0 0
                 _____
                 D 0 1 0 0 0 0
                 Df 0 1 0 1 0 0
                 D 0 1 0 0 0 0

13. Reading f B 1 0 0 0 0 0
                 S 0 0 0 0 0 0
                 _____
                 D 1 0 0 0 0 0
                 Df 1 0 0 1 0 0
                 D 1 0 0 0 0 0

The last bit of D is active, so we report an occurrence ending at text position 13.

4.5.2 Extended BNDM

Figure 4.10 shows pseudo-code for the **BNDM** extension. The preprocessing for **Extended-BNDM** is the same except that the bits in the mask are in reverse order and we also compute ℓmin. Note that the computation of I and F is unaltered even when our pattern is reversed, because the arithmetic operations always work in the same direction.

Extended-BNDM $(p = p_1p_2 \ldots p_m,\ T = t_1t_2 \ldots t_n)$

1.   Preprocessing
2. $L \leftarrow$ number of normal characters in p
3. $\ell min \leftarrow$ minimum length of an occurrence
4. $A \leftarrow 0^L$ /* build B, S and A */
5.   **For** $c \in \Sigma$ **Do** $B[c] \leftarrow 0^L$, $S[c] =\leftarrow 0^L$
6. $i \leftarrow -1$
7.   **For** $j \in 1 \ldots m$ **Do**
8.   **If** $p_j =$ "+" **Then** $S[lastc] \leftarrow S[lastc] \mid 0^i10^{L-i-1}$
9.   **Else If** $p_j =$ "?" **Then** $A \leftarrow A \mid 0^i10^{L-i-1}$
10.   **Else If** $p_j =$ "*" **Then**
11. $S[lastc] \leftarrow S[lastc] \mid 0^i10^{L-i-1}$
12. $A \leftarrow A \mid 0^i10^{L-i-1}$
13.   **Else** /* p_j is a character */
14. $lastc \leftarrow p_j$
15. $i \leftarrow i+1$
16. $B[lastc] \leftarrow B[lastc] \mid 0^i10^{L-i-1}$
17.   **End of if**
18.   **End of for**
19. $I \leftarrow 0^L$, $F \leftarrow 0^L$ /* build I and F */
20.   **For** $i \in 0 \ldots L-1$ **Do**
21.   **If** A & $0^{L-i-1}10^i \neq 0^L$ **Then**
22.   **If** F & $0^{L-i}10^{i-1} = 0^L$ **Then**
23. $I \leftarrow I \mid 0^{L-i}10^{i-1}$
24. $F \leftarrow F \mid 0^{L-i-1}10^i$
25.   **Else**
26. $F \leftarrow F$ & $1^{L-i}01^{i-1}$
27. $F \leftarrow F \mid 0^{L-i-1}10^i$
28.   **End of if**
29.   **End of if**
30.   **End of for**
31.   Searching
32. $pos \leftarrow 0$
33.   **While** $pos \leq n - \ell min$ **Do**
34. $j \leftarrow \ell min - 1$, $last \leftarrow \ell min$
35. $D \leftarrow B[t_{pos+\ell min}]$
36.   **If** D & $10^{L-1} \neq 0^L$ **Then** $last \leftarrow j$
37.   **While** $D \neq 0^L$ AND $j > 0$ **Do**
38. $Df \leftarrow D \mid F$
39. $D \leftarrow D \mid (A$ & $((\sim (Df - I)) \wedge Df))$
40. $D \leftarrow ((D << 1)$ & $B[t_{pos+j}]) \mid (D$ & $S[t_{pos+j}])$
41. $j \leftarrow j - 1$
42.   **If** D & $10^{L-1} \neq 0^L$ **Then** /* prefix recognized */
43.   **If** $j > 0$ **Then** $last \leftarrow j$
44.   **Else** check a possible occurrence starting at pos
45.   **End of if**
46.   **End of while**
47. $pos \leftarrow pos + last$
48.   **End of while**

Fig. 4.10. The extension of **BNDM** to handle patterns with optional and repeatable characters. It assumes $\ell min > 1$.

The search is more complicated. We initialize D using the last character of the window. Then the loop checks for a match and afterward processes the next window character. As for patterns with gaps, we need a forward verification for windows that may match the pattern.

The fact that the maximum length of an occurrence is in general unbounded for extended patterns makes it impossible to know beforehand what the maximum number of characters read will be when checking the occurrence of a pattern in the text window. We have to continue until the automaton runs out of active states, we find the pattern, or the text ends.

Example of Extended-BNDM We search for the initial position of the occurrences of the pattern `"ab?c*de+f"` in the text `"acccdfabdeeef"`.

c	B	S
a	1 0 0 0 0 0	0 0 0 0 0 0
b	0 1 0 0 0 0	0 0 0 0 0 0
c	0 0 1 0 0 0	0 0 1 0 0 0
d	0 0 0 1 0 0	0 0 0 0 0 0
e	0 0 0 0 1 0	0 0 0 0 1 0
f	0 0 0 0 0 1	0 0 0 0 0 0
*	0 0 0 0 0 0	0 0 0 0 0 0

$$
\begin{aligned}
m &= 9 \\
L &= 6 \\
\ell min &= 4 \\[4pt]
A &= 0\,1\,1\,0\,0\,0 \\
I &= 0\,0\,0\,1\,0\,0 \\
F &= 0\,1\,0\,0\,0\,0
\end{aligned}
$$

1. $\boxed{\texttt{accc}}$ `dfabdeeef`

$last \leftarrow 4$

Reading c	B	0 0 1 0 0 0
	D	0 0 1 0 0 0

Reading c	B	0 0 1 0 0 0
	S	0 0 1 0 0 0
	Df	0 1 1 0 0 0
	D	0 1 1 0 0 0
	D	0 0 1 0 0 0

Reading c	B	0 0 1 0 0 0
	S	0 0 1 0 0 0
	Df	0 1 1 0 0 0
	D	0 1 1 0 0 0
	D	0 0 1 0 0 0

Reading a	B	1 0 0 0 0 0
	S	0 0 0 0 0 0
	Df	0 1 1 0 0 0
	D	0 1 1 0 0 0
	D	1 0 0 0 0 0

The last bit of D is set and $j = 0$, so we check forward the pattern in the text window `"acccdfa..."`. At the sixth character the automaton runs out of active states without finding the pattern. So we shift the window by $last = 4$.

2. `accc` $\boxed{\texttt{dfab}}$ `deeef`

$last \leftarrow 4$

Reading b	B	0 1 0 0 0 0
	D	0 1 0 0 0 0

Reading a	B	1 0 0 0 0 0
	S	0 0 0 0 0 0
	Df	0 1 0 0 0 0
	D	0 1 0 0 0 0
	D	1 0 0 0 0 0

The last bit of D is set and $j > 0$, so we set $last \leftarrow 2$.

Reading f	B	0 0 0 0 0 1
	S	0 0 0 0 0 0
	Df	1 1 0 0 0 0
	D	1 0 0 0 0 0
	D	0 0 0 0 0 0

There are no more active states in D, so we shift by $last = 2$.

3. acccdf ⎍abde⎍ eef

     last ← 4

Reading e	B	0 0 0 0 1 0
	D	0 0 0 0 1 0

Reading d	B	0 0 0 1 0 0
	S	0 0 0 0 0 0
	Df	0 1 0 0 1 0
	D	0 0 0 0 1 0
	D	0 0 0 1 0 0

Reading b	B	0 1 0 0 0 0
	S	0 0 0 0 0 0
	Df	0 1 0 1 0 0
	D	0 1 1 1 0 0
	D	0 1 0 0 0 0

Reading a	B	1 0 0 0 0 0
	S	0 0 0 0 0 0
	Df	0 1 0 0 0 0
	D	0 1 0 0 0 0
	D	1 0 0 0 0 0

The last bit of D is active and $j = 0$, so we perform a forward check on the text window "abdeeef". We find an occurrence, so we report the seventh text position as the beginning of an occurrence. Then we shift the window by $last = 4$.

This puts the window outside the text, so we are finished.

4.6 Multipattern searching

Consider now the problem of searching a number of extended strings simultaneously. Since the only techniques that deal well with extended strings are based on bit-parallelism, we need a multipattern search algorithm based on bit-parallelism. Unfortunately, as seen in Chapter 3, most of the techniques for multipattern search do not use bit-parallelism.

The only approach useful for us is the one considered in Sections 3.2.1 and 3.4.1, which packs a number of automata into a single computer word and performs **Shift-And**– or **BNDM**–like searching. If we are searching a number of extended strings of the same kind, we can use the same technique: We pack the bits of many automata in a single computer word and simulate the corresponding type of search on the whole word, thus updating the states of the automata represented in there. As for simple strings, we need to take care of the limits between different patterns and of the initial self-loops of the automata.

This multipattern search capability is extremely limited, as we will be able to represent just a few extended patterns in a single computer word.

When trying to extend **BNDM** in Section 3.4.1 we assumed that all the strings had the same length and otherwise truncated them to the shortest one. Here we do analogously: The ℓmin values of the patterns may be different, and we truncate them to obtain patterns with the same ℓmin value.

The truncation in Section 3.4.1 requires checking forward in the window for the presence of the complete pattern. This does not involve extra complications here, because we *need* to perform a forward verification with the whole patterns that seem to occur in the window.

The easiest way to do the truncation is to take the longest possible pattern prefix whose ℓmin is as chosen, although it is possible to take a pattern factor that has a lower probability of matching. This optimization is pursued in [Nav01b]. Note that the verification is more complex in this case because we have to verify in front of and behind the window in the text.

4.7 Other algorithms and references

The problem of string matching with "don't cares" is a simplification of what we have presented under the name "classes of characters." In this problem there are pattern and text positions whose value is the whole class Σ. An algorithm with time complexity $O(n \log^2 n)$ exists for this problem [FP74]. It is based on convolutions.

The same paper [FP74] presents an $O(n \log^2 m \log \log m \log |\Sigma|)$ time algorithm for patterns with wild cards. For the same problem, an $O(n + m\sqrt{n} \log n \sqrt{\log \log n})$ time algorithm is presented in [Abr87]. The work [Pin85] obtains the same complexity as [FP74] for classes of characters where complements of single characters are permitted. The work [Abr87] considers general classes of characters and obtains subquadratic search algorithms.

All these algorithms are theoretically interesting but are hardly usable in practice. A good survey on the open theoretical problems and existing results in nonstandard stringology is [MP94].

Extensions to patterns with gaps are of great interest in computational biology. For example, one may permit gaps of negative lengths, where some parts of the pattern appear superimposed in the text. These patterns are considered in [MM89, KM95, Mye96], where they also are searched approximately. They are covered in more detail in Chapter 6.

5

Regular expression matching

5.1 Basic concepts

We present in this chapter algorithms to search for regular expressions in texts or biological sequences. Regular expressions are often used in text retrieval or computational biology applications to represent search patterns that are more complex than a string, a set of strings, or an extended string. We begin with a formal definition of a regular expression and the language (set of strings) it represents.

Definition *A regular expression RE is a string on the set of symbols* $\Sigma \cup \{\ \varepsilon,\ |\ ,\ \cdot\ ,* ,(,\ )\ \}$, *which is recursively defined as the empty character* ε; *a character* $\alpha \in \Sigma$; *and* (RE_1), ($RE_1 \cdot RE_2$), ($RE_1 \mid RE_2$), *and* (RE_1*), *where* RE_1 *and* RE_2 *are regular expressions.*

For instance, in this chapter we consider the regular expression (((A·T)|(G·A))·(((A·G)|((A·A)·A))*)). When there is no ambiguity, we simplify our expressions by writing RE_1RE_2 instead of ($RE_1 \cdot RE_2$). This way, we obtain a more readable expression, in our case (AT|GA)((AG|AAA)*). It is usual to use also the precedence order "*", "·", "|" to remove more parentheses, but we do not do this here. The symbols "·", "|", "*" are called *operators*. It is customary to add an extra postfix operator "+" to mean $RE+ = RE \cdot RE*$. We define now the language represented by a regular expression.

Definition *The language represented by a regular expression RE is a set of strings over* Σ, *which is defined recursively on the structure of RE as follows:*

- *If RE is* ε, *then* $L(RE) = \{\varepsilon\}$, *the empty string.*
- *If RE is* $\alpha \in \Sigma$, *then* $L(RE) = \{\alpha\}$, *a single string of one character.*
- *If RE is of the form* (RE_1), *then* $L(RE) = L(RE_1)$.

99

- *If RE is of the form $(RE_1 \cdot RE_2)$, then $L(RE) = L(RE_1) \cdot L(RE_2)$, where $W_1 \cdot W_2$ is the set of strings w such that $w = w_1 w_2$, with $w_1 \in W_1$ and $w_2 \in W_2$. The operator "·" represents the classical concatenation of strings.*
- *If RE is of the form $(RE_1 \mid RE_2)$, then $L(RE) = L(RE_1) \cup L(RE_2)$, the union of the two languages. We call the symbol "$\mid$" the union operator.*
- *If RE is (RE_1*), then $L(RE) = L(RE)^* = \bigcup_{i \geq 0} L(RE_1)^i$, where $L^0 = \{\varepsilon\}$ and $L^i = L \cdot L^{i-1}$ for any L. That is, the result is the set of strings formed by a concatenation of zero or more strings represented by RE_1. We call "$*$" the star operator.*

For instance, $L((\texttt{AT}|\texttt{GA})((\texttt{AG}|\texttt{AAA})*)) = \{$ AT, GA, ATAG, GAAG, ATA-AA, GAAAA, ATAGAG, ATAGAAA, ATAAAAG, ATAAAAAA, GAAGAG, GAAGAAA, ...$\}$. Note that, according to the definition of the star operator, Σ^* denotes the set of all the strings over the alphabet Σ.

The *size* of a regular expression RE is the number of characters of Σ inside it. For instance, the size of $(\texttt{AT}|\texttt{GA})((\texttt{AG}|\texttt{AAA})*)$ is 9. The complexities of the algorithms that we present below are based on this measure.

The problem of searching for a regular expression RE in a text T is to find all the factors of T that belong to the language $L(RE)$. We present in this chapter the main strategies for performing this search.

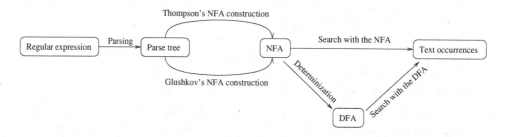

Fig. 5.1. The classical approaches to searching for regular expressions in a text.

Figure 5.1 summarizes the classical approaches. The regular expression is first parsed into an expression tree, which is transformed into a Nondeterministic Finite Automaton (NFA) in several possible ways. In this chapter we first present two NFA constructions, which are the most interesting in practice. The first one is the Thompson construction [Tho68], and the second is the Glushkov construction [Glu61].

It is possible to search directly with the NFA, and there are various ways to do that, but the process is quite slow. The algorithm consists in keeping a list of active states and updating the list each time a new text character is read. The search is normally worst-case time $O(mn)$, but it requires little memory.

Another approach is to convert the NFA into a Deterministic Finite Automaton (DFA), which permits $O(n)$ search time by performing one direct transition per text character. On the other hand, the construction of such an automaton is worst-case time and space $O(2^m)$.

Yet a third strategy is to filter the text using multiple pattern matching or related tools, so as to find anchors around which there might be an occurrence, and then locally verify a possible occurrence using one of the previous strategies. Figure 5.2 illustrates this scheme.

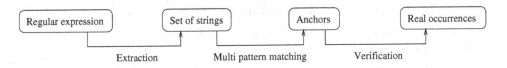

Fig. 5.2. The filtering approach to search for regular expressions in a text.

These strategies can be combined. Moreover, the use of bit-parallelism can accelerate some parts of the search process.

An important point is that most of the automaton constructions use a tree representation of the regular expression RE in order to perform the calculations. The leaves of the tree are labeled with the characters of Σ in RE and also with the symbols ε, if any. The internal nodes are labeled with the operators. The nodes that are labeled "|" or "·" have two children that represent the subexpressions RE_1 and RE_2 (Section 5.1). Nodes labeled "*" have a unique child representing RE_1. The tree representation is usually not unique, since some operators are commutative and/or associative. A tree representation of our example (AT|GA)((AG|AAA)*) is shown in Figure 5.3.

We explain in Section 5.8 how to parse a regular expression in order to obtain a tree representation. We consider below that the parse tree is readily available and identify our regular expressions with any of their tree representations.

When working on the tree representations in our algorithms, we assume that the symbol $\boxed{\cdot}$ (v_l, v_r) means a concatenation tree with root "·" and children v_l and v_r. Similarly, $\boxed{|}$ (v_l, v_r) is the tree rooted with "|". The symbol $\boxed{*}$ (v_*) means a "*" node with a unique child v_*.

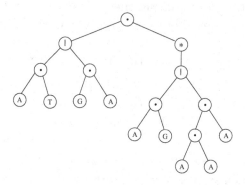

Fig. 5.3. Tree representation of the regular expression (AT|GA)((AG|AAA)*).

5.2 Building an NFA

There exist various ways to build an NFA from a regular expression [Glu61, Tho68, CP92, BS86, BK93, HSW97], among which two are most important because they are practical and often used.

The Thompson construction [Tho68] is simple and leads to an NFA that is linear in the number of states (at most $2m$) and of transitions (at most $4m$). However, this automaton has ε-transitions, that is, "empty" transitions, that can be passed through without reading a character of the text or, alternatively, by reading the empty string ε.

The Glushkov construction [Glu61, BS86], on the other hand, leads to an NFA with exactly $m + 1$ states but a number of transitions that is $O(m^2)$ in the worst case. Nevertheless, this construction produces no ε-transitions. The original construction is $O(m^3)$ time, but it has been shown [BK93] that this can be reduced to $O(m^2)$.

5.2.1 Thompson automaton

The construction of Thompson [Tho68] is an automaton representation of what is recognized by the regular expression. The automaton is a direct transcription of the tree representation of the regular expression. It uses ε-transitions to simplify this transcription.

The idea is to go up the tree representation T_{RE} of the regular expression RE and to compute for each tree node v an automaton $Th(v)$ that recognizes the language RE_v represented by the subtree rooted at v. A specific automaton construction is associated to each type of node and leaf of the tree. These are

(i) Construction for the empty word. The automaton consists of just two nodes joined together by an ε-transition.

$$\Rightarrow \text{I} \cdots \xrightarrow{\varepsilon} \text{F}$$

(ii) For a single character α the construction is similar, except that the transition is labeled with the character rather than with the empty string.

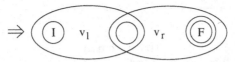

(iii) Construction for a concatenation node. The two Thompson automata of the two children v_l and v_r are merged together, the final state of the first automaton becoming the initial state of the second.

$$\Rightarrow \text{I} \quad v_l \quad \bigcirc \quad v_r \quad \text{F}$$

(iv) The construction for a union node requires ε-transitions. The idea is to transcript the fact that we enter either automaton $Th(v_l)$ or $Th(v_r)$ of the two children. We then add two new states, an initial one I with two ε-transitions to the two initial states of $Th(v_l)$ and $Th(v_r)$, and a final node F that can be reached from the two final states of $Th(v_l)$ and $Th(v_r)$. A path from I to F has to go through one of the two automata, so the language recognized is $RE_{v_l} \mid RE_{v_r}$.

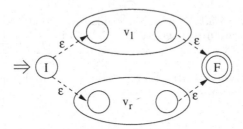

(v) The construction for a star node uses the same idea. First, the language RE_{v_*}, where v_* is the only child node of v, now can be repeated as many times as desired. Hence we create a backward ε-transition from the final state of the automaton $Th(v_*)$ to the initial. But the star also means that the automaton $Th(v_*)$ can be ignored, and hence we create two new nodes, an initial I and a final F, joined together by an ε-transition. With two other ε-transitions we join I to the initial state of $Th(v_*)$, and the final state of $Th(v_*)$ to F. The resulting automaton recognizes the language $(RE_{v_*})^*$.

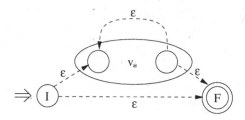

The whole Thompson algorithm consists in performing a bottom-up traversal of the tree representation and keeping the automaton built for the root as the Thompson automaton of the whole expression. The recursive pseudocode of a the algorithm is given in Figure 5.4.

Thompson_recur(v)
1.   **If** $v = [\,|\,]\,(v_l, v_r)$ OR $v = \boxed{\cdot}\,(v_l, v_r)$ **Then**
2. $Th(v_l) \leftarrow$ **Thompson_recur**(v_l)
3. $Th(v_r) \leftarrow$ **Thompson_recur**(v_r)
4.   **Else If** $v = \boxed{*}\,(v_*)$ **Then** $Th(v_*) \leftarrow$ **Thompson_recur**(v_*)
5.   **End of if**
        /* end of the recursive part, we build the automaton for the current node */
6.   **If** $v = (\varepsilon)$ **Then Return** construction *(i)*
7.   **If** $v = (\alpha)$, $\alpha \in \Sigma$ **Then Return** construction *(ii)*
8.   **If** $v = \boxed{\cdot}\,(v_l, v_r)$ **Then Return** construction *(iii)* on $Th(v_l)$ and $Th(v_r)$
9.   **If** $v = [\,|\,]\,(v_l, v_r)$ **Then Return** construction *(iv)* on $Th(v_l)$ and $Th(v_r)$
10.   **If** $v = \boxed{*}\,(v_*)$ **Then Return** construction *(v)* on $Th(v_*)$

Thompson(RE)
11. $v_{RE} \leftarrow$ **Parse**($RE\$,1$) /* parse the regular expression (Section 5.8) */
12. $Th(v_{RE}) \leftarrow$ **Thompson_recur**(v_{RE}) /* build the automaton on the tree */

Fig. 5.4. The Thompson algorithm. The automaton is built recursively on the tree representation of the expression.

Properties of the Thompson automaton The construction for each node of the tree representation adds at most two states and four transitions to the current automaton. Hence, at the end of the construction, the total number of states and transitions is bounded by $2m$ and $4m$, respectively. We can calculate tighter bounds, but the important point is that the number of states and transitions is linear in m. Moreover, each NFA node has at most two incoming and two outgoing edges, and the whole NFA has one initial and one final state.

Another interesting property is that all the arrows that are not labeled by ε go from states numbered i to states numbered $i + 1$. This is always true provided we process the characters of the regular expression from left to right, as in the parser presented at the end of this chapter.

Complexity The time complexity of the whole algorithm is also linear, since we can create each construction in constant time for each node of the tree representation.

Example of a Thompson automaton construction We build the automaton of `(AT|GA)((AG|AAA)*)` from its tree representation (Figure 5.3). The construction is shown in Figure 5.5, except for the basic step of concatenating characters.

5.2.2 Glushkov automaton

The construction of Glushkov [Glu61] has been by popularized Berry and Sethi in [BS86].

We mark the positions of the characters of Σ in RE, counting only characters. For instance, `(AT|GA)((AG|AAA)*)` is marked $(A_1T_2|G_3A_4)-((A_5G_6|\ A_7A_8A_9)*)$. A *marked expression* from a regular expression RE is denoted $\overline{RE}$ and its language, where each character includes its index, is denoted $L(\overline{RE})$. In our example, $L((A_1T_2|G_3A_4)((A_5G_6|A_7A_8A_9)*)) = \{A_1-T_2,\ G_3A_4,\ A_1T_2A_5G_6,\ G_3A_4A_5G_6,\ A_1T_2A_7A_8A_9,\ G_3A_4A_7A_8A_9,\ A_1T_2A_5-G_6A_5\ G_6,\dots\}$. Let $Pos(\overline{RE}) = \{1\dots m\}$ be the set of positions in $\overline{RE}$ and $\overline{\Sigma}$ the marked character alphabet.

The Glushkov automaton is built first on the marked expression $\overline{RE}$ and it recognizes $L(\overline{RE})$. We then derive from it the Glushkov automaton that recognizes $L(RE)$ by erasing the position indices of all the characters (see below).

The set of positions is taken as a reference, becoming the set of states of the resulting automaton in addition to an initial state 0. So we build $m + 1$ states labeled from 0 to m. Each state j represents the fact that we have read in the text a string that ends at NFA position j. Now if we read a new character α, we need to know which positions we can reach from j by α. Glushkov computes from a position (state) j all the other accessible positions.

We need four new definitions to explain in depth the algorithm. We denote below by α_y the indexed character of $\overline{RE}$ that is at position y.

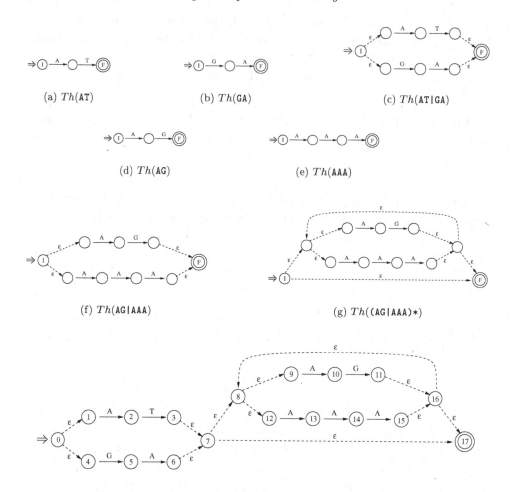

Fig. 5.5. Thompson automaton construction for the regular expression `(AA|AT)((AG|AAA)*)`.

Definition $First(\overline{RE}) = \{x \in Pos(\overline{RE}),\ \exists u \in \overline{\Sigma}^{*},\ \alpha_x u \in L(\overline{RE})\}.$

The set $First(\overline{RE})$ represents the set of initial positions of $L(\overline{RE})$, that is, the set of positions at which the reading can start. In our example, $First((A_1 T_2 | G_3 A_4)((A_5 G_6 | A_7 A_8 A_9)*)) = \{1, 3\}.$

Definition $Last(\overline{RE}) = \{x \in Pos(\overline{RE}),\ \exists u \in \overline{\Sigma}^{*},\ u\alpha_x \in L(\overline{RE})\}.$

The set $Last(\overline{RE})$ represents the set of final positions of $L(\overline{RE})$, that is, the set of positions at which a string read can be recognized. In our example, $Last((A_1 T_2 | G_3 A_4)((A_5 G_6 | A_7 A_8 A_9)*)) = \{2, 4, 6, 9\}.$

Definition $Follow(\overline{RE}, x) = \{y \in Pos(\overline{RE}), \exists u, v \in \Sigma^*, u\alpha_x\alpha_y v \in L(\overline{RE})\}.$

The set $Follow(\overline{RE}, x)$ represents all the positions in $Pos(\overline{RE})$ accessible from x. For instance, in our example, if we consider position 6, the set of accessible positions is $Follow((A_1T_2|G_3A_4)((A_5G_6|A_7A_8A_9)*), 6) = \{7, 5\}.$

We need an extra function $Empty_{RE}$ that indicates whether the empty word ε is in $L(RE)$.

Definition *We define recursively the function $Empty_{RE}$, whose value is $\{\varepsilon\}$ if ε belongs to $L(RE)$ and $\emptyset$ otherwise.*

$$
\begin{aligned}
Empty_\varepsilon &= \{\varepsilon\} \\
Empty_{\alpha \in \Sigma} &= \emptyset \\
Empty_{RE_1|RE_2} &= Empty_{RE_1} \cup Empty_{RE_2} \\
Empty_{RE_1 \cdot RE_2} &= Empty_{RE_1} \cap Empty_{RE_2} \\
Empty_{RE^*} &= \{\varepsilon\}
\end{aligned}
$$

The deterministic Glushkov automaton $\overline{GL}$ that recognizes the language $L(\overline{RE})$ is built in the following way.

$$\overline{GL} = (S, \Sigma, I, F, \overline{\delta})$$

where:

(i) S is the set of states, $S = \{0, 1, \ldots, m\}$, that is, the set of positions $Pos(\overline{RE})$ and the initial state is $I = 0$.

(ii) F is the set of final states, $F = Last(\overline{RE}) \cup (Empty_{RE} \cdot \{0\})$. Informally, a state (position) i is final if it is in $Last(\overline{RE})$. The initial state 0 is also final if the empty word ε belongs to $L(\overline{RE})$, in which case $Empty_{RE} = \{\varepsilon\}$ and hence $Empty_{RE} \cdot \{0\} = \{0\}$. If not, $Empty_{RE} \cdot \{0\} = \emptyset$.

(iii) $\overline{\delta}$ is the transition function of the automaton, defined by

$$\forall x \in Pos(\overline{RE}), \ \forall y \in Follow(\overline{RE}, x), \ \overline{\delta}(x, \alpha_y) = y \qquad (5.1)$$

Informally, there is a transition from state x to y by α_y if y follows x. The transitions from the initial state are defined by

$$\forall y \in First(\overline{RE}), \ \overline{\delta}(0, \alpha_y) = y \qquad (5.2)$$

The Glushkov automaton of our marked regular expression $(A_1T_2|G_3A_4)$ $((A_5G_6|A_7A_8A_9)*)$ is given in Figure 5.6.

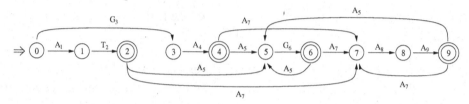

Fig. 5.6. Marked Glushkov automaton built on the marked regular expression (A_1 $T_2|G_3A_4)((A_5G_6|A_7A_8A_9)*)$. The state 0 is initial. Double-circled states are final.

To obtain the Glushkov automaton of the original RE, we simply erase the position indices in the marked automaton. At this step, the automaton usually becomes nondeterministic. The new automaton recognizes the language $L(RE)$. The Glushkov automaton of our example (AT|GA)((AG|AAA)*) is shown in Figure 5.7.

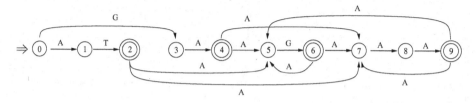

Fig. 5.7. Glushkov automaton built on the regular expression (AT|GA)((AG|AAA)*). The state 0 is initial. Double-circled states are final. The automaton is derived from the marked automaton by simply erasing the position indices.

The algorithm of Glushkov is based on the tree representation T_{RE} of the regular expression (see Figure 5.3). Each node v of this tree represents a subexpression RE_v of RE. We associate the following variables to v:

- $First(v)$: list of positions that represent the set $First(\overline{RE_v})$.
- $Last(v)$: list of positions that represent the set $Last(\overline{RE_v})$.
- $Empty_v$: set to $\{\varepsilon\}$ if $L(RE_v)$ contains the empty string ε, and to $\emptyset$ otherwise.

These variables are computed for each node in postfix order, that is, they are first computed for every child of v and only afterward for v. We denote the two children of v as v_l and v_r if v is "|" or ".", and we denote its unique child as v_* if v represents "*".

The set $Follow(x)$ is a global variable. For each node v we update $Follow(x)$ according to the positions in the subexpression $\overline{RE_v}$.

The recursive algorithm **Glushkov_variables**(v_{RE}, $lpos$) is given in Figure 5.8. It computes the values of $First(v)$, $Last(v)$, $Follow(x)$, and $Empty_v$

Glushkov_variables(v_{RE}, *lpos*)

/* postfix computation, we compute recursively the children first */
1.   **If** $v = \boxed{|}\,(v_l, v_r)$ **OR** $v = \boxed{\cdot}\,(v_l, v_r)$ **Then**
2.   *lpos* ← **Glushkov_variables**(v_l, *lpos*)
3.   *lpos* ← **Glushkov_variables**(v_r, *lpos*)
4.   **Else If** $v = \boxed{*}\,(v_*)$ **Then** *lpos* ← **Glushkov_variables**(v_*, *lpos*)
5.   **End of if**

/* end of the recursive part, we compute the values for the current node */
6.   **If** $v = (\varepsilon)$ **Then**
7. $First(v) \leftarrow \emptyset,\ Last(v) \leftarrow \emptyset,\ Empty_v \leftarrow \{\varepsilon\}$
8.   **Else If** $v = (\alpha)$, $\alpha \in \Sigma$ **Then**
9.   *lpos* ← *lpos* + 1
10. $First(v) \leftarrow \{lpos\},\ Last(v) \leftarrow \{lpos\},\ Empty_v \leftarrow \emptyset,\ Follow(lpos) \leftarrow \emptyset$
11.   **Else If** $v = \boxed{|}\,(v_l, v_r)$ **Then**
12. $First(v) \leftarrow First(v_l) \cup First(v_r)$
13. $Last(v) \leftarrow Last(v_l) \cup Last(v_r)$
14. $Empty_v \leftarrow Empty_{v_l} \cup Empty_{v_r}$
15.   **Else If** $v = \boxed{\cdot}\,(v_l, v_r)$ **Then**
16. $First(v) \leftarrow First(v_l) \cup (Empty_{v_l} \cdot First(v_r))$,
17. $Last(v) \leftarrow (Empty_{v_r} \cdot Last(v_l)) \cup Last(v_r)$,
18. $Empty_v \leftarrow Empty_{v_l} \cap Empty_{v_r}$
19.   **For** $x \in Last(v_l)$ **Do** $Follow(x) \leftarrow Follow(x) \cup First(v_r)$
20.   **Else If** $v = \boxed{*}\,(v_*)$ **Then**
21. $First(v) \leftarrow First(v_*),\ Last(v) \leftarrow Last(v_*),\ Empty_v \leftarrow \{\varepsilon\}$
22.   **For** $x \in Last(v_*)$ **Do** $Follow(x) \leftarrow Follow(x) \cup First(v_*)$
23.   **End of if**
24.   **Return** *lpos*

Fig. 5.8. Recursive part of the Glushkov algorithm. This function computes the values of $First(v)$, $Last(v)$, $Follow(x)$, and $Empty_v$ for each node v of the tree representation of the regular expression $\overline{RE}$.

for each node v of the tree representation of the regular expression RE. We visit the nodes in postfix order. The values of the node v_{RE} are computed from the values obtained for its children. The position of each character is computed on the fly (line 9).

The whole Glushkov algorithm consists in transforming RE into a tree v_{RE}, calculating the variables on it with **Glushkov_variables** (v_{RE},0) and then building the Glushkov automaton from the variables of the root v_{RE} of the tree, following its definition. Pseudo-code for the whole algorithm is given in Figure 5.9.

Properties of the Glushkov automaton Two properties of this automaton are of interest to us. The first one is that the NFA is ε-free. The second

---

Glushkov(RE)

        /* parse the regular expression (Section 5.8) */

1. $v_{RE} \leftarrow$ **Parse**(RE\$,1)

        /* build the variables on the tree */

2. $m \leftarrow$ **Glushkov_variables**(v_{RE},0)

        /* building the automaton */

3. $\Delta = \emptyset$

4.   **For** $i \in 0 \ldots m$ **Do** create state i

5.   **For** $x \in First(v_{RE})$ **Do** $\Delta \leftarrow \Delta \cup \{(0, \alpha_x, x)\}$

6.   **For** $i \in 0 \ldots m$ **Do**

7.   **For** $x \in Follow(i)$ **Do** $\Delta \leftarrow \Delta \cup \{(i, \alpha_x, x)\}$

8.   **End of for**

9.   **For** $x \in Last(v_{RE}) \cup (Empty_{v_{RE}} \cdot \{0\})$ **Do** mark x as terminal

---

Fig. 5.9. The whole Glushkov algorithm. The automaton is nondeterministic in the general case and its transition function is denoted Δ. The initial state is 0.

one is that all the arrows leading to a given state y are labeled by the same character, namely, α_y. This is easily seen in formulas (5.1) and (5.2).

Complexity The worst-case complexity of the whole algorithm is dominated by the function **Glushkov_variables**. In this function, all the unions of sets, except for the star, are disjoint and can be implemented in $O(1)$ time. The **For** loop of line 19 is worst-case $O(m)$. The poor worst-case complexity is due to line 22, that is, the computation of the star. Since $Follow(x)$ and $First(v_*)$ could intersect, the union is worst-case time $O(m)$. As this is inside a **For** loop that can perform $O(m)$ iterations, the whole loop is worst-case time $O(m^2)$. The total complexity of the algorithm is thus worst-case $O(m^3)$, because $O(m)$ stars may exist.

Two variations of this algorithm have been proposed to reduce the worst-case complexity to $O(m^2)$ [BK93, CP92]. Both reduce the complexity of the **For** loop of the star but use different properties. The first one [BK93] uses the fact that

$$Follow(\overline{RE*}, x) = \left[\, Follow(\overline{RE*}, x) \setminus First(\overline{RE*}) \,\right] \cup First(\overline{RE*})$$

while the second [CP92] uses the fact that

$$Follow(\overline{RE*}, x) = Follow(\overline{RE*}, x) \cup \left[\, First(\overline{RE*}) \setminus Follow(\overline{RE*}, x) \,\right]$$

For our purposes, the $O(m^3)$ time algorithm is good enough, since usually the regular expression is small in comparison to the text size. Moreover, by using bit-parallelism to operate the sets of states, one can obtain $O(m^2 \lceil m/w \rceil)$ time, which is in practice $O(m^2)$ for small regular expressions.

5.3 Classical approaches to regular expression searching

We cover in this section the classical ways to search for a regular expression in a text. We first consider the two extremes: pure NFA and pure DFA simulation. We then introduce a third, intermediate approach, which permits trading space for time.

5.3.1 Thompson's NFA simulation

Together with its NFA definition, Thompson proposed in [Tho68] an $O(mn)$ search algorithm based on the direct simulation of his NFA. The resulting algorithm, which we call **NFAThompson**, is not competitive nowadays, but it is the basis of more competitive algorithms seen later in this chapter.

Thompson stores explicitly the set of currently active states. For each new text character read and for each currently active state, he looks at the new states that the current state activates by this character and adds each of them to a new set of active states. From those new active states he follows all the ε-transitions until all the reachable states are obtained.

Since each state has $O(1)$ outgoing transitions under Thompson's construction and there can be $O(m)$ active states, producing the new set of active states takes $O(m)$ time under a suitable representation of the set of states, for example, a bit vector. The propagation by ε-transitions also takes $O(m)$ time if care is taken to not propagate from a state that was already active. On the other hand, the extra space required is just $O(m)$.

Note that it is possible to use bit-parallelism to store the bit vectors. A smarter use of bit-parallelism is considered in Section 5.4.

5.3.2 Using a deterministic automaton

One of the early achievements in string matching was the $O(n)$ time algorithm to search for a regular expression in a text. As explained, the technique consists of converting the regular expression into a DFA and then searching the text using the DFA. The simplest solution is to build first an NFA with a technique like those shown in the previous sections (e.g., Thompson or Glushkov) and then convert the NFA into a DFA.

This algorithm, which we call **DFAClassical**, can be found in any classical book of compilers, such as [ASU86]. The main idea is as follows. When we traverse the text using a nondeterministic automaton, a number of transitions can be followed and a set of states become active. However, a DFA has exactly one active state at a time. So the corresponding deterministic automaton is defined over the *set* of states of the nondeterministic automaton. The key idea is that the unique current state of the DFA is the set of current states of the NFA.

To formalize the concepts, we first need a definition.

Definition *The ε-closure of a state s in an NFA, $E(s)$, is the set of states of the NFA that can be reached from s by ε-transitions.*

Note that in ε-free automata like Glushkov's, $E(s) = \{s\}$ for all states s, but this is not true in Thompson's construction.

We can give now a formal definition of the conversion of the NFA into a DFA. Let the NFA be $(Q, \Sigma, I, F, \Delta)$ according to Section 1.3.3. Then the DFA is defined as

$$(\wp(Q),\ \Sigma,\ E(I),\ F',\ \delta)$$

where

$$F' = \{f \in \wp(Q),\ f \cap F \neq \emptyset\}$$

and

$$\delta(S, \sigma) = \bigcup_{s',\ \exists s \in S,\ (s, \sigma, s') \in \Delta} E(s')$$

that is, for every possible active state s of S we follow all the possible transitions to states s' by the character σ and then follow all the possible ε-transitions from s'.

Since the DFA is built on the set of states of the NFA, its worst-case size is $O(2^m)$ states, which is exponential. This makes the approach suitable for small regular expressions only. In practice, however, most of those states are not reachable from the initial state and therefore do not need to be built.

We now give an algorithm that obtains the DFA from the NFA by building only the reachable states. The algorithm uses sets of NFA states as identifiers for the DFA states. A simple way to represent these sets is to use a boolean array. Note that a bit-parallel representation is also possible, and it permits not only more compact storage but also faster handling of the set union and other required set operations. We give specific bit-parallel algorithms in Section 5.4. For now, we use just an abstract representation of the sets of states.

Figure 5.10 gives pseudo-code to compute the ε-closure $E(s)$ for every state s of the NFA. The result is a set of states for each state s. The algorithm starts with $E(s) = \{s\}$ and then repeatedly traverses the whole automaton looking for ε-transitions. For each of these, it adds the ε-closure of the target state to that of the source state. The process is repeated until no new information is gathered.

EpsClosure$(N = (Q, \Sigma, I, F, \Delta))$
1.   **For** $s \in Q$ **Do** $E(s) \leftarrow \{s\}$
2.   *changed* $\leftarrow$ TRUE
3.   **While** *changed* = TRUE **Do**
4.   *changed* $\leftarrow$ FALSE
5.   **For** $(s, \varepsilon, s') \in \Delta$ **Do**
6.   **If** $E(s') \not\subseteq E(s)$ **Then**
7. $E(s) \leftarrow E(s) \cup E(s')$
8.   *changed* $\leftarrow$ TRUE
9.   **End of if**
10.   **End of for**
11.   **End of while**

Fig. 5.10. Computation of the ε-closure $E(s)$.

The cost of this algorithm is $O(|\Delta|m^2)$, since each complete traversal costs $O(|\Delta|m)$ and it adds 1 to the distance up to which the chains of ε-transitions are considered. Since the maximum distance in the NFA is $O(m)$, it follows that $O(m)$ traversals suffice. Under the Thompson construction we know that $|\Delta| \leq 4m$, so the algorithm is $O(m^3)$ time. Under Glushkov we simply do not need to run the algorithm, as we know that $E(s) = \{s\}$ for every $s \in Q$.

Figure 5.11 shows pseudo-code for the algorithm that builds the DFA. The algorithm builds the initial state I_d and then invokes a recursive procedure **BuildState**, which finds all the target states from a given source state and reinvokes itself on all the target states that do not exist yet. The set of final states, F_d, is built together with the set of all states, Q_d.

It is clear that this algorithm produces only the states that are reachable from the initial state, that is, the states that could be reached when reading the text. Its worst-case time complexity is $O(|Q_d||\Sigma||\Delta| \max_s |E(s)|)$, which is $O(|Q_d|m^2)$ on Thompson's NFA since $|\Delta| = O(m)$ as well as on Glushkov's since $|E(s)| = 1$ always.

Example of DFA construction Let us consider our running example (AT|GA)((AG|AAA)*). Its Thompson NFA is given in Figure 5.5. Table 5.1 gives the corresponding $E(s)$ function built by **EpsClosure**.

For the Glushkov NFA of Figure 5.7, we have that $E(s) = \{s\}$. Figure 5.12 shows the resulting DFAs from both Thompson's and Glushkov's NFAs. Note that, despite the different labeling, both DFAs are the same. Moreover,

BuildState(S)
1. **If** $S \cap F \neq \emptyset$ **Then** $F_d \leftarrow F_d \cup \{S\}$
2. **For** $\sigma \in \Sigma$ **Do**
3. $T \leftarrow \emptyset$
4.   **For** $s \in S$ **Do**
5.   **For** $(s, \sigma, s') \in \Delta$ **Do** $T \leftarrow T \cup E(s')$
6.   **End of for**
7. $\delta(S, \sigma) \leftarrow T$
8.   **If** $T \notin Q_d$ **Then**
9. $Q_d \leftarrow Q_d \cup \{T\}$
10.   **BuildState**(T)
11.   **End of if**
12. **End of for**

BuildDFA($N = (Q, \Sigma, I, F, \Delta)$)
13. **EpsClosure**(N)
14. $I_d \leftarrow E(I)$ /* initial DFA state */
15. $F_d \leftarrow \emptyset$ /* final DFA states */
16. $Q_d \leftarrow \{I_d\}$ /* all the DFA states */
17. **BuildState**(I_d)
18. **Return** $(Q_d, \Sigma, I_d, F_d, \delta)$

Fig. 5.11. Classical computation of the DFA from the NFA.

$E(0)$	$\{0, 1, 4\}$	$E(9)$	$\{9\}$
$E(1)$	$\{1\}$	$E(10)$	$\{10\}$
$E(2)$	$\{2\}$	$E(11)$	$\{8, 9, 11, 12, 16, 17\}$
$E(3)$	$\{3, 7, 8, 9, 12, 17\}$	$E(12)$	$\{12\}$
$E(4)$	$\{4\}$	$E(13)$	$\{13\}$
$E(5)$	$\{5\}$	$E(14)$	$\{14\}$
$E(6)$	$\{6, 7, 8, 9, 12, 17\}$	$E(15)$	$\{8, 9, 12, 15, 16, 17\}$
$E(7)$	$\{7, 8, 9, 12, 17\}$	$E(16)$	$\{8, 9, 12, 16, 17\}$
$E(8)$	$\{8, 9, 12\}$	$E(17)$	$\{17\}$

Table 5.1. *The ε-closure $E(s)$ for the final NFA of Figure 5.5.*

they are minimal, that is, no DFA with fewer states recognizes the same language.

This is not guaranteed in general. Different DFAs may exist to recognize the same language. Moreover, our construction does not guarantee that the result has the minimum size. To ensure this we have to *minimize* the DFA after we build it. Minimization of DFAs is a standard technique that can be found in a classical book such as [ASU86]. We content ourselves with the simple construction, which in most cases produces a DFA of reasonable size.

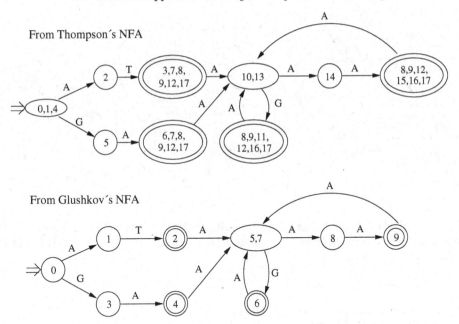

Fig. 5.12. The DFAs resulting from Thompson's and Glushkov's NFAs.

Searching with the DFA The point of building the DFA is to guarantee a linear search time of $O(n)$. This is achievable because we need to cross exactly one transition per text character read. However, we need to modify the automaton in order to use it for text searching. The modification consists of adding a self-loop to the initial state of the NFA, which can be crossed by any character, that is, doing

$$\Delta \leftarrow \Delta \cup \bigcup_{\sigma \in \Sigma}(I, \sigma, I)$$

before converting it into a DFA. If the original automaton recognizes the language $L(RE)$, then after this modification the automaton recognizes $\Sigma^* L(RE)$. Figure 5.13 shows the resulting DFA after adding the self-loop to the Glushkov NFA of Figure 5.7.

The complete search algorithm is depicted in Figure 5.14. The total complexity is $O(m^2 2^m + n)$ in the worst case. The extra space needed to represent the DFA is $O(m 2^m)$ bits.

5.3.3 A hybrid approach

In [Mye92] an approach is proposed which is intermediate between a nondeterministic and a deterministic simulation. The idea is based on Thompson's

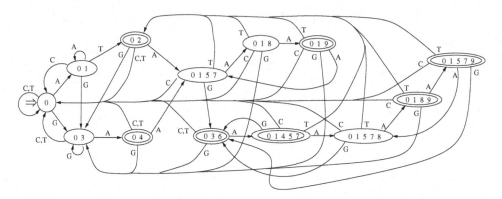

Fig. 5.13. DFA obtained after adding an initial self-loop to the Glushkov automaton of Figure 5.7. It is equivalent to the regular expression (A|C|G|T)* (AT|GA)((AG| AAA)*).

DFAClassical($N = (Q, \Sigma, I, F, \Delta)$, $T = t_1 t_2 \dots t_n$)
1.   Preprocessing
2.   For $\sigma \in \Sigma$ Do $\Delta \leftarrow \Delta \cup (I, \sigma, I)$
3. $(Q_d, \Sigma, I_d, F_d, \delta) \leftarrow$ **BuildDFA**(N)
4.   Searching
5. $s \leftarrow I_d$
6.   For $pos \in 1 \dots n$ Do
7.   If $s \in F_d$ Then report an occurrence ending at $pos - 1$
8. $s \leftarrow \delta(s, t_{pos})$
9.   End of for

Fig. 5.14. Classical search algorithm using a DFA.

construction (Section 5.2.1) and consists in splitting the NFA into *modules* of $O(k)$ nodes each, making them deterministic, and keeping an NFA of the $O(m/k)$ modules. We call this algorithm **DFAModules**.

More specifically, the parse tree of the regular expression is partitioned into modules as follows. First, parse subtrees with k edges are chosen. These subtrees form modules, which are from then on considered as leaves of the parse tree. It is shown that those modules contain between $k/2$ and k leaves. Once the module subtrees have been replaced by leaves, new subtrees are chosen as modules and so on until the root of the whole expression is reached.

The status of each module is represented by a bit mask of length $k + 1$, which is a map of active and inactive NFA states. A transition table is precomputed so that, given a bit mask of active states plus a text character σ, the table delivers the bit mask of active states after processing σ. This is in fact a DFA built on the module with the sets of states represented as bit vectors.

For the lowest level modules it is clear that this DFA can be built. The problem with the higher level modules is that some of their leaves are other submodules. When the bit corresponding to the edge entering the submodule is activated we have to set the initial state of the submodule. And when the final state of the submodule is activated we have to activate the edge leaving the submodule in the higher level module.

Since the construction of modules takes whole subexpressions and Thompson's construction guarantees that there exist just one initial and one final state, the transitions among each module and its parent can be carried out in constant time.

Therefore, to simulate one step of the computation on a higher level module, it is necessary to use the precomputed table to determine which submodules have been reached, and activate their initial state if they have been. Then, we recursively simulate the step on each submodule, and for those that reached their final state we activate the corresponding bit in the higher level module. A final access to the precomputed table yields the final result.

The main problem remaining is the order in which the submodules have to be processed to account for the dependencies between them. Except for the "$*$" operator, which introduces a *back edge*, the NFA can be processed in topological order (i.e., source nodes before target nodes), and a single pass over the NFA is enough. One of the central points of [Mye92] is to show that two passes in topological order, permitting the source of a back edge to influence its target, are enough to account for all the dependencies. Hence, we need only a constant number of passes over the NFA, working $O(1)$ per module.

Since time is proportional to the number of modules, $O(m/k)$ time suffices to process each text character. Each determinized module needs $O(2^k)$ space to perform all its internal transitions in constant time. Hence we need $O(m2^k/k)$ space and $O(mn/k)$ time. Given $O(s)$ space, the algorithm obtains $O(mn/\log s)$ search time.

5.4 Bit-parallel algorithms

As explained in the previous section, a possible way to store the states of the DFA (i.e., the sets of states of the NFA) is to use a bit mask of $O(m)$ bits where the i-th bit is 1 whenever the i-th NFA state belongs to the DFA state. We present in this section two bit-parallel implementations that are hybrids between an NFA and a DFA simulation. As we will see later, they have advantages and disadvantages compared to the classical approaches.

Assume that the NFA $(Q = \{s_0 \ldots s_{|Q|-1}\}, \Sigma, I = s_0, F, \Delta)$ is represented as follows: $Q_n = \{0 \ldots |Q| - 1\}$, $I_n = 0^{|Q|-1}1$, $F_n = |_{s_j \in F} 0^{|Q|-1-j}10^j$ (i.e., the bitwise OR of the final states positions), and the set of transitions Δ is represented by means of two tables B_n and E_n, where

$$B_n[i, \sigma] \;=\; |_{(s_i,\sigma,s_j) \in \Delta}\, 0^{|Q|-1-j}10^j$$

represents the states reachable from state i by character σ without considering ε-transitions, and

$$E_n[i] \;=\; |_{s_j \in E(s_i)}\, 0^{|Q|-1-j}10^j$$

represents $E(i)$, the ε-closure of state s_i (Section 5.3.2).

It is not complicated to produce this representation when applying Thompson's or Glushkov's constructions. Indeed, it is convenient, as we are simply using bit-parallelism to represent sets of states as bit masks of length $|Q|$. Of course E_n is not relevant under Glushkov's construction, since its NFA is ε-free.

5.4.1 Bit-parallel Thompson

A competitive algorithm [WM92b], which we call **BPThompson**, is derived from Thompson's NFA simulation (Section 5.3.1) by a clever use of bit-parallelism. A very important property (Section 5.2.1) is that, except for the ε-transitions, all the arrows go from states numbered i to states numbered $i + 1$.

If we pack the set of states in the bits of a computer word, so that the i-th state is mapped to the i-th bit, then all except the ε-transitions can be simulated using a table B similar to that of the **Shift-And** algorithm (Section 2.2.2). The mechanism to simulate ε-transitions uses a precomputed table E_d. E_d is built such that, for each possible bit mask of active states, it yields the new set of active states that can be reached from the original ones by ε-transitions. This includes the original states and also the initial state 0 and its ε-closure, so as to simulate, without any extra work, the self-loop at the initial state. Formally,

$$E_d[D] \;=\; |_{i,\; i=0 \text{ OR } D\&0^{L-i-1}10^i \neq 0^L}\, E_n[i] \qquad (5.3)$$

where $L = |Q| \leq 2m$ is the number of states in Thompson's NFA.

The mechanism is not completely an NFA simulation, since it precomputes a DFA on the ε-transitions. The simulation of all the other transitions can be seen as the true bit-parallel simulation of an NFA.

Figure 5.15 shows the code to build the tables B and E_d. The idea for B is to ignore the originating states of B_n, that is, we store in $B[\sigma]$ all the states that can be reached by the character σ, from any state:

$$B[\sigma] \quad = \quad |_{i \in 0...m} \, B_n[i, \sigma] \tag{5.4}$$

The idea for E_d is to iteratively add a new highest bit to the masks and use the results already computed for smaller masks. The overall process takes time $O(2^L + m|\Sigma|)$.

BuildEps$(N = (Q_n, \Sigma, I_n, F_n, B_n, E_n))$
1.   **For** $\sigma \in \Sigma$ **Do**
2. $B[\sigma] \leftarrow 0^L$
3.   **For** $i \in 0 \ldots L - 1$ **Do** $B[\sigma] \leftarrow B[\sigma] \mid B_n[i, \sigma]$
4.   **End of for**
        /* B is already built, now build E_d */
5. $E_d[0] \leftarrow E_n[0]$ /* the initial state and its closure */
6.   **For** $i \in 0 \ldots L - 1$ **Do**
7.   **For** $j \in 0 \ldots 2^i - 1$ **Do** /* recall that $E_n[i]$ includes i */
8. $E_d[2^i + j] \leftarrow E_n[i] \mid E_d[j]$
9.   **End of for**
10.   **End of for**
11.   **Return** (B, E_d)

Fig. 5.15. Bit-parallel construction of E_d and B from Thompson's NFA. We use a numeric notation for the arguments of E_d.

Figure 5.16 shows the search algorithm. Each transition is simulated in two steps: First we use a **Shift-And**–like mechanism for the normal transitions using B, and second we use E_d to simulate all the ε-transitions.

Reducing space A table of size 2^L may be too large depending on the machine and the pattern. However, a *horizontal partitioning* scheme can be used to fit the available memory. We split E_d into two tables, E_d^1 and E_d^2, each of them defined over half of the bits. This exploits the following property, which comes directly from equation (5.3):

$$E_d[D_1 D_2] \quad = \quad E_d[D_1 0^{|D_2|}] \mid E_d[0^{|D_1|} D_2]$$

BPThompson$(N = (Q_n, \Sigma, I_n, F_n, B_n, E_n), T = t_1 t_2 \ldots t_n)$
1.   Preprocessing
2. $(B, E_d) \leftarrow$ **BuildEps**(N)
3.   Searching
4. $D \leftarrow E_d[I_n]$ /* the initial state */
5.   **For** $pos \in 1 \ldots n$ **Do**
6.   **If** D & $F_n \neq 0^L$ **Then** report an occurrence ending at $pos - 1$
7. $D \leftarrow E_d [(D << 1)$ & $B[t_{pos}]]$
8.   **End of for**

Fig. 5.16. Thompson's bit-parallel search algorithm.

that is, we can decompose the argument of E_d in two parts. Hence E_d^1 and E_d^2 are defined as follows, over masks of length $\lfloor L/2 \rfloor$ and $\lceil L/2 \rceil$, respectively:

$$E_d^1[D] = E_d[0^{\lceil L/2 \rceil} D] \; , \; E_d^2[D] = E_d[D 0^{\lfloor L/2 \rfloor}]$$

and hence it holds

$$E_d[d_m \ldots d_0] \;\; = \;\; E_d^1[d_{\lfloor L/2 \rfloor - 1} \ldots d_0] \;\; | \;\; E_d^2[d_m \ldots d_{\lfloor L/2 \rfloor}]$$

For instance, in Figure 5.5 we would have $E_n[3] = 100001001110001000$ and $E_n[11] = 111001101100000000$, so $E_d^1[000001000] = 100001001110001000$ and $E_d^2[000000100] = 111001101100000000$. Thus, $E_d[000000100000001000]$ $= 111001101110001000$.

The net result is that, instead of having a table of size $O(2^L)$, we have two much smaller tables, of size $O(2^{L/2})$. The cost is that we have to pay two accesses to memory in order to perform each transition.

The scheme can be generalized as follows. Assume that we have $O(s)$ space available for the tables. We split our table E_d into k tables $E_d^1 \ldots E_d^k$, each one addressing $\lfloor L/k \rfloor$ or $\lceil L/k \rceil$ bits of the argument mask. The total space required is $O(k 2^{L/k})$. If this space is s, then we have that $k \approx L/\log_2 s$. Therefore, the scheme permits a search time of $O(mn/\log s)$ using $O(s)$ space. This trade-off cannot be achieved with the classical DFA algorithm. Note that the complexity has to be multiplied by m/w for long patterns.

Depending on the architecture, even when a large table fits in memory, the cache optimization mechanism can make it advisable to use two smaller tables, which have more locality of reference.

Example of BPThompson We search for the pattern (AT|GA)((AG|AAA) *) in the text AAAGATAAGATAGAAAA, marking the final positions of occurrences. The states have been numbered according to Figure 5.5. As it is not practical to show the whole table E_d of $2^{18} = 262,144$ entries, we show the table E_n. Remember that the E_d rows are obtained by OR-ing the E_n rows corresponding to the bits set in the argument of E_d. We only show the E_n entries where $E(s) \neq \{s\}$; otherwise $E_n[s]$ contains $E(0) \cup \{s\}$.

For each character read we show two steps in the update of D, namely, before and after the ε-closure.

Table E_n

0	0 0 0 0 0 0 0 0 0 0 0 0 1 0 0 1 1
3	1 0 0 0 0 1 0 0 1 1 1 0 0 1 1 0 1 1
6	1 0 0 0 0 1 0 0 1 1 1 1 0 1 0 0 1 1
7	1 0 0 0 0 1 0 0 1 1 1 0 0 1 0 0 1 1
8	0 0 0 0 0 1 0 0 1 1 0 0 0 1 0 0 1 1
11	1 1 0 0 0 1 1 0 1 1 0 0 0 1 0 0 1 1
15	1 1 1 0 0 1 0 0 1 1 0 0 0 1 0 0 1 1
16	1 1 0 0 0 1 0 0 1 1 0 0 0 1 0 0 1 1

A	0 0 1 1 1 0 0 1 0 0 0 1 0 0 0 1 0 0
C	0 0 0 0 0 0 0 0 0 0 0 0 0 0 0 0 0 0
G	0 0 0 0 0 0 1 0 0 0 0 0 1 0 0 0 0 0
T	0 0 0 0 0 0 0 0 0 0 0 0 0 1 0 0 0
*	0 0 0 0 0 0 0 0 0 0 0 0 0 0 0 0 0 0

Table B

$F_n =$ 1 0 0 0 0 0 0 0 0 0 0 0 0 0 0 0 0 0

$D =$ 0 0 0 0 0 0 0 0 0 0 0 0 0 1 0 0 1 1

1. Reading A

$B[A]$ 0 0 1 1 1 0 0 1 0 0 0 1 0 0 0 1 0 0
$D =$ 0 0 0 0 0 0 0 0 0 0 0 0 0 0 0 1 0 0
$D =$ 0 0 0 0 0 0 0 0 0 0 0 0 0 1 0 1 1 1

2. Reading A

$B[A]$ 0 0 1 1 1 0 0 1 0 0 0 1 0 0 0 1 0 0
$D =$ 0 0 0 0 0 0 0 0 0 0 0 0 0 0 0 1 0 0
$D =$ 0 0 0 0 0 0 0 0 0 0 0 0 0 1 0 1 1 1

3. Reading A

$B[A]$ 0 0 1 1 1 0 0 1 0 0 0 1 0 0 0 1 0 0
$D =$ 0 0 0 0 0 0 0 0 0 0 0 0 0 0 0 1 0 0
$D =$ 0 0 0 0 0 0 0 0 0 0 0 0 0 1 0 1 1 1

4. Reading G

$B[G]$ 0 0 0 0 0 0 1 0 0 0 0 0 1 0 0 0 0 0
$D =$ 0 0 0 0 0 0 0 0 0 0 0 0 1 0 0 0 0 0
$D =$ 0 0 0 0 0 0 0 0 0 0 0 0 1 1 0 0 1 1

5. Reading A

$B[A]$ 0 0 1 1 1 0 0 1 0 0 0 1 0 0 0 1 0 0
$D =$ 0 0 0 0 0 0 0 0 0 0 0 1 0 0 0 1 0 0
$D =$ 1 0 0 0 0 1 0 0 1 1 1 1 0 1 0 1 1 1

D & $F_n \neq 0^L$, so we mark an occurrence.

6. Reading T

$B[T]$ 0 0 0 0 0 0 0 0 0 0 0 0 0 1 0 0 0
$D =$ 0 0 0 0 0 0 0 0 0 0 0 0 0 1 0 0 0
$D =$ 1 0 0 0 0 1 0 0 1 1 1 1 0 0 1 1 0 1 1

D & $F_n \neq 0^L$, so we mark an occurrence.

7. Reading A

$B[A]$ 0 0 1 1 1 0 0 1 0 0 0 1 0 0 0 1 0 0
$D =$ 0 0 0 0 1 0 0 1 0 0 0 0 0 0 0 1 0 0
$D =$ 0 0 0 0 1 0 0 1 0 0 0 0 0 0 1 0 1 1 1

8. Reading A

$B[A]$ 0 0 1 1 1 0 0 1 0 0 0 1 0 0 0 1 0 0
$D =$ 0 0 0 1 0 0 0 0 0 0 0 0 0 0 0 1 0 0
$D =$ 0 0 0 1 0 0 0 0 0 0 0 0 0 1 0 1 1 1

9. Reading G

$B[G]$ 0 0 0 0 0 0 1 0 0 0 0 0 1 0 0 0 0 0
$D =$ 0 0 0 0 0 0 0 0 0 0 0 0 1 0 0 0 0 0
$D =$ 0 0 0 0 0 0 0 0 0 0 0 0 1 1 0 0 1 1

10. Reading A

$B[A]$ 0 0 1 1 1 0 0 1 0 0 0 1 0 0 0 1 0 0
$D =$ 0 0 0 0 0 0 0 0 0 0 1 0 0 0 1 0 0
$D =$ 1 0 0 0 0 1 0 0 1 1 1 1 0 1 0 1 1 1

D & $F_n \neq 0^L$, so we mark an occurrence.

11. Reading T

$B[T]$ 0 0 0 0 0 0 0 0 0 0 0 0 0 1 0 0 0
$D =$ 0 0 0 0 0 0 0 0 0 0 0 0 0 1 0 0 0
$D =$ 1 0 0 0 0 1 0 0 1 1 1 0 0 1 1 0 1 1

D & $F_n \neq 0^L$, so we mark an occurrence.

12. Reading A

$B[A]$ 0 0 1 1 1 0 0 1 0 0 0 1 0 0 0 1 0 0
$D =$ 0 0 0 0 1 0 0 1 0 0 0 0 0 0 0 1 0 0
$D =$ 0 0 0 0 1 0 0 1 0 0 0 0 0 0 1 0 1 1 1

13. Reading G

$$\frac{B[\text{G}] \quad 0\,0\,0\,0\,0\,0\,1\,0\,0\,0\,0\,0\,1\,0\,0\,0\,0\,0}{\begin{array}{l} D = \quad 0\,0\,0\,0\,0\,0\,1\,0\,0\,0\,0\,0\,1\,0\,0\,0\,0\,0 \\ D = \quad 1\,1\,0\,0\,0\,1\,1\,0\,1\,1\,0\,0\,1\,1\,0\,0\,1\,1 \end{array}}$$

    $D \,\&\, F_n \neq 0^L$, so we mark an occurrence.

16. Reading A

$$\frac{B[\text{A}] \quad 0\,0\,1\,1\,1\,0\,0\,1\,0\,0\,0\,1\,0\,0\,0\,1\,0\,0}{\begin{array}{l} D = \quad 0\,0\,1\,1\,0\,0\,0\,0\,0\,0\,0\,0\,0\,0\,0\,1\,0\,0 \\ D = \quad 1\,1\,1\,1\,0\,1\,0\,0\,1\,1\,0\,0\,0\,1\,0\,1\,1\,1 \end{array}}$$

    $D \,\&\, F_n \neq 0^L$, so we mark an occurrence.

14. Reading A

$$\frac{B[\text{A}] \quad 0\,0\,1\,1\,1\,0\,0\,1\,0\,0\,0\,1\,0\,0\,0\,1\,0\,0}{\begin{array}{l} D = \quad 0\,0\,0\,0\,1\,0\,0\,1\,0\,0\,0\,1\,0\,0\,0\,1\,0\,0 \\ D = \quad 1\,0\,0\,0\,1\,1\,0\,1\,1\,1\,1\,1\,0\,1\,0\,1\,1\,1 \end{array}}$$

    $D \,\&\, F_n \neq 0^L$, so we mark an occurrence.

17. Reading A

$$\frac{B[\text{A}] \quad 0\,0\,1\,1\,1\,0\,0\,1\,0\,0\,0\,1\,0\,0\,0\,1\,0\,0}{\begin{array}{l} D = \quad 0\,0\,1\,0\,1\,0\,0\,1\,0\,0\,0\,0\,0\,0\,0\,1\,0\,0 \\ D = \quad 1\,1\,1\,0\,1\,1\,0\,1\,1\,1\,0\,0\,0\,1\,0\,1\,1\,1 \end{array}}$$

    $D \,\&\, F_n \neq 0^L$, so we mark an occurrence.

15. Reading A

$$\frac{B[\text{A}] \quad 0\,0\,1\,1\,1\,0\,0\,1\,0\,0\,0\,1\,0\,0\,0\,1\,0\,0}{\begin{array}{l} D = \quad 0\,0\,0\,1\,1\,0\,0\,1\,0\,0\,0\,0\,0\,0\,0\,1\,0\,0 \\ D = \quad 0\,0\,0\,1\,1\,0\,0\,1\,0\,0\,0\,0\,0\,1\,0\,1\,1\,1 \end{array}}$$

5.4.2 Bit-parallel Glushkov

Another bit-parallel algorithm [NR99a, Nav01b, NR01a] uses Glushkov's NFA, which has exactly $m + 1$ states. We call it **BPGlushkov**.

The reason to choose Glushkov over Thompson is that we need to build and store a table whose size is $2^{|Q|}$, and Thompson's automaton has more states than Glushkov's. The price is that now the transitions of the automaton cannot be decomposed into forward ones plus ε-transitions. In Glushkov's construction there are no ε-transitions, but the transitions by characters do not follow a simple forward pattern.

However, there is another property enforced by Glushkov's construction that can be successfully exploited (Section 5.2.2): All the arrows arriving at a given state are labeled by the same character. So we can compute the transitions by using two tables: $B[\sigma]$ (formula (5.4)) tells which states can be reached by character σ, and

$$T_d[D] \;=\; \big|_{(i,\sigma),\; D\,\&\,0^{m-i}10^i \neq 0^{m+1},\; \sigma \in \Sigma}\; B_n[i,\sigma]$$

tells which states can be reached from D by any character.

Thus $\delta(D, \sigma) \;=\; T_d[D] \,\&\, B[\sigma]$. We use this property to build and store only T_d and B instead of a complete transition table. Figure 5.17 shows the necessary preprocessing. The ideas are similar to those used to build E_d and B in Section 5.4.1. This time the cost is $O(2^m + m|\Sigma|)$ by using an intermediate table $A[i] = |_{\sigma \in \Sigma}\, B[i,\sigma]$, which is essentially a bit-parallel representation of the *Follow* set (Section 5.2.2). Figure 5.18 shows the search algorithm, which is similar to **BPThompson**.

BuildTran $(N = (Q_n, \Sigma, I_n, F_n, B_n))$
1.   **For** $i \in 0 \ldots m$ **Do** $A[i] \leftarrow 0^{m+1}$
2.   **For** $\sigma \in \Sigma$ **Do** $B[\sigma] \leftarrow 0^{m+1}$
3.   **For** $i \in 0 \ldots m$, $\sigma \in \Sigma$ **Do**
4. $A[i] \leftarrow A[i] \mid B_n[i, \sigma]$
5. $B[\sigma] \leftarrow B[\sigma] \mid B_n[i, \sigma]$
6.   **End of for**
             /* B and A are built, now build T_d */
7. $T_d[0] \leftarrow 0^{m+1}$
8.   **For** $i \in 0 \ldots m$ **Do**
9.   **For** $j \in 0 \ldots 2^i - 1$ **Do**
10. $T_d[2^i + j] \leftarrow A[i] \mid T_d[j]$
11.   **End of for**
12.   **End of for**
13.   **Return** (B, T_d)

Fig. 5.17. Bit-parallel construction of B and T_d from Glushkov's NFA. We use a numeric notation for the argument of T_d.

BPGlushkov$(N = (Q_n, \Sigma, I_n, F_n, B_n), T = t_1 t_2 \ldots t_n)$
1.   Preprocessing
2.   **For** $\sigma \in \Sigma$ **Do** $B_n[0, \sigma] \leftarrow B_n[0, \sigma] \mid 0^m 1$ /* initial self-loop */
3. $(B, T_d) \leftarrow$ **BuildTran**(N)
4.   Searching
5. $D \leftarrow 0^m 1$ /* the initial state */
6.   **For** $pos \in 1 \ldots n$ **Do**
7.   **If** $D \text{ \& } F_n \neq 0^{m+1}$ **Then** report an occurrence ending at $pos - 1$
8. $D \leftarrow T_d[D] \text{ \& } B[t_{pos}]$
9.   **End of for**

Fig. 5.18. Glushkov's bit-parallel search algorithm.

Compared to **BPThompson**, **BPGlushkov** has the advantage of needing $O(2^m)$ space instead of up to $O(2^{2m})$. Just as for E_d, it is possible to split T_d horizontally to obtain $O(mn/\log s)$ time with $O(s)$ space. Therefore, **BPGlushkov** should be always preferred over **BPThompson**.

Example of BPGlushkov We search for the pattern (AT|GA)((AG|AAA)*) in the text AAAGATAAGATAGAAAA, marking the final position of occurrences. We use Glushkov's simulation, where the states have been numbered according to Figure 5.7. Since it is not practical to show the whole table T_d of $2^{10} = 1024$ entries, we show only the tables B_n, B, and the rows of T_d that are needed in the search. Remember that the T_d rows are obtained by OR-ing the B_n rows corresponding to the bits set in the argument of T_d over every character. In B_n we only show the entries leading to a nonzero result.

$$B_n = \begin{cases} \begin{array}{|c|c|l|} \hline 0 & \text{A} & 0\,0\,0\,0\,0\,0\,0\,0\,1\,1 \\ 0 & \text{C} & 0\,0\,0\,0\,0\,0\,0\,0\,0\,1 \\ 0 & \text{G} & 0\,0\,0\,0\,0\,0\,1\,0\,0\,1 \\ 0 & \text{T} & 0\,0\,0\,0\,0\,0\,0\,0\,0\,1 \\ 1 & \text{T} & 0\,0\,0\,0\,0\,0\,0\,1\,0\,0 \\ 2 & \text{A} & 0\,0\,1\,0\,1\,0\,0\,0\,0\,0 \\ 3 & \text{A} & 0\,0\,0\,0\,0\,1\,0\,0\,0\,0 \\ 4 & \text{A} & 0\,0\,1\,0\,1\,0\,0\,0\,0\,0 \\ 5 & \text{G} & 0\,0\,0\,1\,0\,0\,0\,0\,0\,0 \\ 6 & \text{A} & 0\,0\,1\,0\,1\,0\,0\,0\,0\,0 \\ 7 & \text{A} & 0\,1\,0\,0\,0\,0\,0\,0\,0\,0 \\ 8 & \text{A} & 1\,0\,0\,0\,0\,0\,0\,0\,0\,0 \\ 9 & \text{A} & 0\,0\,1\,0\,1\,0\,0\,0\,0\,0 \\ \hline \end{array} \end{cases}$$

$$B = \begin{cases} \begin{array}{|c|l|} \hline \text{A} & 1\,1\,1\,0\,1\,1\,0\,0\,1\,1 \\ \text{C} & 0\,0\,0\,0\,0\,0\,0\,0\,0\,1 \\ \text{G} & 0\,0\,0\,1\,0\,0\,1\,0\,0\,1 \\ \text{T} & 0\,0\,0\,0\,0\,0\,0\,1\,0\,1 \\ \hline \end{array} \end{cases}$$

$F_n = 1\,0\,0\,1\,0\,1\,0\,1\,0\,0$

$D = 0\,0\,0\,0\,0\,0\,0\,0\,0\,1$

1. Reading A
$$\begin{aligned} T_d[D] &= 0\,0\,0\,0\,0\,0\,1\,0\,1\,1 \\ B[\text{A}] &= 1\,1\,1\,0\,1\,1\,0\,0\,1\,1 \\ D &= 0\,0\,0\,0\,0\,0\,0\,0\,1\,1 \end{aligned}$$

2. Reading A
$$\begin{aligned} T_d[D] &= 0\,0\,0\,0\,0\,0\,1\,1\,1\,1 \\ B[\text{A}] &= 1\,1\,1\,0\,1\,1\,0\,0\,1\,1 \\ D &= 0\,0\,0\,0\,0\,0\,0\,0\,1\,1 \end{aligned}$$

3. Reading A
$$\begin{aligned} T_d[D] &= 0\,0\,0\,0\,0\,0\,1\,1\,1\,1 \\ B[\text{A}] &= 1\,1\,1\,0\,1\,1\,0\,0\,1\,1 \\ D &= 0\,0\,0\,0\,0\,0\,0\,0\,1\,1 \end{aligned}$$

4. Reading G
$$\begin{aligned} T_d[D] &= 0\,0\,0\,0\,0\,0\,1\,1\,1\,1 \\ B[\text{G}] &= 0\,0\,0\,1\,0\,0\,1\,0\,0\,1 \\ D &= 0\,0\,0\,0\,0\,0\,1\,0\,0\,1 \end{aligned}$$

5. Reading A
$$\begin{aligned} T_d[D] &= 0\,0\,0\,0\,0\,1\,1\,0\,1\,1 \\ B[\text{A}] &= 1\,1\,1\,0\,1\,1\,0\,0\,1\,1 \\ D &= 0\,0\,0\,0\,0\,1\,0\,0\,1\,1 \end{aligned}$$

D & $F_n \neq 0^{m+1}$, so we mark an occurrence.

6. Reading T
$$\begin{aligned} T_d[D] &= 0\,0\,1\,0\,1\,0\,1\,1\,1\,1 \\ B[\text{T}] &= 0\,0\,0\,0\,0\,0\,0\,1\,0\,1 \\ D &= 0\,0\,0\,0\,0\,0\,0\,1\,0\,1 \end{aligned}$$

D & $F_n \neq 0^{m+1}$, so we mark an occurrence.

7. Reading A
$$\begin{aligned} T_d[D] &= 0\,0\,1\,0\,1\,0\,1\,0\,1\,1 \\ B[\text{A}] &= 1\,1\,1\,0\,1\,1\,0\,0\,1\,1 \\ D &= 0\,0\,1\,0\,1\,0\,0\,0\,1\,1 \end{aligned}$$

8. Reading A
$$\begin{aligned} T_d[D] &= 0\,1\,0\,1\,0\,0\,1\,1\,1\,1 \\ B[\text{A}] &= 1\,1\,1\,0\,1\,1\,0\,0\,1\,1 \\ D &= 0\,1\,0\,0\,0\,0\,0\,0\,1\,1 \end{aligned}$$

9. Reading G
$$\begin{aligned} T_d[D] &= 1\,0\,0\,0\,0\,0\,1\,1\,1\,1 \\ B[\text{G}] &= 0\,0\,0\,1\,0\,0\,1\,0\,0\,1 \\ D &= 0\,0\,0\,0\,0\,0\,1\,0\,0\,1 \end{aligned}$$

10. Reading A
$$\begin{aligned} T_d[D] &= 0\,0\,0\,0\,0\,1\,1\,0\,1\,1 \\ B[\text{A}] &= 1\,1\,1\,0\,1\,1\,0\,0\,1\,1 \\ D &= 0\,0\,0\,0\,0\,1\,0\,0\,1\,1 \end{aligned}$$

D & $F_n \neq 0^{m+1}$, so we mark an occurrence.

11. Reading T
$$\begin{aligned} T_d[D] &= 0\,0\,1\,0\,1\,0\,1\,1\,1\,1 \\ B[\text{T}] &= 0\,0\,0\,0\,0\,0\,0\,1\,0\,1 \\ D &= 0\,0\,0\,0\,0\,0\,0\,1\,0\,1 \end{aligned}$$

D & $F_n \neq 0^{m+1}$, so we mark an occurrence.

12. Reading A
$$\begin{aligned} T_d[D] &= 0\,0\,1\,0\,1\,0\,1\,0\,1\,1 \\ B[\text{A}] &= 1\,1\,1\,0\,1\,1\,0\,0\,1\,1 \\ D &= 0\,0\,1\,0\,1\,0\,0\,0\,1\,1 \end{aligned}$$

13. Reading G

$$T_d[D] = 0101001111$$
$$B[\texttt{G}] = 0001001001$$
$$D = 0001001001$$

D & $F_n \neq 0^{m+1}$, so we mark an occurrence.

14. Reading A

$$T_d[D] = 0010111011$$
$$B[\texttt{A}] = 1110110011$$
$$D = 0010110011$$

D & $F_n \neq 0^{m+1}$, so we mark an occurrence.

15. Reading A

$$T_d[D] = 0111101111$$
$$B[\texttt{A}] = 1110110011$$
$$D = 0110100011$$

16. Reading A

$$T_d[D] = 1101001111$$
$$B[\texttt{A}] = 1110110011$$
$$D = 1100000011$$

D & $F_n \neq 0^{m+1}$, so we mark an occurrence.

17. Reading A

$$T_d[D] = 1010101111$$
$$B[\texttt{A}] = 1110110011$$
$$D = 1010100011$$

D & $F_n \neq 0^{m+1}$, so we mark an occurrence.

5.5 Filtration approaches

All the approaches seen so far needed to examine every text character. It is natural to ask whether any of the approaches seen in previous chapters for simple, multiple, or extended string matching can be applied to regular expression searching. Our goal in this section is to avoid reading every text character.

The algorithms that use filtration are generally newer than those of the previous sections, and they achieve in general much faster searching when the regular expression permits it. As we will see shortly, not every regular expression is amenable to filtration, so there are cases where we have to resort to the previous techniques.

For technical reasons, it will be more interesting to reverse our example pattern in this section. Its Glushkov automaton is shown in Figure 5.19.

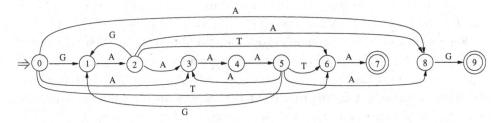

Fig. 5.19. Glushkov automaton built on the regular expression `((GA|AAA)*)` `(TA|AG)`.

Given a regular expression, we compute the length ℓmin of its shortest occurrence. Any method based on skipping text characters must examine at least one out of every ℓmin characters to avoid missing an occurrence. Hence, in general we will use a window of length ℓmin.

Figure 5.20 gives the recursive algorithm to compute ℓmin in $O(m)$ time using the parse tree of the regular expression. A shortest path algorithm from the initial to a final NFA state is also possible.

Lmin(v)
1.   **If** $v = \boxed{|}\ (v_l, v_r)$ **Then Return** $min(\mathbf{Lmin}(v_l), \mathbf{Lmin}(v_r))$
2.   **If** $v = \boxed{\cdot}\ (v_l, v_r)$ **Then Return** $\mathbf{Lmin}(v_l) + \mathbf{Lmin}(v_r)$
3.   **If** $v = \boxed{*}\ (v_*)$ **Then Return** 0
4.   **If** $v = (\alpha)\ ,\ \alpha \in \Sigma$ **Then Return** 1
5.   **If** $v = (\varepsilon)$ **Then Return** 0

Fig. 5.20. Computation of ℓmin.

5.5.1 Multistring matching approach

This method [Wat96], which we call **MultiStringRE**, consists of generating the prefixes of length ℓmin for all the strings matching the regular expression $Pref(RE)$. In the regular expression $RE = ((GA | AAA) *) (TA | AG)$ we have $\ell min(RE) = 2$, and the set of length-2 prefixes of strings matching the pattern is $Pref(RE) = \{$ GA, AA, TA, AG $\}$. A more complex example would be $RE = (AT | GA)(AG | AAA)((AG | AAA)+)$, where $\ell min(RE) = 6$ and the set of prefixes is $Pref(RE) = \{$ ATAGAG, ATAGAA, ATAAAA, GAAGAG, GAAGAA, GAAAAA $\}$.

Figure 5.21 gives pseudo-code that generates the set of prefixes from a regular expression. A very convenient way of representing $Pref$ is as a trie, because it is easier to generate and to use later for searching. For simplicity we assume that the NFA is ε-free. The time is worst-case $O(|\Delta|^{\ell min})$.

For reasons that will become clear soon, we also store at each trie leaf x the DFA state $Active(x)$ that is reached by reading each trie path. In this case we represent the DFA state as the set of NFA states. It is also possible to write a version of **Compute_Pref** that works on the DFA, and in this case any other representation for DFA states can be used as well.

Once the set of prefixes is computed, the algorithm uses a multipattern search for the set $Pref(RE)$ (Chapter 3). In particular, [Wat96] focuses on **Commentz-Walter**–like algorithms. Since every occurrence of the regular

```
Pref(s, Δ, ℓmin, Trie)
 1.     If ℓmin = 0 Then /* trie leaf */
 2.         Active(Trie) ← Active(Trie) ∪ {s}
 3.         Return Trie
 4.     End of if
 5.     For (s, σ, s') ∈ Δ Do
 6.         If δ(Trie, σ) = θ Then
 7.             Create new state Next = δ(Trie, σ)
 8.             Active(Next) ← ∅
 9.         End of if
10.         Pref(s', Δ, ℓmin − 1, Next)
11.     End of for

Compute_Pref(N = (Q, Σ, I, F, Δ), ℓmin)
12.     Trie ← θ
13.     Pref(I, Δ, ℓmin, Trie)
14.     Return (Trie, Active)
```

Fig. 5.21. Computation of *Pref*. It receives an ε-free NFA and *ℓmin* and returns *Pref* in trie form and *Active* at the leaves.

expression must start with the occurrence of a string in *Pref*(*RE*), it is enough to check for the occurrences of *RE* that start at the initial positions of *Pref*(*RE*) in the text. To check for an occurrence starting at a given position we can use any of the methods seen earlier in this chapter, except that we do *not* add the initial self-loop. This forces the occurrence to start at the position specified. Since the length of a string matching a regular expression is in general unbounded, we have to run the automaton until it reaches a final state, it runs out of active states, or we reach the end of the text.

To avoid re-reading the first *ℓmin* characters of the window at verification time, we initialize the automaton with the states in *Active*(*x*) and start reading the characters after the window. In particular, if we use a bit-parallel representation of the DFA, then *Active* can be stored as a bit mask and used directly to initialize the automaton.

The effectiveness of this method depends basically on two values: *ℓmin* (the search is faster for larger *ℓmin*) and the size of *Pref*(*RE*) (the search is faster for less prefixes). Note that the size of *Pref*(*RE*) can be exponential in *m*, for example, searching for (a|b)(a|b) ... (a|b). It is possible to artificially reduce *ℓmin* to avoid an excessively large trie. We see in Section 5.5.3 a method that avoids this problem.

MultiStringRE($N = (Q, \Sigma, I, F, \Delta)$, ℓmin)
1.   Preprocessing
        /* Construction of *Pref* */
2.   (*Pref*, *Active*) $\leftarrow$ **Compute_Pref**($N, \ell min$)
        /* Construction of the DFA (Figure 5.17) without initial self-loop */
3.   Produce bit-parallel version $N' = (Q_n, \Sigma, I_n, F_n, B_n)$ of N
4. $(B, T_d) \leftarrow$ **BuildTran**(N')
5.   Searching
        /* Multipattern search of *Pref*. Check each occurrence with the DFA */
6.   **For** (*pos*, *i*) $\in$ output of multipattern search of *Pref* **Do**
7. $D \leftarrow Active(i)$, $j \leftarrow pos + 1$
8.   **While** $j \leq n$ AND $D \,\&\, F_n = 0^{m+1}$ AND $D \neq 0^{m+1}$ **Do**
9. $D \leftarrow T_d[D] \,\&\, B[t_j]$
10.   **End of while**
11.   **If** $D \,\&\, F_n \neq 0^{m+1}$ **Then**
12.   Report an occurrence beginning at $pos + 1 - \ell min$
13.   **End of if**
14.   **End of for**

Fig. 5.22. MultiStringRE search algorithm. It receives an NFA and the minimum length of a string accepted by it and reports the initial positions of occurrences. We assume that the verification is done with the bit-parallel Glushkov simulation of Section 5.4.2. Consequently, we assume a bit map representation of *Active*.

Example of MultiStringRE search We search for the pattern ((GA|AAA)*)(TA|AG) in the text AAAAGATAGAATAGAAA, the reverse of the example text used earlier in this chapter, and mark the initial positions of occurrences.

We use as our verification engine the bit-parallel Glushkov simulation of Section 5.4.2, where the states have been numbered according to Figure 5.19. As before, we only show the nonzero B_n entries.

The example may look clumsy because our search pattern and text permit little filtering. However, the example shows all the cases that may occur.

$$B_n = \begin{cases}
\begin{array}{|c|c|l|}
\hline
0 & A & 0\,1\,0\,0\,0\,0\,1\,0\,0\,0 \\
0 & G & 0\,0\,0\,0\,0\,0\,0\,0\,1\,0 \\
0 & T & 0\,0\,0\,1\,0\,0\,0\,0\,0\,0 \\
\hline
1 & A & 0\,0\,0\,0\,0\,0\,0\,1\,0\,0 \\
\hline
2 & A & 0\,1\,0\,0\,0\,0\,1\,0\,0\,0 \\
2 & G & 0\,0\,0\,0\,0\,0\,0\,0\,1\,0 \\
2 & T & 0\,0\,0\,1\,0\,0\,0\,0\,0\,0 \\
\hline
3 & A & 0\,0\,0\,0\,0\,1\,0\,0\,0\,0 \\
\hline
4 & A & 0\,0\,0\,0\,1\,0\,0\,0\,0\,0 \\
\hline
5 & A & 0\,1\,0\,0\,0\,0\,1\,0\,0\,0 \\
5 & G & 0\,0\,0\,0\,0\,0\,0\,0\,1\,0 \\
5 & T & 0\,0\,0\,1\,0\,0\,0\,0\,0\,0 \\
\hline
6 & A & 0\,0\,1\,0\,0\,0\,0\,0\,0\,0 \\
\hline
8 & G & 1\,0\,0\,0\,0\,0\,0\,0\,0\,0 \\
\hline
\end{array}
\end{cases}$$

$$B = \begin{cases}
\begin{array}{|c|l|}
\hline
A & 0\,1\,1\,0\,1\,1\,1\,1\,0\,0 \\
C & 0\,0\,0\,0\,0\,0\,0\,0\,0\,0 \\
G & 1\,0\,0\,0\,0\,0\,0\,0\,1\,0 \\
T & 0\,0\,0\,1\,0\,0\,0\,0\,0\,0 \\
\hline
\end{array}
\end{cases}$$

$$Pref = \begin{cases}
\begin{array}{|c|l|}
\hline
\text{prefix} & Active \\
\hline
\text{GA} & 0\,0\,0\,0\,0\,0\,0\,1\,0\,0 \\
\text{AA} & 0\,0\,0\,0\,0\,1\,0\,0\,0\,0 \\
\text{TA} & 0\,0\,1\,0\,0\,0\,0\,0\,0\,0 \\
\text{AG} & 1\,0\,0\,0\,0\,0\,0\,0\,0\,0 \\
\hline
\end{array}
\end{cases}$$

$$F_n = 1\,0\,1\,0\,0\,0\,0\,0\,0\,0$$

$$\ell min = 2$$

1. $\boxed{\text{AA}}$ AAGATAGAATAGAAA

   $D = \quad 0\ 0\ 0\ 0\ 0\ 1\ 0\ 0\ 0\ 0$
Reading A	0 0 0 0 1 0 0 0 0 0
Reading A	0 1 0 0 0 0 1 0 0 0
Reading G	1 0 0 0 0 0 0 0 0 0

   $D \,\&\, F_n \neq 0^{m+1}$, so we report an occurrence beginning at 1.

2. A $\boxed{\text{AA}}$ AGATAGAATAGAAA

   $D = \quad 0\ 0\ 0\ 0\ 0\ 1\ 0\ 0\ 0\ 0$
Reading A	0 0 0 0 1 0 0 0 0 0
Reading G	0 0 0 0 0 0 0 0 1 0
Reading A	0 0 0 0 0 0 0 1 0 0
Reading T	0 0 0 1 0 0 0 0 0 0
Reading A	0 0 1 0 0 0 0 0 0 0

   $D \,\&\, F_n \neq 0^{m+1}$, so we report an occurrence beginning at 2.

3. AA $\boxed{\text{AA}}$ GATAGAATAGAAA

   $D = \quad 0\ 0\ 0\ 0\ 0\ 1\ 0\ 0\ 0\ 0$
Reading G	0 0 0 0 0 0 0 0 0 0

   $D = 0^{m+1}$, so we discard position 3.

4. AAA $\boxed{\text{AG}}$ ATAGAATAGAAA

   $D = \quad 1\ 0\ 0\ 0\ 0\ 0\ 0\ 0\ 0\ 0$

   $D \,\&\, F_n \neq 0^{m+1}$, so we report an occurrence beginning at 4.

5. AAAA $\boxed{\text{GA}}$ TAGAATAGAAA

   $D = \quad 0\ 0\ 0\ 0\ 0\ 0\ 0\ 1\ 0\ 0$
Reading T	0 0 0 1 0 0 0 0 0 0
Reading A	0 0 1 0 0 0 0 0 0 0

   $D \,\&\, F_n \neq 0^{m+1}$, so we report an occurrence beginning at 5.

6. AAAAGA $\boxed{\text{TA}}$ GAATAGAAA
   (we skipped position 6).

   $D = \quad 0\ 0\ 1\ 0\ 0\ 0\ 0\ 0\ 0\ 0$

   $D \,\&\, F_n \neq 0^{m+1}$, so we report an occurrence beginning at 7.

7. AAAAGAT $\boxed{\text{AG}}$ AATAGAAA

   $D = \quad 1\ 0\ 0\ 0\ 0\ 0\ 0\ 0\ 0\ 0$

   $D \,\&\, F_n \neq 0^{m+1}$, so we report an occurrence beginning at 8.

8. AAAAGATA $\boxed{\text{GA}}$ ATAGAAA

   $D = \quad 0\ 0\ 0\ 0\ 0\ 0\ 0\ 1\ 0\ 0$
Reading A	0 1 0 0 0 0 1 0 0 0
Reading T	0 0 0 0 0 0 0 0 0 0

   $D = 0^{m+1}$, so we discard position 9.

9. AAAAGATAG $\boxed{\text{AA}}$ TAGAAA

   $D = \quad .0\ 0\ 0\ 0\ 0\ 1\ 0\ 0\ 0\ 0$
Reading T	0 0 0 0 0 0 0 0 0 0

   $D = 0^{m+1}$, so we discard position 10.

10. AAAAGATAGAA $\boxed{\text{TA}}$ GAAA

    $D = \quad 0\ 0\ 1\ 0\ 0\ 0\ 0\ 0\ 0\ 0$

    $D \,\&\, F_n \neq 0^{m+1}$, so we report an occurrence beginning at 12.

11. AAAAGATAGAAT $\boxed{\text{AG}}$ AAA

    $D = \quad 1\ 0\ 0\ 0\ 0\ 0\ 0\ 0\ 0\ 0$

    $D \,\&\, F_n \neq 0^{m+1}$, so we report an occurrence beginning at 13.

12. AAAAGATAGAATA $\boxed{\text{GA}}$ AA

    $D = \quad 0\ 0\ 0\ 0\ 0\ 0\ 0\ 1\ 0\ 0$
Reading A	0 1 0 0 0 0 1 0 0 0
Reading A	0 0 0 0 0 1 0 0 0 0

    The text finishes without an occurrence, so we discard text position 14.

13. AAAAGATAGAATAG $\boxed{\text{AA}}$ A

    $D = \quad 0\ 0\ 0\ 0\ 0\ 1\ 0\ 0\ 0\ 0$
Reading A	0 0 0 0 1 0 0 0 0 0

    The text finishes without an occurrence, so we discard text position 15.

14. AAAAGATAGAATAGA $\boxed{\text{AA}}$

    $D = \quad 0\ 0\ 0\ 0\ 0\ 1\ 0\ 0\ 0\ 0$

    The text finishes without an occurrence, so we discard text position 16.

5.5.2 Gnu's heuristic based on necessary factors

A heuristic used in *Gnu Grep* consists of selecting a *necessary set of factors*. We call it **MultiFactRE**. In the simplest case, we may find that a given string must appear in every occurrence of the regular expression. For example, if we look for (AG|GA)ATA((TT)*), then the string ATA is a necessary factor.

The idea in general is to find a set of necessary factors and perform a multipattern search for all of them. There are many ways to choose a suitable set, and *Grep*'s documentation is insufficient to determine its technique. Note that *Pref* is just a particular case of this approach. The advantage of *Pref* is that we know where the match should start, while the general method may need a verification in both directions starting from the factor found.

The selection of the best set of necessary factors has two parts. The first part is an algorithm that detects the correct candidate sets. The second part is a function that evaluates the cost to search using a candidate set and the number of potential matches it produces. A good measure for evaluating a set is its overall probability of occurrence, but finer considerations may include knowledge of the search algorithm used.

Figure 5.23 gives an algorithm that finds sets of necessary factors and selects the best one, assuming that a function *best* to compare sets has been defined. The code works recursively on the parse tree of the regular expression and returns $(all, pref, suff, fact)$, where *all* is the set of all the strings matching the expression, *pref* is the best set of prefixes, *suff* is the best set of suffixes, and *fact* is the best set of factors. Our answer is the fourth element of the tuple returned. If this is θ, then no finite set of necessary factors exists.

The easiest cases are single characters and ε. For a "*" operator, the strings inside can be repeated an unbounded number of times, so we cannot guarantee a finite set for *all*. So we return $\{\varepsilon\}$ for *pref*, *suff* and *fact*, and θ for *all*. For a "|" operator, we need to make the union of the two children for each of the four values. Note that we have to keep any θ present at the children. Finally, the most interesting operator is ".". To obtain $all(RE_1 RE_2)$ we concatenate any string of $all(RE_1)$ to any string of $all(RE_2)$. To obtain the best $pref(RE_1 RE_2)$ we choose the best among $pref(RE_1)$ and $pref(RE_2)$, with the understanding that this last set has to be preceded by $all(RE_1)$. The case of *suff* is symmetrical. Finally, for $fact(RE_1 RE_2)$ we can choose between $fact(RE_1)$, $fact(RE_2)$, and $suff(RE_1)$ concatenated to $pref(RE_2)$.

BestFactor(v)
1. **If** $v = [\,|\,](v_l, v_r)$ OR $v = \boxed{\cdot}\,(v_l, v_r)$ **Then**
2. $(all_l, pref_l, suff_l, fact_l) \leftarrow$ **BestFactor**(v_l)
3. $(all_r, pref_r, suff_r, fact_r) \leftarrow$ **BestFactor**(v_r)
4. **End of if**
5. **If** $v = [\,|\,](v_l, v_r)$ **Then**
6.   **Return** $(all_l \cup all_r,\ pref_l \cup pref_r,\ suff_l \cup suff_r,\ fact_l \cup fact_r)$
7. **Else If** $v = \boxed{\cdot}\,(v_l, v_r)$ **Then**
8.   **Return** $(all_l \cdot all_r,\ best(pref_l, all_l \cdot pref_r),$
              $best(suff_r, suff_l \cdot all_r),\ best(fact_l, fact_r, suff_l \cdot pref_r)$
9. **Else If** $v = \boxed{*}\,(v_*)$ **Then Return** $(\theta, \theta, \theta, \theta)$
10. **Else If** $v = \boxed{\alpha}\,,\ \alpha \in \Sigma$ **Then Return** $(\{\alpha\}, \{\alpha\}, \{\alpha\}, \{\alpha\})$
11. **Else If** $v = \boxed{\varepsilon}$ **Then Return** $(\{\varepsilon\}, \{\varepsilon\}, \{\varepsilon\}, \{\varepsilon\})$
12. **End of if**

Fig. 5.23. Computation of the best set of necessary factors. We assume that θ acts as Σ^*, so that $\theta \cup A = A \cup \theta = \theta \cdot A = A \cdot \theta = \theta$ for any A. Also, $best$ always considers θ the worst option.

This method gives better results than **MultiStringRE** because it has the potential of choosing the best set. In the example $(\texttt{(GA|AAA)*})(\texttt{TA|AG})$, instead of choosing a set of four strings as **MultiStringRE** does, it can choose $\{\texttt{TA},\texttt{AG}\}$, which is smaller.

5.5.3 An approach based on BNDM

Our final technique able to skip characters [NR99a, Nav01b] is an extension of **BNDM** (Sections 2.4.2, 4.3.2, and 4.2.2) to regular expressions. We call it **RegularBNDM**. It has the benefit of using the same space as a forward search.

The idea is based on the bit-parallel DFA simulation of Glushkov's construction (Section 5.4.2). We modify the DFA by reversing the arrows and making all states initial, so that the resulting automaton recognizes every reverse prefix of RE and is alive as long as we have read a reverse factor of RE. Note that this automaton does not have an initial self-loop. Figure 5.24 shows the result on $(\texttt{(GA|AAA)*})(\texttt{TA|AG})$.

We slide a window of length ℓmin along the text. The window is read backwards with the automaton. Each time we recognize a prefix we store in a variable *last* the window position where this happened. When the window is shifted, it is aligned so as to start at position *last*. The backward traversal inside the window may finish because the DFA runs out of active states, in

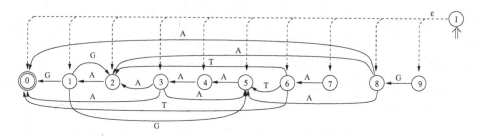

Fig. 5.24. Automaton to recognize all the reverse prefixes of the regular expression `((GA|AAA)*)(TA|AG)`.

which case we shift the window and restart the process, or because we reach the beginning of the window.

In the latter case, as for extended patterns (Chapter 4), we cannot guarantee an occurrence of the regular expression, just a factor of it. So, if the final state of the automaton has been reached at the beginning of the window, we start a forward verification using the normal DFA without an initial self-loop.

The above scheme can be improved. If we are at window position $j \le \ell min$, it is not relevant whether an automaton state at a distance greater than j from the initial state 0 is still active, because that state can never activate state 0 within the window. So we keep masks $Reach_j$ for $j \in 0 \ldots \ell min$, which contain the states that can influence the final result from window position j. By removing active states that are not in $Reach_j$, we are able to shift the window sooner.

Figure 5.24 makes it clear that the Glushkov property of all the arrows arriving at a given state being labeled by the same character does not hold when we reverse the arrows. Therefore, the **BPGlushkov** simulation cannot be applied directly. However, we can obtain a similar result by noticing that a dual property holds after we reverse the arrows: All the arrows leaving a given state are labeled by the same character.

Therefore we can use again tables T_d and B as before, but this time we have to mask with B *before* using T_d. That is, we keep the active states whose arrows leave by the current character and then take all the transitions leaving them. Formally, $\delta(D, \sigma) = T_d[\, D\ \&\ B[\sigma]\,]$, where B corresponds to the *forward* transitions.

Figure 5.25 shows the preprocessing algorithm, which yields a forward automaton (B, Tf_d), a backward automaton Tb_d, and the table $Reach$. Table Tf_d is obtained by making the input NFA deterministic without adding a

Compute_Reach $(T_d, I, \ell min)$
1. $Reach_0 \leftarrow I$ /* the initial state */
2.   **For** $j \in 1 \ldots \ell min$ **Do**
3. $Reach_j \leftarrow Reach_{j-1} \mid T_d[Reach_{j-1}]$
4.   **Return** $Reach$

Reverse_Arrows $(N = (Q_n, \Sigma, I_n, F_n, Bf_n))$
5.   **For** $i \in 0 \ldots m, \; \sigma \in \Sigma$ **Do**
6. $Bb_n[i, \sigma] \leftarrow 0^{m+1}$
7.   **For** $j \in 0 \ldots m$ **Do**
8.   **If** $Bf_n[j, \sigma] \; \& \; 0^{m-i}10^i \neq 0^{m+1}$ **Then**
9. $Bb_n[i, \sigma] \leftarrow Bb_n[i, \sigma] \mid 0^{m-j}10^j$
10.   **End of if**
11.   **End of for**
12.   **End of for**
13.   **Return** Bb_n

BNDM_Preproc $(N = (Q_n, \Sigma, I_n, F_n, B_n), \; \ell min)$
            /* (B, Tf_d) (no initial self-loop) is used for verification */
14. $(B, Tf_d) \leftarrow$ **BuildTran**(N)
            /* Reach tells reachable states */
15. $Reach \leftarrow$ **Compute_Reach**$(Tf_d, I_n, \ell min)$
            /* Tb_d is a DFA for recognizing reverse prefixes */
16. $Bb_n \leftarrow$ **Reverse_Arrows**(N)
17. $(Bb, Tb_d) \leftarrow$ **BuildTran**$(Nb = (Q_n, \Sigma, 1^{m+1}, 0^m1, Bb_n))$
18.   **Return** $(B, Tf_d, Tb_d, Reach)$

Fig. 5.25. Preprocessing for the BNDM-based algorithm.

self-loop at the initial state. *Reach* is obtained by starting at the initial state of (B, Tf_d) and performing up to ℓmin transitions by any character. Finally, Tb_d is obtained by reversing all the arrows of the NFA and then making it deterministic. The overall process takes time $O(2^m + m^2|\Sigma|)$. Figure 5.26 shows the search algorithm.

An extra space improvement is possible: Since we are interested only in the states that can be reached in at most ℓmin steps from state 0, it is not necessary to use the whole automaton with the reverse arrows; only the states belonging to $Reach_{\ell min}$ are relevant. By discarding the others we can save space.

Since at window position j we remove the states that cannot reach state 0, we keep a given state active only if it can become a prefix of length ℓmin of an occurrence. Hence, the algorithm is just another mechanism to search for *Pref* (Section 5.5.1). However, it uses the same automaton with the arrows reversed to represent the state of the search instead of the full trie as in the **MultiStringRE** algorithm.

RegularBNDM$(N = (Q, \Sigma, I, F, \Delta),\ \ell min)$
1.   Preprocessing
2. $(B, Tf_d, Tb_d, Reach) \leftarrow$ **BNDM_Preproc**$(N, \ell min)$
3.   Searching
4. $pos \leftarrow 0$
5.   **While** $pos \leq n - \ell min$ **Do**
6. $j \leftarrow \ell min,\ last \leftarrow \ell min$
7. $D \leftarrow Reach_{\ell min}$
8.   **While** $D \neq 0^{m+1}$ AND $j > 0$ **Do**
9. $D \leftarrow Tb_d[D\ \&\ B[t_{pos+j}]]\ \&\ Reach_{j-1}$
10. $j \leftarrow j - 1$
11.   **If** $D\ \&\ 0^m 1 \neq 0^{m+1}$ **Then** /* prefix recognized */
12.   **If** $j > 0$ **Then** $last \leftarrow j$
13.   **Else** /* check a possible occurrence starting at $pos + 1$ */
14. $D \leftarrow 0^m 1,\ j \leftarrow pos + 1$
15.   **While** $j \leq n$ AND $D \& F_n = 0^{m+1}$ AND $D \neq 0^{m+1}$ **Do**
16. $D \leftarrow Tf_d[D]\ \&\ B[t_j]$
17.   **End of while**
18.   **If** $D\ \&\ F_n \neq 0^{m+1}$ **Then**
19.   Report an occurrence beginning at $pos + 1$
20.   **End of if**
21.   **End of if**
22.   **End of if**
23.   **End of while**
24. $pos \leftarrow pos + last$
25.   **End of while**

Fig. 5.26. Extension of **BNDM** for regular expressions.

In [Nav01b] it is shown that this scheme can be improved by finding good "necessary factors" of the regular expression, just as in **MultiFactRE**. In this case the result is a subgraph of the NFA, so that any path from the initial to a final state needs to traverse the subgraph.

Example of RegularBNDM search We search for the pattern ((GA|AAA)*)(TA|AG) in the text AAAAGATAGAATAGAAA, marking the initial positions of occurrences. The states have been numbered according to Figure 5.19. We show the nonzero entries of Bb_n with the rows of table Tb_d that are needed in the search. We omit the details of the forward verification.

Again, the code is slower than a simple forward scan, but this is because our particular pattern is difficult to search for in this manner.

$$Bb_n = \begin{cases} \begin{array}{|c|c|c|} \hline 1 & \text{G} & 0\,0\,0\,0\,1\,0\,0\,1\,0\,1 \\ \hline 2 & \text{A} & 0\,1\,0\,0\,0\,0\,0\,0\,1\,0 \\ \hline 3 & \text{A} & 0\,0\,0\,0\,1\,0\,0\,1\,0\,1 \\ \hline 4 & \text{A} & 0\,0\,0\,0\,0\,0\,1\,0\,0\,0 \\ \hline 5 & \text{A} & 0\,0\,0\,0\,0\,1\,0\,0\,0\,0 \\ \hline 6 & \text{T} & 0\,0\,0\,0\,1\,0\,0\,1\,0\,1 \\ \hline 7 & \text{A} & 0\,0\,0\,1\,0\,0\,0\,0\,0\,0 \\ \hline 8 & \text{A} & 0\,0\,0\,0\,1\,0\,0\,1\,0\,1 \\ \hline 9 & \text{G} & 0\,1\,0\,0\,0\,0\,0\,0\,0\,0 \\ \hline \end{array} \end{cases}$$

$$B = \begin{cases} \begin{array}{|c|c|} \hline \text{A} & 0\,1\,1\,0\,1\,1\,1\,1\,0\,0 \\ \hline \text{C} & 0\,0\,0\,0\,0\,0\,0\,0\,0\,0 \\ \hline \text{G} & 1\,0\,0\,0\,0\,0\,0\,0\,1\,0 \\ \hline \text{T} & 0\,0\,0\,1\,0\,0\,0\,0\,0\,0 \\ \hline \end{array} \end{cases}$$

$Reach_0 = 0\,0\,0\,0\,0\,0\,0\,0\,0\,1$
$Reach_1 = 0\,1\,0\,1\,0\,0\,1\,0\,1\,1$
$Reach_2 = 1\,1\,1\,1\,0\,1\,1\,1\,1\,1$

$\ell min = 2$

1. $\boxed{\text{AA}}$ AAGATAGAATAGAAA

$D =$	$1\,1\,1\,1\,0\,1\,1\,1\,1\,1$
Reading A	
$D \,\&\, B[\text{A}] =$	$0\,1\,1\,0\,0\,1\,1\,1\,0\,0$
$Tb_d =$	$0\,1\,0\,1\,1\,0\,1\,1\,1\,1$
$\&\, Reach_1 =$	$0\,1\,0\,1\,0\,0\,1\,0\,1\,1$
$last =$	1 $(D \,\&\, I_n \neq 0^{m+1})$
Reading A	
$D \,\&\, B[\text{A}] =$	$0\,1\,0\,0\,0\,0\,1\,0\,0\,0$
$Tb_d =$	$0\,0\,0\,0\,1\,0\,0\,1\,0\,1$
$\&\, Reach_0 =$	$0\,0\,0\,0\,0\,0\,0\,0\,0\,1$

$D \,\&\, I_n \neq 0^{m+1}$, so we start a verification at position 1. After 5 steps we find the pattern and report it. Then we shift the window by $last = 1$.

2. A $\boxed{\text{AA}}$ AGATAGAATAGAAA

As for Step 1, $D \,\&\, I_n \neq 0^{m+1}$, so we start a verification at position 2. After 7 steps we find the pattern and report it. Then we shift the window by $last = 1$.

3. AA $\boxed{\text{AA}}$ GATAGAATAGAAA

As for Step 1, $D \,\&\, I_n \neq 0^{m+1}$, so we start a verification at position 3. After 3 steps the automaton runs out of active states, so we discard position 3 and shift by $last = 1$.

4. AAA $\boxed{\text{AG}}$ ATAGAATAGAAA

$D =$	$1\,1\,1\,1\,0\,1\,1\,1\,1\,1$
Reading G	
$D \,\&\, B[\text{G}] =$	$1\,0\,0\,0\,0\,0\,0\,0\,1\,0$
$Tb_d =$	$0\,1\,0\,0\,1\,0\,0\,1\,0\,1$
$\&\, Reach_1 =$	$0\,1\,0\,0\,0\,0\,0\,0\,0\,1$
$last =$	1 $(D \,\&\, I_n \neq 0^{m+1})$

$D =$	$0\,1\,0\,0\,0\,0\,0\,0\,0\,1$
Reading A	
$D \,\&\, B[\text{A}] =$	$0\,1\,0\,0\,0\,0\,0\,0\,0\,0$
$Tb_d =$	$0\,0\,0\,0\,1\,0\,0\,1\,0\,1$
$\&\, Reach_0 =$	$0\,0\,0\,0\,0\,0\,0\,0\,0\,1$

$D \,\&\, I_n \neq 0^{m+1}$, so we start a verification at position 4. After 2 steps we find the pattern and report it. Then we shift the window by $last = 1$.

5. AAAA $\boxed{\text{GA}}$ TAGAATAGAAA

$D =$	$1\,1\,1\,1\,0\,1\,1\,1\,1\,1$
Reading A	
$D \,\&\, B[\text{A}] =$	$0\,1\,1\,0\,0\,1\,1\,1\,0\,0$
$Tb_d =$	$0\,1\,0\,1\,1\,0\,1\,1\,1\,1$
$\&\, Reach_1 =$	$0\,1\,0\,1\,0\,0\,1\,0\,1\,1$
$last =$	1 $(D \,\&\, I_n \neq 0^{m+1})$
Reading G	
$D \,\&\, B[\text{G}] =$	$0\,0\,0\,0\,0\,0\,0\,0\,1\,0$
$Tb_d =$	$0\,0\,0\,0\,1\,0\,0\,1\,0\,1$
$\&\, Reach_0 =$	$0\,0\,0\,0\,0\,0\,0\,0\,0\,1$

$D \,\&\, I_n \neq 0^{m+1}$, so we start a verification at position 5. After 4 steps we find the pattern and report it. Then we shift the window by $last = 1$.

6. AAAAG $\boxed{\text{AT}}$ AGAATAGAAA

$D =$	$1\,1\,1\,1\,0\,1\,1\,1\,1\,1$
Reading T	
$D \,\&\, B[\text{T}] =$	$0\,0\,0\,1\,0\,0\,0\,0\,0\,0$
$Tb_d =$	$0\,0\,0\,0\,1\,0\,0\,1\,0\,1$
$\&\, Reach_1 =$	$0\,0\,0\,0\,0\,0\,0\,0\,0\,1$
$last =$	1 $(D \,\&\, I_n \neq 0^{m+1})$
Reading A	
$D \,\&\, B[\text{A}] =$	$0\,0\,0\,0\,0\,0\,0\,0\,0\,0$
$Tb_d =$	$0\,0\,0\,0\,0\,0\,0\,0\,0\,0$
$\&\, Reach_0 =$	$0\,0\,0\,0\,0\,0\,0\,0\,0\,0$

$D \,\&\, I_n = 0^{m+1}$, so we shift by $last = 1$.

7. AAAAGA ‖TA‖ GAATAGAAA

$D =$	1 1 1 1 0 1 1 1 1 1

Reading **A**	
$D \ \& \ B[\text{A}] =$	0 1 1 0 0 1 1 1 0 0
$Tb_d =$	0 1 0 1 1 0 1 1 1 1
$\& \ Reach_1 =$	0 1 0 1 0 0 1 0 1 1
$last =$	1 $(D \ \& \ I_n \ \neq \ 0^{m+1})$

Reading **T**	
$D \ \& \ B[\text{T}] =$	0 0 0 1 0 0 0 0 0 0
$Tb_d =$	0 0 0 0 1 0 0 1 0 1
$\& \ Reach_0 =$	0 0 0 0 0 0 0 0 0 1

$D \ \& \ I_n \ \neq \ 0^{m+1}$, so we start a verification at position 7. After 2 steps we find the pattern and report it. Then we shift the window by $last = 1$.

8. AAAAGAT ‖AG‖ AATAGAAA

As for Step 4, $D \ \& \ I_n \ \neq \ 0^{m+1}$, so we start a verification at position 8. After 2 steps we find the pattern and report it. Then we shift the window by $last = 1$.

9. AAAAGATA ‖GA‖ ATAGAAA

As for Step 5, $D \ \& \ I_n \ \neq \ 0^{m+1}$, so we start a verification at position 9. After 4 steps the automaton runs out of active states and we shift the window by $last = 1$.

10. AAAAGATAG ‖AA‖ TAGAAA

As for Step 1, $D \ \& \ I_n \ \neq \ 0^{m+1}$, so we start a verification at position 10. After 3 steps the automaton runs out of active states, so we shift by $last = 1$.

11. AAAAGATAGA ‖AT‖ AGAAA

As for Step 6, $D \ \& \ I_n \ = \ 0^{m+1}$, so we shift by $last = 1$.

12. AAAAGATAGAA ‖TA‖ GAAA

As for Step 7, $D \ \& \ I_n \ \neq \ 0^{m+1}$, so we start a verification at position 12. After 2 steps we find the pattern and report it. Then we shift the window by $last = 1$.

13. AAAAGATAGAAT ‖AG‖ AAA

As for Step 4, $D \ \& \ I_n \ \neq \ 0^{m+1}$, so we start a verification at position 13. After 2 steps we find the pattern and report it. Then we shift the window by $last = 1$.

14. AAAAGATAGAATA ‖GA‖ AA

As for Step 5, $D \ \& \ I_n \ \neq \ 0^{m+1}$, so we start a verification at position 14. After 4 steps the text finishes without recognizing the pattern, so we shift the window by $last = 1$.

15. AAAAGATAGAATAG ‖AA‖ A

As for Step 1, $D \ \& \ I_n \ \neq \ 0^{m+1}$, so we start a verification at position 15. After 3 steps the text finishes without recognizing the pattern, so we shift the window by $last = 1$.

16. AAAAGATAGAATAGA ‖AA‖

As for Step 1, $D \ \& \ I_n \ \neq \ 0^{m+1}$, so we start a verification at position 16. After 2 steps the text finishes without recognizing the pattern, so we shift the window by $last = 1$.

5.6 Experimental map

Determining the best search algorithm for a regular expression is more difficult than for simple patterns, because the structure of the regular expression plays a complex role in the efficiency.

An obvious disadvantage of the bit-parallel versions compared to **DFA-Classical** is that the bit-parallel algorithms build all the $2^{|Q|}$ possible combinations, while **DFAClassical** builds only the reachable states. Thus **DFA-Classical** may produce a much smaller automaton.

On the other hand, there are important advantages to the bit-parallel versions. One is that they are simpler to code. Another is that they are more flexible. For example, we will see in Chapter 6 that this scheme can be extended to permit differences between the pattern and its occurrences, which is hard to do with **DFAClassical**. Finally, bit-parallel versions are amenable to horizontal partitioning, which permits reducing the space as much as necessary.

Among bit-parallel versions, **BPGlushkov** is preferable to **BPThompson** because it needs less space and has more locality of reference as it addresses a smaller table.

Finally, **NFAModules** obtains the same space-dependent complexity as **BPGlushkov**, $O(mn/\log s)$, but it is more complicated to implement and slower in practice. However, when the regular expression needs more than, say, four or more computer words, it becomes attractive in comparison to bit-parallel algorithms. Moreover, **NFAModules** can also be extended to handle classes of characters and approximate searching (Chapter 6).

Filtration approaches, depending on the regular expression structure, can be better or worse than the previous approaches. It is difficult to define a parameter that always works well at predicting the behavior of filtration, but a good approximation is

$$Prob\text{-}verif = \frac{|Pref|}{|\Sigma|^{\ell min}}$$

which is an approximation of the probability of matching a string in *Pref*, defined in Section 5.5.1. Each time an element in *Pref* matches, we have to perform a verification whose cost is difficult to bound, but on average it can be approximated by

$$Cost\text{-}verif = \sum_{\ell \geq 0} \frac{|Pref_\ell|}{|\Sigma|^\ell}$$

where $Pref_\ell$ is the set of all prefixes of length ℓ of possible occurrences of the regular expression. Those sets can be obtained with the same algorithm that computes *Pref* (Section 5.5.1).

A general rule of thumb is that filtration should be used only when

$$Cost\text{-}filter \ = \ Prob\text{-}verif \ \times \ Cost\text{-}verif \ \leq 1$$

The value *Pref* used works well with **MultiStringRE** and **RegularBNDM** based approaches, but for **MultiFactRE** it must be changed to the set of strings chosen there.

With respect to the different filtration approaches, **MultiStringRE** and **RegularBNDM** are similar in terms of text characters considered, especially if **Multiple BNDM** or **SBDM** is used for **MultiStringRE** (Section 3.4). **RegularBNDM** uses a compact representation of the set *Pref* by cleverly using the automaton itself instead of a fully developed trie of all alternatives. But, when the regular expression is too large **RegularBNDM** takes too much time and it is a good idea to resort to **MultiStringRE**. Another advantage of **MultiStringRE** is that it does not need to re-read the window.

Finally, **MultiFactRE**–like filtration can be seen as an improvement over the previous approaches. In particular, *Gnu Grep* (Section 7.1.1) works better than the plain **MultiStringRE** approach, and *Nrgrep* (Section 7.1.3) contains an implementation of **RegularBNDM** that also finds the best necessary factor of the regular expression.

Even for small patterns it sometimes happens that *Gnu Grep* is faster than *Nrgrep*, but **RegularBNDM** can be extended to approximate searching, while search algorithms based on classical multipattern matching normally cannot.

Table 5.2 summarizes our recommendations.

	Low *Cost-filter* (below 1.0)	High *Cost-filter* (above 1.0)
Small size ($m \leq 4w$)	**RegularBNDM** / **MultiFactRE**	**DFAClassical** / **BPGlushkov**
Large size ($m > 4w$)	**MultiFactRE**	**NFAModules**

Table 5.2. *The algorithms we recommend to search for a regular expression according to some parameters of the pattern.*

5.7 Other algorithms and references

NFA construction A theoretic lower bound to the number of transitions needed to build an ε-free NFA is $O(m \log m)$ [HSW97]. Reaching the lower bound is still an open issue. An $O(m^2)$ time algorithm producing an NFA with $O(m \log^2 m)$ transitions was proposed in [HSW97]. It was improved to $O(m \log^2 m)$ time in [HM98]. Unfortunately, this algorithm is too complicated for our purposes.

Set of regular expressions A natural extension of the regular expression search problem is that of searching for a set of regular expressions RE_1, RE_2, ... , RE_r. In principle, this can be converted into the basic single-pattern problem by searching for $RE_1 \mid RE_2 \mid ... \mid RE_r$. However, many of the algorithms presented do not work well with very large expressions.

One algorithm that is able to deal with large expressions is **NFAModules**, but its cost grows linearly with the size of the pattern, in our case, with r. Much better algorithms are **MultiStringRE** and **MultiFactRE**, provided the expressions can be searched for efficiently by filtration algorithms.

5.8 Building a parse tree

We show in this section how to parse a regular expression to obtain its parse tree, which in general is not unique. In the tree, each leaf is labeled by a character of $\Sigma \cup \{\varepsilon\}$ and each internal node by an operator in the set $\{\mid, \cdot, *\}$.

The general approach is to consider a regular expression as a string generated by a grammar, and then use the classical Unix tools *Lex* and *Yacc* or Gnu *Flex* and *Bison* to generate from the grammar the automaton that recognizes the regular expression and transforms it into a tree. The theory behind these tools can be found in books on compilers, such as [ASU86].

This general approach is valuable for large grammars, for instance, for parsers of programming languages, and for very simple grammars that need just lexical analyzers like *Lex* or *Flex*. The grammar for regular expressions is too complex to be addressed by a lexical analyzer and too simple to deserve a full bottom-up parser. The best approach is to build a simple parser by hand, and this is what we do in Figure 5.27. It assumes that the regular expression is well written and that it terminates with a special character '$'. It also assumes that the concatenation operator "." is implicit. Of course, this simple parser has to be modified to handle various types of errors when used in a real application, but this pseudo-code should be a useful starting point, and enough for simple applications.

Parse$(p = p_1 p_2 \ldots p_m, last)$
1. $v \leftarrow \theta$
2.   **While** $p_{last} \neq \$$ **Do**
3.   **If** $p_{last} \in \Sigma$ OR $p_{last} = \varepsilon$ **Then**   /* normal character */
4. $v_r \leftarrow$ Create a node with p_{last}
5.   **If** $v \neq \theta$ **Then** $v \leftarrow \boxed{\cdot}\,(v, v_r)$
6.   **Else** $v \leftarrow v_r$
7. $last \leftarrow last + 1$
8.   **Else If** $p_{last} = \,'|'$ **Then**   /* union operator */
9. $(v_r, last) \leftarrow$ **Parse**$(p, last + 1)$
10. $v \leftarrow \boxed{|}\,(v, v_r)$
11.   **Else If** $p_{last} = \,'*'$ **Then**   /* star operator */
12. $v \leftarrow \boxed{*}\,(v)$
13. $last \leftarrow last + 1$
14.   **Else If** $p_{last} = \,'('$ **Then**   /* open parenthesis */
15. $(v_r, last) \leftarrow$ **Parse**$(p, last + 1)$
16. $last \leftarrow last + 1$
17.   **If** $v \neq \theta$ **Then** $v \leftarrow \boxed{\cdot}\,(v, v_r)$
18.   **Else** $v \leftarrow v_r$
19.   **Else If** $p_{last} = \,')'$ **Then**   /* close parenthesis */
20.   **Return** $(v, last)$
21.   **End of if**
22.   **End of while**
23.   **Return** $(v, last)$

Fig. 5.27. A basic recursive parser for a well-written regular expression. θ is the empty tree.

Instead of explaining in depth how this parser works, we show its behavior on our regular expression `(AT|GA)((AG|AAA)*)`.

Parsing example We parse the regular expression `(AT|GA)((AG|AAA)*)` using **Parse**`((AT|GA)((AG|AAA)*)$`,1). We number the recursive calls using **Parse**[1], **Parse**[2], and so on. The corresponding variables are marked the same way.

1. **Parse**[1]`((AT|GA)((AG|AAA)*)` , 1)
   $last^1 = 1$, $v^1 = \theta$,
   we read $\boxed{(}$ `AT|GA)((AG|AAA)*)$`.
   Line 15. We call:

2. **Parse**[2]`((AT|GA)((AG|AAA)*)` , 2)
   $last^2 = 2$, $v^2 = \theta$,
   we read ($\boxed{A}$ `T|GA)((AG|AAA)*)$`.
   Line 4. $v_r^2 \leftarrow ⒜$
   Line 6. $v^2 \leftarrow v_r^2$.
   Line 7. $last^2 = 3$.
   We return to the while loop of **Parse**[2], line 2.

3. As $p_{last^2} \neq$ \$,
   we read (A $\boxed{\text{T}}$ |GA)((AG|AAA)*)\$.
   Line 4. $v_r^2 \leftarrow \text{T}$
   Line 5. $v^2 \leftarrow$
   Line 7. $last^2 = 4$.

4. We enter line 8,
   we read (AT [|] GA)((AG|AAA)*)\$.
   Line 9. We call:

5. **Parse**^{3}((AT|GA)((AG|AAA)*) , 5)
   $last^3 = 5$, $v^3 = \theta$,
   we read (AT| $\boxed{\text{G}}$ A)((AG|AAA)*)\$.
   Line 4. $v_r^3 \leftarrow \text{G}$
   Line 6. $v^3 \leftarrow v_r^3$.
   Line 7. $last^3 = 6$.
   We return to the while loop of **Parse**^{3},
   line 2.

6. As $p_{last^3} \neq$ \$,
   we read (AT|G $\boxed{\text{A}}$)((AG|AAA)*)\$.
   Line 4. $v_r^3 \leftarrow \text{A}$
   Line 5. $v^3 \leftarrow$
   Line 7. $last^3 = 7$.

7. We enter line 19,
   we read (AT|GA $\boxed{)}$ ((AG|AAA)*)\$.
   Line 20. We quit the function **Parse**^{3}.
   We return $(v^3, 7)$.
   Coming back to **Parse**^{2} line 9,
   $v_r^2 \leftarrow$, $last^2 \leftarrow 7$.
   Line 10. $v^2 \leftarrow$

   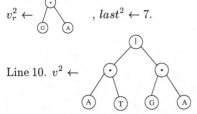

8. We enter line 19,
   we read again (AT|GA $\boxed{)}$ ((AG|AAA)*)\$.
   Line 20. We quit the function **Parse**^{2}.
   We return $(v^2, 7)$.
   Coming back to **Parse**^{1} line 15,

$v_r^1 \leftarrow$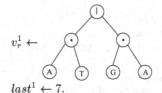

$last^1 \leftarrow 7$.
Line 16. $last^1 \leftarrow 8$.
Line 18. $v^1 \leftarrow v_r^1$.
We return to the while loop of **Parse**^{1},
line 2.

9. As $p_{last^1} \neq$ \$,
   we read (AT|GA) $\boxed{(}$ (AG|AAA)*)\$.
   Line 15. We call:

10. **Parse**^{2}((AT|GA)((AG|AAA)*) , 9)
    $last^2 = 9$, $v^2 = \theta$.
    As $p_{last^2} \neq$ \$,
    we read (AT|GA)($\boxed{(}$ AG|AAA)*)\$.
    Line 15. We call:

11. **Parse**^{3}((AT|GA)((AG|AAA)*) , 10)
    $last^3 = 10$, $v^3 = \theta$,

    we read (AT|GA)(($\boxed{\text{A}}$ G|AAA)*)\$.
    Line 4. $v_r^3 \leftarrow \text{A}$
    Line 6. $v^3 \leftarrow v_r^3$.
    Line 7. $last^3 = 11$.
    We return to the while loop of **Parse**^{3},
    line 2.

12. As $p_{last^3} \neq$ \$,
    we read (AT|GA)((A $\boxed{\text{G}}$ |AAA)*)\$.
    Line 4. $v_r^3 \leftarrow \text{G}$
    Line 5. $v^3 \leftarrow$
    Line 7. $last^3 = 12$.

13. We enter line 8,
    we read (AT|GA)((AG [|] AAA)*)\$.
    Line 9. We call:

14. **Parse**^{4}((AT|GA)((AG|AAA)*) , 13)
$last^4 = 13$, $v^4 = \theta$,
we read (AT|GA)((AG| A AA)*)\$.
Line 4. $v_r^4 \leftarrow$ Ⓐ
Line 6. $v^4 \leftarrow v_r^4$.
Line 7. $last^4 = 14$.
We return to the while loop of **Parse**^{4},
line 2.

15. As $p_{last^4} \neq \$$,
we read (AT|GA)((AG|A A A)*)\$.
Line 4. $v_r^4 \leftarrow$ Ⓐ

Line 5. $v^4 \leftarrow$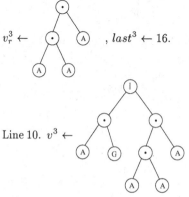

Line 7. $last^4 = 15$.
We return to the while loop of **Parse**^{4},
line 2.

16. As $p_{last^4} \neq \$$,
we read (AT|GA)((AG|AA A)*)\$.
Line 4. $v_r^4 \leftarrow$ Ⓐ

Line 5. $v^4 \leftarrow$

Line 7. $last^4 = 16$.

17. We enter line 19,
we read (AT|GA)((AG|AAA) *)\$.
Line 20. We quit the function **Parse**^{4}.
We return $(v^4, 16)$.
Coming back to **Parse**^{3} line 9,

$v_r^3 \leftarrow$, $last^3 \leftarrow 16$.

Line 10. $v^3 \leftarrow$

18. We enter line 19,
we read again (AT|GA)((AG|AAA) *)\$.
Line 20. We quit the function **Parse**^{3}.
We return $(v^3, 16)$.
Coming back to **Parse**^{2} line 15,

$v_r^2 \leftarrow$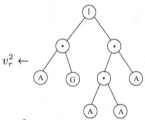

$last^2 \leftarrow 16$
Line 16. $last^2 \leftarrow 17$.
Line 18. $v^2 \leftarrow v_r^2$.
We return to the while loop of **Parse**^{2},
line 2.

19. As $p_{last^2} \neq \$$,
we read (AT|GA)((AG|AAA [*])\$.

Line 12. $v^2 \leftarrow$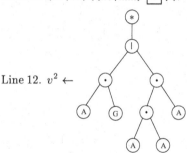

Line 13. $last^2 \leftarrow 18$.

20. We enter line 19,
    we read (AT|GA)((AG|AAA)*) $.
    Line 20. We quit the function **Parse**^{2}.
    We return $(v^2, 18)$.
    Coming back to **Parse**^{1} line 15,

$v_r^1 \leftarrow$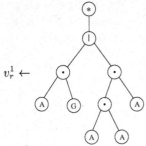

$last^1 \leftarrow 18$
Line 16. $last^1 \leftarrow 19$.

Line 17. $v^1 \leftarrow$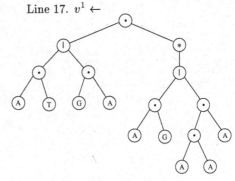

We return to the while loop of **Parse**^{1},
line 2.

21. As $p_{last^1} = \$$,
    We stop the function and return
    $(v^1, 19)$.

6

Approximate matching

6.1 Basic concepts

Approximate string matching, also called "string matching allowing errors," is the problem of finding a pattern p in a text T when a limited number k of *differences* is permitted between the pattern and its occurrences in the text.

From the many existing models defining a "difference," we focus on the most popular one, called *Levenshtein distance* or *edit distance* [Lev65]. Other more complex models exist, especially in computational biology, but the edit distance model has received the most attention and the most effective algorithms have been developed for it. Some of these algorithms can be extended to more complex models.

Under edit distance, one difference equals one *edit operation*: a character insertion, deletion, or substitution. That is, the edit distance between two strings x and y, $ed(x, y)$, is the minimum number of edit operations required to convert x into y, or vice versa. For example, $ed(\texttt{annual}, \texttt{annealing}) = 4$. The approximate string matching problem becomes that of finding all occurrences in T of every p' that satisfies $ed(p, p') \leq k$. To ensure a linear size output it is customary to report only the starting or ending positions of the occurrences.

Note that the problem only makes sense for $0 < k < m$, because otherwise every text substring of length m can be converted into p by substituting the m characters. The case $k = 0$ corresponds to exact string matching. We call $\alpha = k/m$ the "error level." It gives a measure of the "fraction" of the pattern that can be altered.

We concentrate on algorithms that are the fastest in the cases that are likely to be of use in some foreseeable application, particularly text retrieval and computational biology. In particular, $\alpha < 1/2$ in most cases of interest.

We present four approaches. The first approach, which is also the oldest

145

and most flexible, adapts a dynamic programming algorithm that computes edit distance. The second uses an automaton-based formulation of the problem and deals with the ways to simulate the automaton. The third, one of the most successful approaches, is based on the bit-parallel simulation of other approaches. Finally, the fourth approach uses a simple necessary condition to filter out large text areas and another algorithm to search the areas that cannot be discarded. Filtration is the most successful approach for low error levels.

6.2 Dynamic programming algorithms

The oldest solution to the problem relies on dynamic programming. Discovered and rediscovered many times since the 1960s, the final search algorithm is attributed to Sellers [Sel80]. Although the algorithm is not very efficient, taking $O(mn)$ time, it is among the most adaptable to more complex distance functions.

We first show how to compute the edit distance between two strings. Later, we extend the algorithm to search for a pattern in a text allowing errors. We then show how this algorithm can be made faster on average. Finally, we discuss alternative algorithms based on dynamic programming.

6.2.1 Computing edit distance

We need to compute $ed(x, y)$. A matrix $M_{0...|x|,0...|y|}$ is filled, where $M_{i,j}$ represents the minimum number of edit operations needed to match $x_{1...i}$ to $y_{1...j}$, that is, $M_{i,j} = ed(x_{1...i}, y_{1...j})$. This is computed as follows:

$$M_{0,0} \leftarrow 0$$
$$M_{i,j} \leftarrow \min(M_{i-1,j-1} + \delta(x_i, y_j), M_{i-1,j} + 1, M_{i,j-1} + 1)$$

where $\delta(a, b) = 0$ if $a = b$ and 1 otherwise, and M is assumed to take the value ∞ when accessed outside its bounds. At the end, $M_{|x|,|y|} = ed(x, y)$.

The rationale of the formula is as follows. $M_{0,0}$ is the edit distance between two empty strings. For two strings of length i and j, we assume inductively that all the edit distances between shorter strings have already been computed, and try to convert $x_{1...i}$ into $y_{1...j}$.

Consider the last characters x_i and y_j. If they are equal, we do not need to consider them, just convert $x_{1...i-1}$ into $y_{1...j-1}$ at a cost $M_{i-1,j-1}$. On the other hand, if they are not equal, we must deal with them. Following the three allowed operations, we can substitute x_i by y_j and convert $x_{1...i-1}$ into $y_{1...j-1}$ at a cost $M_{i-1,j-1} + 1$, delete x_i and convert $x_{1...i-1}$ into $y_{1...j}$ at a cost $M_{i-1,j}+1$, or insert y_j at the end of $x_{1...i}$ and convert $x_{1...i}$ into $y_{1...j-1}$ at a cost $M_{i,j-1}+1$. Note that the insertions in one string are equivalent to deletions in the other.

Therefore, the algorithm is $O(|x||y|)$ time in the worst and average cases. An alternative formulation that yields faster coding is as follows:

$$M_{i,0} \leftarrow i, \qquad M_{0,j} \leftarrow j \qquad\qquad (6.1)$$

$$M_{i,j} \leftarrow \begin{cases} M_{i-1,j-1} & \text{if } x_i = y_j, \\ 1 + \min(M_{i-1,j-1}, M_{i-1,j}, M_{i,j-1}) & \text{otherwise} \end{cases}$$

which is equivalent to the previous one because neighboring cells in M differ at most by 1. Therefore, when $\delta(x_i, y_j) = 0$, we have that $M_{i-1,j-1}$ cannot be larger than $M_{i-1,j}+1$ or $M_{i,j-1}+1$.

From the matrix it is possible to determine an *optimal path*, that is, a minimum cost sequence of matrix cells that goes from cell $M_{0,0}$ to $M_{|x|,|y|}$. Multiple paths may exist. Each path is related to an *alignment*, which is a mapping between the characters of x and y that shows how characters should be matched, substituted, and deleted to make x and y equal. A complete reference on alignments is [Gus97].

Figure 6.1 illustrates the algorithm to compute $ed(\text{annual}, \text{annealing})$.

		a	n	n	e	a	l	i	n	g
	0	1	2	3	4	5	6	7	8	9
a	1	**0**	1	2	3	4	5	6	7	8
n	2	1	**0**	1	2	3	4	5	6	7
n	3	2	1	**0**	1	2	3	4	5	6
u	4	3	2	1	**1**	2	3	4	5	6
a	5	4	3	2	2	**1**	2	3	4	5
l	6	5	4	3	3	2	**1**	**2**	**3**	4

a n n e a l i n g

a n n u a l

Fig. 6.1. Example of the dynamic programming algorithm to compute the edit distance between "annual" and "annealing". The path in bold yields the only optimal alignment. On the right we show the alignment, where the dashed line means a substitution.

6.2.2 Text searching

Searching a pattern p in a text T is basically similar to computing edit distance, with $x = p$ and $y = T$. The only difference is that we must allow an occurrence to begin at any text position. This is achieved by setting $M_{0,j} = 0$ for all $j \in 0\ldots n$. That is, the empty pattern occurs with zero errors at any text position because it matches with a text substring of length zero.

The resulting algorithm needs $O(mn)$ time. If we use a matrix M, it also needs $O(mn)$ space. However, we can work with just $O(m)$ space. The key observation is that to compute $M_{*,j}$ we only need the values of $M_{*,j-1}$. Therefore, instead of building the whole matrix M, we process T character by character and maintain a column C of M, which is updated after reading each new text position j to keep the invariant $C_i = M_{i,j}$.

The algorithm initializes its column $C_{0...m}$ with the values $C_i \leftarrow i$ and processes the text character by character. At each new text character t_j, its column vector is updated to $C'_{0...m}$. The update formula is

$$C'_i \leftarrow \begin{cases} C_{i-1} & \text{if } p_i = t_j \text{ ,} \\ 1 + \min(C_{i-1}, C'_{i-1}, C_i) & \text{otherwise} \end{cases}$$

and the text positions where $C_m \leq k$ are reported as ending positions of occurrences. Observe that since $C = M_{*,j-1}$ is the old column and $C' = M_{*,j}$ is the new one, C_{i-1} corresponds to $M_{i-1,j-1}$, C'_{i-1} to $M_{i-1,j}$ and C_i to $M_{i,j-1}$ in formula (6.1).

Figure 6.2 applies this algorithm to search for the pattern "annual" in the text "annealing" with at most $k = 2$ errors. In this case there are three occurrences.

		a	n	n	e	a	l	i	n	g
	0	0	0	0	0	0	0	0	0	0
a	1	0	1	1	1	0	1	1	1	1
n	2	1	0	1	2	1	1	2	1	2
n	3	2	1	0	1	2	2	2	2	2
u	4	3	2	1	1	2	3	3	3	3
a	5	4	3	2	2	1	2	3	4	4
l	6	5	4	3	3	**2**	**1**	**2**	3	4

Fig. 6.2. Example of the dynamic programming algorithm to search for "annual" in the text "annealing" with two errors. Each column of this matrix is a value of the column C at some point in time. Bold entries indicate ending positions of occurrences in the text.

6.2.3 Improving the average case

A simple twist to the dynamic programming algorithm [Ukk85], which retains all its flexibility, takes $O(kn)$ time on average [CL92, BYN99]. We call it **DP**. The idea is that, since a pattern does not normally match in the text, the values at each column read from top to bottom quickly reach $k+1$ (i.e., mismatch), and that if a cell has a value larger than $k+1$, the result of the search does not depend on its exact value. A cell is called *active* if its value is at most k. The algorithm keeps count of the last active cell and avoids working on subsequent cells.

The last active cell must be recomputed for each new column. When moving from one text position to the next, the last active cell can be incremented by at most one since neighbors in M differ by at most one, so we check in constant time whether we have activated the next cell. However, it is also possible that the formerly last active cell becomes inactive now. In this case we have to search upwards in the column for the new last active cell. Although we can work $O(m)$ at a given column, we cannot work more than $O(n)$ overall, because there are at most n increments of this value in the whole process, and hence there are no more than n decrements. So, the last active cell is maintained at $O(1)$ worst-case amortized cost per column.

Figure 6.3 shows pseudo-code for this algorithm. Its basic idea of avoiding to compute some inactive cells has been used extensively in other algorithms. In particular, the bit-parallel algorithms that we cover later profit from this technique to reduce their average search time.

DP $(p = p_1 p_2 \ldots p_m, \ T = t_1 t_2 \ldots t_n, \ k)$
1.　　**Preprocessing**
2.　　　　**For** $i \in 0 \ldots m$ **Do** $C_i \leftarrow i$
3.　　　　$lact \leftarrow k + 1$ /* last active cell */
4.　　**Searching**
5.　　　　**For** $pos \in 1 \ldots n$ **Do**
6.　　　　　　$pC \leftarrow 0, \ nC \leftarrow 0$
7.　　　　　　**For** $i \in 1 \ldots lact$ **Do**
8.　　　　　　　　**If** $p_i = t_{pos}$ **Then** $nC \leftarrow pC$
9.　　　　　　　　**Else**
10.　　　　　　　　　　**If** $pC < nC$ **Then** $nC \leftarrow pC$
11.　　　　　　　　　　**If** $C_i < nC$ **Then** $nC \leftarrow C_i$
12.　　　　　　　　　　$nC \leftarrow nC + 1$
13.　　　　　　　　**End of if**
14.　　　　　　　　$pC \leftarrow C_i, \ C_i \leftarrow nC$
15.　　　　　　**End of for**
16.　　　　　　**While** $C_{lact} > k$ **Do** $lact \leftarrow lact - 1$
17.　　　　　　**If** $lact = m$ **Then** report an occurrence at pos
18.　　　　　　**Else** $lact \leftarrow lact + 1$
19.　　　　**End of for**

Fig. 6.3. An $O(kn)$ expected time dynamic programming algorithm. Note that it works with just one column vector.

6.2.4 Other algorithms based on dynamic programming

There are many other algorithms based on this scheme. From the practical point of view, the most interesting is "column partitioning" [CL92], which obtains $O(kn/\sqrt{|\Sigma|})$ expected time [Nav01a]. This is the fastest algorithm based on dynamic programming. But it is hard to extend to more complex distance functions, and in this case newer bit-parallel algorithms are faster.

From the theoretical point of view, some of the most important algorithms are based on dynamic programming. If we are restricted to polynomial space in m and k, then the best existing algorithms use this technique and achieve $O(kn)$ worst-case search time with $O(m)$ extra space. The most competitive in practice are [GP90, CL94], which are still slower than algorithms that do not offer such a worst-case guarantee. When k is much smaller than m, an $O(n(1 + k^4/m))$ time algorithm [CH98] becomes of interest. The worst-case lower bound for the problem when only polynomial space in m and k can be used is an open issue.

6.3 Algorithms based on automata

An alternative and very useful way to consider the approximate search problem is to model the search with a nondeterministic finite automaton (NFA). This automaton, in its deterministic form, was proposed first in [Ukk85], and later explicitly presented in [BY91, WM92b, BYN99].

Consider the NFA for $k = 2$ errors under edit distance shown in Figure 6.4. Every row denotes the number of errors seen. Every column represents matching a pattern prefix. Horizontal arrows represent matching a character (i.e., if the pattern and text characters match, we advance in the pattern and in the text). All the others increment the number of errors by moving to the next row: Vertical arrows insert a character in the pattern (we advance in the text but not in the pattern), solid diagonal arrows substitute a character (we advance in the text and pattern), and dashed diagonal arrows delete a character of the pattern (they are ε-transitions, since we advance in the pattern without advancing in the text). The initial self-loop allows an occurrence to start anywhere in the text. The automaton signals (the end of) an occurrence whenever a rightmost state is active.

It is not hard to see that once a state in the automaton is active, all the states in the same column and higher numbered rows are active too. Moreover, at a given text position, if we collect the smallest active rows at each NFA column, we obtain the current vertical vector of the dynamic programming matrix. For example, after reading the text **"anneal"**, the seventh column in Figure 6.2 shows that $C = [0, 1, 1, 2, 3, 2, 1]$. Compare it with the least active row per NFA column in Figure 6.4.

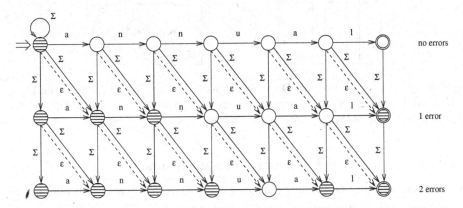

Fig. 6.4. An NFA for approximate string matching of the pattern "annual" with two errors. The shaded states are those active after reading the text "anneal".

The original proposal of [Ukk85] was to make this automaton deterministic using the classical algorithm to convert an NFA into a DFA. This way, $O(n)$ worst-case search time is obtained, which is optimal. The main problem then becomes the construction and storage requirements of the DFA. An upper bound to the number of states of the DFA is $O(\min(3^m, m(2m|\Sigma|)^k))$ [Ukk85]. In practice, this automaton cannot be used for $m > 20$, and nowadays it is not the best choice even for small m: Bit-parallel algorithms are simpler and faster thanks to their higher locality of reference.

An alternative way to look at the DFA is to consider that each DFA state is a possible column of the dynamic programming matrix, so the preprocessing precomputes the transitions among columns for each possible input character.

Later developments [WMM96] based on the Four-Russians approach tackled the space and preprocessing cost problem by cutting columns into "regions" and building a DFA of regions. Figure 6.5 shows a schematic view of the automaton.

Given $O(s)$ space, the algorithm obtains $O(kn/\log s)$ expected time and $O(mn/\log s)$ worst-case time. Although it is the fastest choice in practice for long patterns and high error level ($\alpha > 0.7$), we do not include the details of this algorithm because it is complicated and because it is not the fastest in the most interesting cases: 0.7 is too high an error level for most applications.

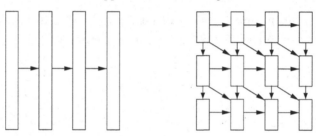

Fig. 6.5. On the left is the full DFA, where each column is a state. On the right is the Four-Russians version, where each region of a column is a state. The arrows show dependencies between consecutive regions.

6.4 Bit-parallel algorithms

Bit-parallelism has been heavily used for approximate searching, and many of the best results are obtained using this approach. The results are most useful for short patterns, and in many cases these are the patterns of interest. In cases when the representation does not fit in a single computer word, standard techniques permit the simulation of a virtual computer word formed from a number of physical words. Then, the techniques developed in Section 6.2.3 for the algorithm **DP** can be applied, so that only the computer words holding "active" data are updated.

Bit-parallel algorithms simulate "classical" algorithms. In approximate searching we find some that parallelize the work of the NFA and others that parallelize the work of the dynamic programming matrix.

6.4.1 Parallelizing the NFA

If we consider the first row of Figure 6.4, we are left with an NFA for exact string matching, the same one that is simulated using the **Shift-And** approach (Section 2.2.2). Different techniques have been proposed to extend this idea to the more general automaton.

6.4.1.1 Row-wise bit-parallelism

The simplest technique [WM92b], which we call **BPR**, packs each row i of the NFA in a different machine word R_i, with each state represented by a bit. For each new text character, all the transitions of the automaton are simulated using bit operations among the $k + 1$ bit masks. Notice that all $k + 1$ bit masks have the same structure, that is, the same bit is aligned to the same text position. The update formula to obtain the new R_i' values at text position j from the current R_i values is

$$R'_0 \leftarrow ((R_0 << 1) \mid 0^{m-1}1) \& B[t_j]$$
$$R'_i \leftarrow ((R_i << 1) \& B[t_j]) \mid R_{i-1} \mid (R_{i-1} << 1) \mid (R'_{i-1} << 1)$$

where B is the table from the **Shift-And** algorithm. We start the search with $R_i = 0^{m-i}1^i$, which is equivalent to $C_i = i$ in the **DP** algorithm. As expected, R_0 undergoes a simple **Shift-And** process, while the other rows receive ones (i.e., active states) from previous rows as well. The formula for R'_i expresses horizontal, vertical, diagonal, and dashed diagonal arrows, respectively. Figure 6.6 gives pseudo-code for this algorithm.

BPR $(p = p_1 p_2 \ldots p_m,\ T = t_1 t_2 \ldots t_n,\ k)$
1.   Preprocessing
2.   **For** $c \in \Sigma$ **Do** $B[c] \leftarrow 0^m$
3.   **For** $j \in 1 \ldots m$ **Do** $B[p_j] \leftarrow B[p_j] \mid 0^{m-j}10^{j-1}$
4.   Searching
5.   **For** $i \in 0 \ldots k$ **Do** $R_i \leftarrow 0^{m-i}1^i$
6.   **For** $pos \in 1 \ldots n$ **Do**
7. $oldR \leftarrow R_0$
8. $newR \leftarrow ((oldR << 1) \mid 0^{m-1}1) \& B[t_{pos}]$
9. $R_0 \leftarrow newR$
10.   **For** $i \in 1 \ldots k$ **Do**
11. $newR \leftarrow ((R_i << 1) \& B[t_{pos}]) \mid oldR \mid ((oldR \mid newR) << 1)$
12. $oldR \leftarrow R_i,\ R_i \leftarrow newR$
13.   **End of for**
14.   **If** $newR \& 10^{m-1} \neq 0^m$ **Then** report an occurrence at pos
15.   **End of for**

Fig. 6.6. Row-wise bit-parallel simulation of the NFA. The length of the pattern must be less than w.

The cost of this simulation is $O(k\lceil m/w \rceil n)$ in the worst and average cases, which is $O(kn)$ for patterns typical in text searching (i.e., $m \leq w$). Notice that for short patterns this is competitive with the best worst-case algorithms. As we see next, one can do much better, but this algorithm has maximum flexibility when it comes to adapting it to more complex cases such as wild cards or regular expression searching allowing errors.

Example of BPR We search for the string "annual" in the text "annea-ling" allowing $k = 2$ errors. Note that, at any point, the bit representations of R_0, R_1, and R_2 resemble the active states in the NFA of Figure 6.4, provided we read the states right to left and discard the first column of the NFA, which is never represented because it is known to be active all the time. In particular, compare the bit map after reading the text `"anneal"` with the active states of Figure 6.4. It is also interesting to compare the bit maps to the column values of Figure 6.2 to check that C_i is the least active row at NFA column i.

$$B = \begin{cases} \begin{array}{c|c} a & 0\,1\,0\,0\,0\,1 \\ 1 & 1\,0\,0\,0\,0\,0 \\ n & 0\,0\,0\,1\,1\,0 \\ u & 0\,0\,1\,0\,0\,0 \\ * & 0\,0\,0\,0\,0\,0 \end{array} \end{cases}$$

$R_0 = 0\,0\,0\,0\,0\,0$
$R_1 = 0\,0\,0\,0\,0\,1$
$R_2 = 0\,0\,0\,0\,1\,1$

1. Reading a $0\,1\,0\,0\,0\,1$
   $$\begin{aligned} R_0 &= & 0\,0\,0\,0\,0\,1 \\ R_1 &= & 0\,0\,0\,0\,1\,1 \\ R_2 &= & 0\,0\,0\,1\,1\,1 \end{aligned}$$

2. Reading n $0\,0\,0\,1\,1\,0$
   $$\begin{aligned} R_0 &= & 0\,0\,0\,0\,1\,0 \\ R_1 &= & ,0\,0\,0\,1\,1\,1 \\ R_2 &= & 0\,0\,1\,1\,1\,1 \end{aligned}$$

3. Reading n $0\,0\,0\,1\,1\,0$
   $$\begin{aligned} R_0 &= & 0\,0\,0\,1\,0\,0 \\ R_1 &= & 0\,0\,1\,1\,1\,1 \\ R_2 &= & 0\,1\,1\,1\,1\,1 \end{aligned}$$

4. Reading e $0\,0\,0\,0\,0\,0$
   $$\begin{aligned} R_0 &= & 0\,0\,0\,0\,0\,0 \\ R_1 &= & 0\,0\,1\,1\,0\,1 \\ R_2 &= & 0\,1\,1\,1\,1\,1 \end{aligned}$$

5. Reading a $0\,1\,0\,0\,0\,1$
   $$\begin{aligned} R_0 &= & 0\,0\,0\,0\,0\,1 \\ R_1 &= & 0\,1\,0\,0\,1\,1 \\ R_2 &= & 1\,1\,1\,1\,1\,1 \end{aligned}$$

The last bit of R_2 is set, so we mark an occurrence.

6. Reading 1 $1\,0\,0\,0\,0\,0$
   $$\begin{aligned} R_0 &= & 0\,0\,0\,0\,0\,0 \\ R_1 &= & 1\,0\,0\,0\,1\,1 \\ R_2 &= & 1\,1\,0\,1\,1\,1 \end{aligned}$$

The last bit of R_2 is set again, so we mark an occurrence. Note that the position matches even in R_1, i.e., with $k = 1$ errors.

7. Reading i $0\,0\,0\,0\,0\,0$
   $$\begin{aligned} R_0 &= & 0\,0\,0\,0\,0\,0 \\ R_1 &= & 0\,0\,0\,0\,0\,1 \\ R_2 &= & 1\,0\,0\,1\,1\,1 \end{aligned}$$

The last bit of R_2 is set, so we mark an occurrence. Note that this occurrence is just a consequence of having matched with $k < 2$ errors at the previous positions, since no more matches of pattern letters are involved.

8. Reading n $0\,0\,0\,1\,1\,0$
   $$\begin{aligned} R_0 &= & 0\,0\,0\,0\,0\,0 \\ R_1 &= & 0\,0\,0\,0\,1\,1 \\ R_2 &= & 0\,0\,0\,1\,1\,1 \end{aligned}$$

9. Reading g $0\,0\,0\,0\,0\,0$
   $$\begin{aligned} R_0 &= & 0\,0\,0\,0\,0\,0 \\ R_1 &= & 0\text{-}0\,0\,0\,0\,1 \\ R_2 &= & 0\,0\,0\,1\,1\,1 \end{aligned}$$

6.4.1.2 Diagonal-wise bit-parallelism

In light of the row-wise parallelization presented above, the classical dynamic programming algorithm can be thought of as a column-wise parallelization of the automaton where, as explained, each NFA column corresponds to a cell in C that stores the smallest active row at that column. Neither algorithm is able to increase the parallelism even if all the NFA states fit in a computer word, because the ε-transitions of the automaton cause *zero-*

time dependencies. That is, the current values of two rows or two columns depend on each other and hence cannot be computed in parallel.

In [BYN99] the bit-parallel formula for a *diagonal-wise* parallelization was found. We call **BPD** the resulting algorithm. They pack the states of the automaton along diagonals instead of rows or columns, running in the direction of the diagonal arrows. There are $m - k + 1$ complete diagonals, which are numbered left to right from 0 to $m - k$. Let D_i be the row number of the first active state in diagonal i. All the subsequent states in the diagonal are active because of the ε-transitions. The new D_i' values after reading text position j are

$$D_i' \leftarrow \min (D_i + 1, \ D_{i+1} + 1, \ g(i - 1, t_j)) \tag{6.2}$$

where the first term represents the substitutions, the second term the insertions, and the last term the matches. Deletions are implicit since only the lowest-row active state of each diagonal is represented. The main problem is how to compute the function g, defined as

$$g(i, c) = \min (\ \{k + 1\} \ \cup \ \{ r, \ r \geq D_i \ \text{AND} \ p_{i+1+r} = c \ \})$$

which expresses the fact that from all active states at diagonal i, namely, $r \in \{D_i, \ D_i + 1, \ \ldots, \ k\}$, those that can follow a horizontal arrow (i.e., $p_{i+1+r} = c$) move to diagonal $i + 1$. We take the minimum over those r. Another way to understand g is to note that an active state that crosses a horizontal edge has to propagate all the way down along the diagonal.

This process is simulated in [BYN99] by representing the D_i values in unary and using arithmetic operations on the bits to produce the desired propagation effect (in Section 4.4 a similar flooding problem is solved in detail). The update formula can be understood either numerically (operating on the D_i) or logically (simulating the arrows of the automaton). A computer word D holds $m - k$ blocks, one per diagonal excluding D_0 because it is known to be always active. From left to right, D_1 to D_{m-k} are represented. Inside each block there are $k + 2$ bits. The rightmost bit is always zero to avoid propagation of arithmetic operations to adjacent blocks, and the other $k + 1$ bits are used to represent D_i in unary: The leftmost D_i bits of block i are 1 and the others are 0. The typical B table is used, except that its bits are reversed. A table BB is computed from B in order to align the corresponding horizontal arrows to the arrangement made in D.

Figure 6.7 shows the algorithm. The representation does not include the states to the right of the last full diagonal. As a result, some occurrences are lost. However, those occurrences are uninteresting in most applications since they are trivial extensions of occurrences already found, in the sense that no new pattern characters match the text (such as the one found after processing `"anneali"` in the example of **BPR**). To ensure that those occurrences are consistently discarded, line 14 removes all the active states in the last diagonal after an occurrence is reported. Hence the algorithm reports any occurrence that ends with a text character matching the pattern.

Line 11 updates D according to formula (6.2), by AND-ing four expressions, an operation that corresponds to minimization in unary. The first expression represents $D_i + 1$, the second $D_{i+1} + 1$, the third $g(i - 1, t_{pos})$, and the last cleans up separators. About the third expression, note that x holds the states of the previous diagonal that arrive by horizontal transitions, and we make the last zero flood the block to the right.

BPD $(p = p_1 p_2 \ldots p_m,\ T = t_1 t_2 \ldots t_n,\ k)$

1.	Preprocessing
2.	For $c \in \Sigma$ **Do** $B[c] \leftarrow 1^m$
3.	For $j \in 1 \ldots m$ **Do** $B[p_j] \leftarrow B[p_j]$ & $1^{m-j} 0 1^{j-1}$
4.	For $c \in \Sigma$ **Do**
5.	$BB[c] \leftarrow 0\ s_{k+1}(B[c], 0)\ \ 0\ s_{k+1}(B[c], 1)\ \ \ldots\ \ 0\ s_{k+1}(B[c], m - k - 1)$
6.	**End of for**
7.	Searching
8.	$D \leftarrow (0 1^{k+1})^{m-k}$
9.	For $pos \in 1 \ldots n$ **Do**
10.	$x \leftarrow (D >> (k + 2))\ |\ BB[t_{pos}]$
11.	$D \leftarrow ((D << 1)\ |\ (0^{k+1} 1)^{m-k})$
	$\quad$ & $((D << (k + 3))\ |\ (0^{k+1} 1)^{m-k-1} 0 1^{k+1})$
	$\quad$ & $(((x + (0^{k+1} 1)^{m-k}) \wedge x) >> 1)$ & $(0 1^{k+1})^{m-k}$
12.	**If** D & $0^{(m-k-1)(k+2)} 0 1 0^k = 0^{(m-k)(k+2)}$ **Then**
13.	Report an occurrence at pos
14.	$D \leftarrow D\ |\ 0^{(m-k-1)(k+2)} 0 1^{k+1}$
15.	**End of if**
16.	**End of for**

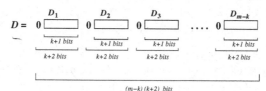

Fig. 6.7. Diagonal-wise bit-parallel simulation of the NFA. It requires that $(m - k)(k + 2) \le w$. The function $s_\ell(D, j)$ extracts the j-th to the $(j + \ell - 1)$-th bits of D, that is, $s_\ell(D, j) = (D >> j)$ & $0^{(m-k)(k+2)-\ell} 1^\ell$. On the bottom we show how the unary D_i values are arranged in the mask D.

The resulting algorithm is $O(n)$ worst-case time and very fast in practice if all the bits of the automaton fit in a computer word, while the row-wise simulation remains $O(kn)$. In general, it is $O(\lceil k(m-k)/w\rceil n)$ worst-case time. It can be made $O(\lceil k^2/w\rceil n)$ on average by updating only the computer words holding active states, using an adaptation of the technique for active cells presented for **DP**. The scheme can handle classes of characters, wild cards, and different integral costs in the edit operations [BYN99], but it is less flexible than row-wise simulation.

Example of BPD We search for the string "annual" in the text "annealing" allowing $k = 2$ errors. This time the bit representation for D is harder to relate visually to the NFA of Figure 6.4. The rule is to read full NFA diagonals, excluding the first, and to map them to blocks. Each diagonal must be read from top to bottom and its active states mapped to the zeros of its block, read from right to left.

$$B = \begin{cases} \text{a} & 1\,0\,1\,1\,1\,0 \\ \text{l} & 0\,1\,1\,1\,1\,1 \\ \text{n} & 1\,1\,1\,0\,0\,1 \\ \text{u} & 1\,1\,0\,1\,1\,1 \\ \text{*} & 1\,1\,1\,1\,1\,1 \end{cases}$$

$D = 0\,1\,1\,1\ \ 0\,1\,1\,1\ \ 0\,1\,1\,1\ \ 0\,1\,1\,1$

Table BB

a	0101	0011	0111	0110
l	0011	0111	0111	0111
n	0111	0110	0100	0001
u	0110	0101	0011	0111
*	0111	0111	0111	0111

1. Reading a

$$\frac{BB[\text{a}]\quad 0101\ \ 0011\ \ 0111\ \ 0110}{D=\quad\ \ 0000\ \ 0111\ \ 0111\ \ 0111}$$

2. Reading n

$$\frac{BB[\text{n}]\quad 0111\ \ 0110\ \ 0100\ \ 0001}{D=\quad\ \ 0001\ \ 0000\ \ 0111\ \ 0111}$$

3. Reading n

$$\frac{BB[\text{n}]\quad 0111\ \ 0110\ \ 0100\ \ 0001}{D=\quad\ \ 0001\ \ 0001\ \ 0000\ \ 0111}$$

4. Reading e

$$\frac{BB[\text{e}]\quad 0111\ \ 0111\ \ 0111\ \ 0111}{D=\quad\ \ 0011\ \ 0001\ \ 0001\ \ 0111}$$

5. Reading a

$$\frac{BB[\text{a}]\quad 0101\ \ 0011\ \ 0111\ \ 0110}{D=\quad\ \ 0000\ \ 0011\ \ 0011\ \ 0001}$$

The highest bit of $D_{m-k} = D_4$ (third bit read right to left in D) is zero, so we mark an occurrence and clean the last diagonal:

$D = 0000\ \ 0011\ \ 0011\ \ 0111$

6. Reading l

$$\frac{BB[\text{l}]\quad 0011\ \ 0111\ \ 0111\ \ 0111}{D=\quad\ \ 0001\ \ 0111\ \ 0011\ \ 0011}$$

The highest bit of D_4 is zero again, so we mark an occurrence and clean the last diagonal:

$D = 0001\ \ 0111\ \ 0011\ \ 0111$

7. Reading i   8. Reading n

$$\frac{BB[\mathtt{i}] \quad 0111 \; 0111 \; 0111 \; 0111}{D = \quad 0011 \; 0111 \; 0111 \; 0111}$$

Unlike the classical algorithm, we do not mark an occurrence here, because it does not involve any new matching pattern character. This is a consequence of having cleaned the last diagonal in the previous step.

$$\frac{BB[\mathtt{n}] \quad 0111 \; 0110 \; 01000001}{D = \quad 0001 \; 0111 \; 0111 \; 0111}$$

9. Reading g

$$\frac{BB[\mathtt{g}] \quad 0111 \; 0111 \; 0111 \; 0111}{D = \quad 0011 \; 0111 \; 0111 \; 0111}$$

6.4.2 Parallelizing the DP matrix

A better way to parallelize the computation [Mye99] is to represent the differences between consecutive rows or columns of the dynamic programming matrix instead of the absolute values. Let us call

$$\Delta h_{i,j} \;=\; M_{i,j} - M_{i,j-1} \;\in\; \{-1,0,+1\}$$
$$\Delta v_{i,j} \;=\; M_{i,j} - M_{i-1,j} \;\in\; \{-1,0,+1\}$$
$$\Delta d_{i,j} \;=\; M_{i,j} - M_{i-1,j-1} \;\in\; \{0,1\}$$

the horizontal, vertical, and diagonal differences among consecutive cells. Their range of values comes from the properties of the dynamic programming matrix.

We present a version [Hyy01] that differs slightly from that of [Mye99]: Although both perform the same number of operations per text character, the one we present is easier to understand.

Let us introduce the following boolean variables. The first four refer to horizontal/vertical positive/negative differences and the last to the diagonal difference being zero:

$$VP_{i,j} \;\equiv\; \Delta v_{i,j} = +1 \qquad VN_{i,j} \;\equiv\; \Delta v_{i,j} = -1$$
$$HP_{i,j} \;\equiv\; \Delta h_{i,j} = +1 \qquad HN_{i,j} \;\equiv\; \Delta h_{i,j} = -1$$
$$D0_{i,j} \;\equiv\; \Delta d_{i,j} = 0$$

Note that $\Delta v_{i,j} = VP_{i,j} - VN_{i,j}$, $\Delta h_{i,j} = HP_{i,j} - HN_{i,j}$, and $\Delta d_{i,j} = 1 - D0_{i,j}$. It is clear that these values completely define $M_{i,j} = \sum_{r=1...i} \Delta v_{r,j}$. The key idea is to notice some dependencies among the above values:

- If $HN_{i,j}$, then $\Delta h_{i,j} = -1$. Therefore, the only possibility is that $\Delta v_{i,j-1} = +1$ and hence $\Delta d_{i,j} = 0$, otherwise the Δ ranges of values would be violated. The last two conditions are equivalent to $VP_{i,j-1}$ AND $D0_{i,j}$. On the other hand, if these two conditions hold, $HN_{i,j}$ holds.

- By symmetric arguments it can be seen that $VN_{i,j}$ is logically equivalent to $HP_{i-1,j}$ AND $D0_{i,j}$.

- If $HP_{i,j}$ holds, then $VP_{i,j-1}$ cannot hold without violating the ranges of the Δ values. So the choices for $\Delta v_{i,j-1}$ are -1 and 0. In the first case we have $VN_{i,j-1}$, whereas in the second we have that neither $VP_{i,j-1}$ nor $D0_{i,j}$ hold. Moreover, this is a logical equivalence: If $VN_{i,j-1}$, then $HP_{i,j}$ has to hold; and if both $VP_{i,j-1}$ and $D0_{i,j}$ are false, then $HP_{i,j}$ has to hold as well.

- Symmetrically, we can see that $VP_{i,j}$ is logically equivalent to $HN_{i-1,j}$ OR (NOT $HP_{i-1,j}$ AND NOT $D0_{i,j}$).

- Finally, $D0_{i,j}$ can be true for three possible reasons, which correspond to formula (6.1). First, it may happen that $P_i = T_j$. Second, it may be the case that $M_{i,j} = 1 + M_{i,j-1} = M_{i-1,j-1}$, which means $HP_{i,j}$ AND $VN_{i,j-1}$. Third, it may occur that $M_{i,j} = 1 + M_{i-1,j} = M_{i-1,j-1}$, which means $VP_{i,j}$ AND $HN_{i-1,j}$. From these conditions we use only $(P_i = T_j)$ OR $VN_{i,j-1}$ OR $HN_{i-1,j}$. Note again that if any of these three conditions hold, then $D0_{i,j}$ holds, so we have a logical equivalence.

Hence we have proved the following equivalences:

$$
\begin{aligned}
HN_{i,j} &\equiv VP_{i,j-1} \text{ AND } D0_{i,j} \\
VN_{i,j} &\equiv HP_{i-1,j} \text{ AND } D0_{i,j} \\
HP_{i,j} &\equiv VN_{i,j-1} \text{ OR NOT } (VP_{i,j-1} \text{ OR } D0_{i,j}) \\
VP_{i,j} &\equiv HN_{i-1,j} \text{ OR NOT } (HP_{i-1,j} \text{ OR } D0_{i,j}) \\
D0_{i,j} &\equiv (P_i = T_j) \text{ OR } VN_{i,j-1} \text{ OR } HN_{i-1,j} \; .
\end{aligned}
$$

The algorithm traverses the text and, at each text position j, keeps track of the five values above for every i. Since each value needs only one bit, we keep bit masks HN, VN, HP, VP, and $D0$ and update them for every new text character T_j read. Hence, for example, the i-th bit of the bit mask HN will correspond to the value $HN_{i,j}$. The index $j-1$ refers to the previous value of the bit mask (before processing T_j), whereas j refers to the new value, after processing T_j.

Under this light, it is clear that we can first compute $D0$, then HN and HP, and finally VN and VP. However, there is a circular dependency regarding $D0_{i,j}$; it depends on $HN_{i-1,j}$, which in turn depends on $D0_{i-1,j}$. That is, current $D0_{i,j}$ values depend on other current $D0_{i',j}$ values. This corresponds, again, to the zero-time dependency problem and complicates computing $D0$ in one shot. However, a solution exists.

Let us expand the formula for $D0_{i,j}$:

$$D0_{i,j} \equiv (P_i = T_j) \text{ OR } VN_{i,j-1} \text{ OR } (VP_{i-1,j-1} \text{ AND } D0_{i-1,j}) ,$$

which has the form $D_i \equiv X_i$ OR $(Y_{i-1}$ AND $D_{i-1})$. Unrolling the first values we get

$$D_1 \equiv X_1$$
$$D_2 \equiv X_2 \text{ OR } (Y_1 \text{ AND } X_1)$$
$$D_3 \equiv X_3 \text{ OR } (Y_2 \text{ AND } X_2) \text{ OR } (Y_2 \text{ AND } Y_1 \text{ AND } X_1)$$
$$D_i \equiv \text{ OR } _{r=1}^{i}(X_r \text{ AND } Y_r \text{ AND } Y_{r+1} \text{ AND } \ldots \text{ AND } Y_{i-1}) .$$

Let s be such that $Y_s \ldots Y_{i-1} = 1$ and $Y_{s-1} = 0$. It should be clear that D_i will be activated if $X_r = 1$ for some $s \leq r \leq i$. In other words, D_i will be activated if there is a bit set in X in the area covered by the last contiguous block of bits set in Y. If we compute $(Y + (X \& Y))$, the result is that every $X_r = 1$ that is aligned to a $Y_r = 1$ will propagate a change until one position after the end of the block. This covers all the positions i that should be set in D because of X_r being aligned to a block of 1's in Y. If we compute $(Y + (X \& Y)) \wedge Y$, the bits that changed will be on. Note that, since there may be several X_r bits under the same block of Y, all but the first such r positions will remain unchanged and hence not marked by the XOR operation. To fix this and to account for the case $X_i = 1$, we OR the final result with X. An example is as follows:

$$
\begin{aligned}
Y &= 0\,0\,0\,1\,1\,1\,1\,1\,0\,0\,0\,0\,1\,1 \\
X &= 0\,0\,0\,0\,1\,0\,1\,0\,0\,0\,0\,1\,0\,1 \\
X \& Y &= 0\,0\,0\,0\,1\,0\,1\,0\,0\,0\,0\,0\,0\,1 \\
(Y + (X \& Y)) &= 0\,0\,1\,0\,1\,0\,0\,1\,0\,0\,0\,1\,0\,0 \\
(Y + (X \& Y)) \wedge Y &= 0\,0\,1\,1\,0\,1\,1\,0\,0\,0\,0\,1\,1\,1 \\
D0 = ((Y + (X \& Y)) \wedge Y) \mid X &= 0\,0\,1\,1\,1\,1\,1\,0\,0\,0\,0\,1\,1\,1
\end{aligned}
$$

Once the solution to $D0$ is obtained, the rest flows easily. Figure 6.8 gives pseudo-code. The value err stores $C_m = M_{m,j}$ explicitly and is updated using $HP_{m,j}$ and $HN_{m,j}$. Note that the shifts correctly introduce zeros.

We call this algorithm **BPM**. It uses the bits of the computer word better than the previous bit-parallel algorithms, with a worst case of $O(\lceil m/w \rceil n)$ and an average case of $O(\lceil k/w \rceil n)$, achieved by updating only the computer words having "active" cells, as for **DP**. The update formula is a little more complex than that of **BPD** and the algorithm is a bit slower, but it adapts better to longer patterns because fewer computer words are needed. On the

BPM $(p = p_1p_2 \ldots p_m, \; T = t_1t_2 \ldots t_n, \; k)$
1.   Preprocessing
2.   **For** $c \in \Sigma$ **Do** $B[c] \leftarrow 0^m$
3.   **For** $j \in 1 \ldots m$ **Do** $B[p_j] \leftarrow B[p_j] \mid 0^{m-j}10^{j-1}$
4. $VP \leftarrow 1^m, \; VN \leftarrow 0^m$
5. $err \leftarrow m$
6.   Searching
7.   **For** $pos \in 1 \ldots n$ **Do**
8. $X \leftarrow B[t_{pos}] \mid VN$
9. $D0 \leftarrow ((VP + (X \; \& \; VP)) \wedge VP) \mid X$
10. $HN \leftarrow VP \; \& \; D0$
11. $HP \leftarrow VN \mid \sim (VP \mid D0)$
12. $X \leftarrow HP << 1$
13. $VN \leftarrow X \; \& \; D0$
14. $VP \leftarrow (HN << 1) \mid \sim (X \mid D0)$
15.   **If** $HP \; \& \; 10^{m-1} \neq 0^m$ **Then** $err \leftarrow err + 1$
16.   **Else If** $HN \; \& \; 10^{m-1} \neq 0^m$ **Then** $err \leftarrow err - 1$
17.   **If** $err \leq k$ **Then** report an occurrence at pos
18.   **End of for**

Fig. 6.8. Bit-parallel simulation of the dynamic programming matrix. It requires $m \leq w$.

other hand, **BPM** is even less flexible than **BPD** when it comes to searching for complex patterns or different distance functions.

Note that the algorithm can be adapted to compute edit distance simply by adding "$\mid 0^{m-1}1$" at the end of line 12 in Figure 6.8, since this time there is a horizontal increment at row zero (not represented in the bit masks).

Example of BPM We search for the string `"annual"` in the text `"annealing"` allowing $k = 2$ errors. The easiest way to understand what is going on is to relate the bit masks to the Δ values and these in turn to those of the dynamic programming matrix of Figure 6.2.

It is interesting to verify that err correctly maintains the value of the last cell of the current column of the **DP** matrix.

a	0 1 0 0 0 1	
l	1 0 0 0 0 0	
n	0 0 0 1 1 0	
u	0 0 1 0 0 0	
*	0 0 0 0 0 0	

$$B = \begin{cases} \end{cases}$$

$VN \;\; = \;\; 0\,0\,0\,0\,0\,0$
$VP \;\; = \;\; 1\,1\,1\,1\,1\,1$
$err \;\; = \;\; 6$

1.   Reading a $0\,1\,0\,0\,0\,1$
      $D0 = \;\; 1\,1\,1\,1\,1\,1$
      $HN = \;\; 1\,1\,1\,1\,1\,1$
      $HP = \;\; 0\,0\,0\,0\,0\,0$
      $VN = \;\; 0\,0\,0\,0\,0\,0$
      $VP = \;\; 1\,1\,1\,1\,1\,0$
      $err = \;\;\;\;\;\; 5$

2. Reading n   0 0 0 1 1 0
    —————————————————————————
    $D0 =$ 1 1 1 1 1 0
    $HN =$ 1 1 1 1 1 0
    $HP =$ 0 0 0 0 0 1
    $VN =$ 0 0 0 0 1 0
    $VP =$ 1 1 1 1 0 1
    $err =$ 4

3. Reading n   0 0 0 1 1 0
    —————————————————————————
    $D0 =$ 1 1 1 1 1 0
    $HN =$ 1 1 1 1 0 0
    $HP =$ 0 0 0 0 1 0
    $VN =$ 0 0 0 1 0 0
    $VP =$ 1 1 1 0 0 1
    $err =$ 3

4. Reading e   0 0 0 0 0 0
    —————————————————————————
    $D0 =$ 0 0 0 1 0 0
    $HN =$ 0 0 0 0 0 0
    $HP =$ 0 0 0 1 1 0
    $VN =$ 0 0 0 1 0 0
    $VP =$ 1 1 0 0 1 1
    $err =$ 3

5. Reading a   0 1 0 0 0 1
    —————————————————————————
    $D0 =$ 1 1 0 1 1 1
    $HN =$ 1 1 0 0 1 1
    $HP =$ 0 0 1 1 0 0
    $VN =$ 0 1 0 0 0 0
    $VP =$ 1 0 0 1 1 0
    $err =$ 2

We mark an occurrence since $err \leq 2$.

6. Reading l   1 0 0 0 0 0
    —————————————————————————
    $D0 =$ 1 1 0 0 0 0
    $HN =$ 1 0 0 0 0 0
    $HP =$ 0 1 1 0 0 1
    $VN =$ 1 1 0 0 0 0
    $VP =$ 0 0 1 1 0 1
    $err =$ 1

We mark an occurrence since $err \leq 2$.

7. Reading i   0 0 0 0 0 0
    —————————————————————————
    $D0 =$ 1 1 0 0 0 0
    $HN =$ 0 0 0 0 0 0
    $HP =$ 1 1 0 0 1 0
    $VN =$ 1 0 0 0 0 0
    $VP =$ 0 0 1 0 1 1
    $err =$ 2

We mark an occurrence since $err \leq 2$.

8. Reading n   0 0 0 1 1 0
    —————————————————————————
    $D0 =$ 1 0 0 1 1 0
    $HN =$ 0 0 0 0 1 0
    $HP =$ 1 1 0 0 0 0
    $VN =$ 1 0 0 0 0 0
    $VP =$ 0 1 1 1 0 1
    $err =$ 3

9. Reading g   0 0 0 0 0 0
    —————————————————————————
    $D0 =$ 1 0 0 0 0 0
    $HN =$ 0 0 0 0 0 0
    $HP =$ 1 0 0 0 1 0
    $VN =$ 0 0 0 0 0 0
    $VP =$ 0 1 1 0 1 1
    $err =$ 4

6.5 Algorithms for fast filtering the text

The idea behind filtration algorithms is that it may be easier to tell that a text position does *not* match than to tell that it does. So these algorithms filter the text, discarding areas that cannot match. They are unable on their own to tell that there *is* a match, so every filtration algorithm needs to be coupled with a nonfiltration algorithm to check the nondiscarded text areas for potential occurrences.

Filtering algorithms only improve the average-case performance, and their major attraction is the potential for algorithms that do not inspect every text character. The performance of filtration algorithms is related to the amount of text that they are able to discard, and it is very sensitive to the error level. Most filters work very well on low error levels and poorly otherwise, so when evaluating filtration algorithms it is important to consider not only their time efficiency but also their tolerance to errors.

There are many filtration algorithms, among which we have selected the two that are the best in most cases. The first, **PEX**, is the best when the alphabet size is not too small, for example, on English text. The second one, **ABNDM**, is the best on DNA and other small-alphabet texts.

6.5.1 Partitioning into $k+1$ pieces

The idea behind this algorithm, which we call **PEX**, is that if a pattern is cut into $k+1$ pieces, then at least *one* of the pieces must appear unchanged in an approximate occurrence. This is evident, since k errors cannot alter $k+1$ pieces, at least under the edit distance model. Indeed, a more general lemma turns out to be useful [Mye94, BYN99]:

Lemma 1 *Let Occ match p with k errors, $p = p^1 \ldots p^j$ be a concatenation of subpatterns, and $a_1 \ldots a_j$ be nonnegative integers such that $A = \sum_{i=1}^{j} a_i$. Then, for some $i \in 1 \ldots j$, Occ includes a substring that matches p^i with $\lfloor a_i k / A \rfloor$ errors.*

To see this, note that if each p^i matches only with $1 + \lfloor a_i k / A \rfloor$ errors, then the whole p cannot match with less than $k+1$ errors. If we set $A = j = k+1$ and $a_i = 1$, then the simpler case shows up.

The proposal in [WM92b, BYN99, NBY99] is to split the pattern into $k+1$ approximately equal length pieces, search the pieces in the text with a multipattern search algorithm, and then check the neighborhood of their occurrences. Some care has to be exercised to report the occurrences in order and to avoid reporting the same occurrences more than once.

The "neighborhood" must be large enough to hold any occurrence. Occurrences are of length at most $m + k$ under edit distance. If pattern piece $p_{i_1 \ldots i_2}$ matches at text position $t_{j \ldots j+(i_2-i_1)}$, then the occurrence can start at most $i_1 - 1 + k$ positions before t_j since the insertions can all occur at the beginning of the occurrence, and it can finish at most $m - i2 + k$ positions after $t_{j+(i_2-i_1)}$ since the insertions can all occur at the end of the occurrence. Hence we need to check the text area $T_{j-(i_1-1)-k \ldots j+(m-i_1)+k}$, which is of length $m + 2k$. Note that if two pieces happen to be equal, each occurrence must trigger two verifications with different areas.

Two choices need to be made to obtain a concrete algorithm. The most important one is which multipattern search algorithm to use (Chapter 3). **Multiple Shift-And** is used in [WM92b], while [BYN99, NBY99] use **Set Horspool**.

The second choice is the verification algorithm. Although many authors care little about this choice and resort to plain dynamic programming, a faster technique such as **BPM** reduces the cost per verification from $O(m^2)$ to $O(m^2/w)$.

It is shown in [BYN99] that the cost of the multipattern search dominates for $\alpha < 1/(3\log_{|\Sigma|} m)$. Above that error level, the cost of verifying candidate text positions starts to dominate and the filter efficiency deteriorates abruptly. In the area where the filter behaves well, its search cost is about $O(kn\log_{|\Sigma|}(m)/m)$.

Hierarchical verification To reduce unnecessary verification costs, "hierarchical verification" is introduced in [NBY99]. The idea is that, since the verification cost is quadratic in the pattern length, we pay too much verifying the whole pattern each time a small piece matches. We could reject the occurrence with a cheaper test for a shorter pattern piece.

Assume that the pattern is partitioned into $j = k+1 = 2^r$ pieces. Instead of splitting it into $k + 1$ pieces in one shot, we do it hierarchically. The pattern is first split in half, each half to be searched with $\lfloor k/2 \rfloor$ errors due to Lemma 1. The halves are then recursively split in two, until the number of errors allowed becomes zero.

Figure 6.9 illustrates the resulting tree. The leaves of this tree are the pieces actually searched. When a leaf occurs in the text, instead of checking the whole pattern as in the basic technique, the parent of the leaf is checked (with $k = 1$ errors in the example) in a small area around the piece that matched. The extension of this area is computed as before, according to the piece length and the error level permitted. If that parent node is not found, then the verification stops and the multipattern scanning resumes. Otherwise the verification continues with the grandparent of the leaf and so on, until the root (i.e., the whole pattern) is found.

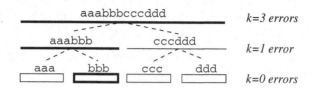

Fig. 6.9. The hierarchical verification method for a pattern split into four parts. The boxes (leaves) are the elements that are really searched, and the root represents the whole pattern. At least one pattern at each level must appear in any occurrence of the complete pattern. If the bold box is found, all the bold lines may be verified.

This technique is correct because Lemma 1 applies to each level of the tree: The grandparent cannot appear if none of its children appear, even if a grandchild appeared.

Let us go back to Figure 6.9. If one searches for the pattern "aaabbbcc-cddd" with three errors in the text "xxxbbbxxxxxx", and splits the pattern into four pieces to be searched for without errors, then the piece "bbb" will be found in the text. In the original approach, one would verify the complete pattern with $k = 3$ errors in the text area, while with hierarchical verification one checks only its parent "aaabbb" with one error and immediately determines that there cannot be a complete occurrence. This latter check is much cheaper.

The analysis in [NBY99] shows that with hierarchical verification the area of applicability of the algorithm grows to $\alpha < 1/\log_{|\Sigma|} m$.

When $k + 1$ is not a power of 2, it is advisable to keep the binary tree as balanced as possible. For example, if $k + 1 = 3$, then we split the pattern into three pieces (leaves) of length $\lfloor m/3 \rfloor$. In the binary tree, the left child of the root has length $2\lfloor m/3 \rfloor$ and is searched with $\lfloor 2k/3 \rfloor = 1$ errors, while the second child is the leftmost leaf with length $\lfloor m/3 \rfloor$ to be searched with $\lfloor k/3 \rfloor = 0$ errors. The node that is searched with one error is then split into its two leaves. Pseudo-code for the algorithm that builds this tree is shown in Figure 6.10 together with the resulting tree for the pattern "annual" with $k = 2$. Pseudo-code for the **PEX** algorithm is shown in Figure 6.11.

Example of PEX We search for the string "annual" in the text "any_annealing" allowing $k = 2$ errors. The corresponding partition is given in Figure 6.10. As can be seen, the same occurrences can be found many times.

1. Found $\boxed{\text{an}}$ y_annealing

Search for	"annu" with $k = 1$
inside	$\boxed{\text{any\_a}}$ nnealing
failed	(so abort verification)

2. Found any_ $\boxed{\text{an}}$ nealing

Search for	"annu" with $k = 1$
inside	any $\boxed{\text{\_annea}}$ ling
found	(so go upper in the tree)

Search for	"annual" with $k = 2$
inside	an $\boxed{\text{y\_annealin}}$ g
found	(report positions 9,10,11)

3. Found any_anne $\boxed{\text{al}}$ ing

Search for	"annual" with $k = 2$
inside	an $\boxed{\text{y\_annealin}}$ g
found	(report positions 9,10,11)

CreateTree $(p = p_i p_{i+1} \ldots p_j,\ k,\ myParent,\ idx,\ plen)$
1.   Create new *node*
2. $from(node) \leftarrow i$
3. $to(node) \leftarrow j$
4. $left \leftarrow \lceil (k+1)/2 \rceil$
5. $parent(node) \leftarrow myParent$
6. $err(node) \leftarrow k$
7.   **If** $k = 0$ **Then** $leaf_{idx} \leftarrow node$
8.   **Else**
9.   **CreateTree**$(p_{i \ldots i+left \cdot plen - 1},\ \lfloor (left \cdot k)/(k+1) \rfloor,\ node,\ idx,\ plen)$
10.   **CreateTree**$(p_{i+left \cdot plen \ldots j},\ \lfloor ((k+1-left) \cdot k)/(k+1) \rfloor,$
                                $node,\ idx + left,\ plen)$

11.   **End of if**

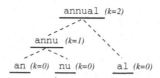

Fig. 6.10. Recursive algorithm to build the hierarchical verification tree on $p_{i \ldots j}$ with k errors. The other variables are *myParent* (parent of the node to be built), *idx* (next leaf index to assign), and *plen* (length of the pieces). At the bottom is an example for the pattern "annual" with $k = 2$.

6.5.2 *Approximate BNDM*

Just as **BDM/BNDM** is better than **Boyer-Moore** algorithms for small alphabet sizes, an extension of **BNDM** proposed in [NR00] works better than **PEX** on DNA. We call it **ABNDM**.

The modification is to build an NFA to search the *reversed* pattern allowing errors, modify it to match any pattern suffix, and apply essentially **BNDM** (Section 2.4.2) using this automaton. Figure 6.12 shows the resulting automaton.

This automaton recognizes any reverse prefix of p allowing k errors. The text window will be abandoned when no pattern factor matches with k errors what was read. At that point, the window is shifted to the next pattern prefix found with k errors (position *last*).

The occurrences must start exactly at the initial window position. This makes it easier to report initial rather than final positions of the pattern occurrences, although with some care we can report the sorted final positions without repetitions.

PEX $(p = p_1p_2 \ldots p_m,\; T = t_1t_2 \ldots t_n,\; k)$
1.   **Preprocessing**
2.   **CreateTree**$(p,\; k,\; \theta,\; 0,\; \lfloor m/(k+1)\rfloor)$
3.   Preprocess multipattern search for
               $\{p_{from(node)} \cdots p_{to(node)},\; node = leaf_i,\; i \in \{0 \ldots k\}\}$
4.   **Searching**
5.   **For** $(pos, i) \in$ output of multipattern search **Do**
6. $node \leftarrow leaf_i$
7. $in \leftarrow from(node)$
8. $node \leftarrow parent(node)$
9. $cand \leftarrow$ TRUE
10.   **While** $cand$ = TRUE   AND $node \neq \theta$ **Do**
11. $p_1 \leftarrow pos - (in - from(node)) - err(node)$
12. $p_2 \leftarrow pos + (to(node) - in + 1) + err(node)$
13.   Verify text area $T_{p_1 \ldots p_2}$ for pattern piece $p_{from(node) \ldots to(node)}$
                     allowing $err(node)$ errors
14.   **If** pattern piece was not found **Then** $cand \leftarrow$ FALSE
15.   **Else** $node \leftarrow parent(node)$
16.   **End of while**
17.   **If** $cand$ = TRUE **Then**
18.   Report the positions where the whole p was found
19.   **End of if**
20.   **End of for**

Fig. 6.11. Filtration algorithm based on partitioning into exact searches. It assumes that the multipattern search algorithm delivers its results in the form $(text\_position, piece\_that\_matched)$.

The window length is $m - k$, not m, to ensure that if there is an occurrence starting at the window position then a factor of the pattern occurs in any suffix of the window.

Reaching the beginning of the window does not guarantee an occurrence, however. Since the occurrences are of varying length, we only know that a factor of the pattern has occurred with at most k errors. In particular, if no pattern *prefix* has been read with k errors or less, no match can start at the initial window position. On the other hand, if we found such a pattern prefix, we would have to check the area by computing the edit distance from the beginning of the window, reading at most $m + k$ text characters.

This verification can be done with the algorithm to compute edit distance given in Section 6.2.1. Another choice is to use **BPR**, where we remove the initial self-loop in Figure 6.4. The formula is the same except for R_0, where it becomes

$$R_0' \;\leftarrow\; (R_0 << 1)\; \&\; B[t_j]$$

The other bit-parallel algorithms are more complicated to adapt.

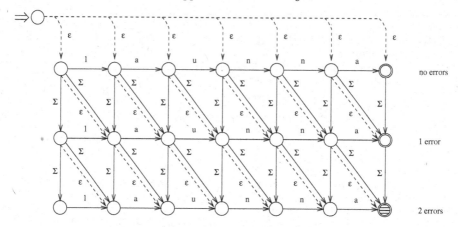

Fig. 6.12. The NFA to search for any reverse prefix of "annual" allowing two errors. We show the active states after reading the text window "any_".

As with the original NFA of Figure 6.4, there are many ways to simulate the automaton of Figure 6.12. Given that this algorithm works well for small k values, using row-wise parallelization is a good choice. In particular, specializing the code for constant k values is a good idea. The only change is that we have to initialize the automaton with all the states active and remove the self-loop.

Other schemes, such as **BPD** and **BPM**, are more complicated to use. **BPD** needs more bits than for searching, because the whole automaton needs to be represented, not just the full diagonals. In principle $(m + k + 2)(k + 2)$ bits are necessary. **BPM** was not designed to tell whether the automaton has any active state (there is, however, recent work on this [HN01]). This is the first example where the flexibility of **BPR** pays off.

Figure 6.13 shows the algorithm. We initialize it after reading the first character of the window.

The algorithm works well for small alphabets and short patterns; it needs $m \le w$ because of bit-parallelism. With longer patterns it is possible to use more computer words, but the results quickly deteriorate because the trick of only updating the computer words holding active states does not work well. The reason is that, since we initialize the NFA with all the states activated, the active states tend to be distributed uniformly over the whole pattern. On the other hand, making the automaton deterministic as with **BDM** generates an exponential number of states, just as the DFA construction reviewed in Section 6.3.

ABNDM $(p = p_1 p_2 \ldots p_m, \ T = t_1 t_2 \ldots t_n, \ k)$

1.	Preprocessing
2.	For $c \in \Sigma$ Do $B[c] \leftarrow 0^m$
3.	For $j \in 1 \ldots m$ Do $B[p_j] \leftarrow B[p_j] \mid 0^{j-1} 1 0^{m-j}$
4.	Searching
5.	$pos \leftarrow 0$
6.	While $pos \leq n - (m - k)$ Do
7.	$j \leftarrow m - k - 1, \ last \leftarrow m - k - 1$
8.	$R_0 \leftarrow B[t_{pos+m-k}]$
9.	$newR \leftarrow 1^m$
10.	For $i \in 1 \ldots k$ Do $R_i \leftarrow newR$
11.	While $newR \neq 0^m$ AND $j \neq 0$ Do
12.	$oldR \leftarrow R_0$
13.	$newR \leftarrow (oldR << 1) \ \& \ B[t_{pos+j}]$
14.	$R_0 \leftarrow newR$
15.	For $i \in 1 \ldots k$ Do
16.	$newR \leftarrow ((R_i << 1) \ \& \ B[t_{pos+j}])$
	$\mid oldR \mid ((oldR \mid newR) << 1)$
17.	$oldR \leftarrow R_i, \ R_i \leftarrow newR$
18.	End of for
19.	$j \leftarrow j - 1$
20.	If $newR \ \& \ 10^{m-1} \neq 0^m$ Then /* prefix recognized */
21.	If $j > 0$ Then $last \leftarrow j$
22.	Else check a possible occurrence starting at $pos + 1$
23.	End of if
24.	End of while
25.	$pos \leftarrow pos + last$
26.	End of while

Fig. 6.13. The extension of **BNDM** to approximate searching. It assumes $m - k > 1$.

Example of ABNDM We search for the string `"annual"` in the text `"any_annealing"` allowing $k = 1$ errors. We have reduced the error level because $k = 2$ is too high to be illustrative.

$$
B = \begin{cases}
\begin{array}{|c|c|}
\hline
\text{a} & 1\,0\,0\,0\,1\,0 \\
\hline
\text{l} & 0\,0\,0\,0\,0\,1 \\
\hline
\text{n} & 0\,1\,1\,0\,0\,0 \\
\hline
\text{u} & 0\,0\,0\,1\,0\,0 \\
\hline
* & 0\,0\,0\,0\,0\,0 \\
\hline
\end{array}
\end{cases}
$$

Reading _	$0\,0\,0\,0\,0\,0$
$R_0 =$	$0\,0\,0\,0\,0\,0$
$R_1 =$	$1\,0\,0\,1\,1\,0$

The last bit of R_1 is set, so $last \leftarrow 3$.

Reading y	$0\,0\,0\,0\,0\,0$
$R_0 =$	$0\,0\,0\,0\,0\,0$
$R_1 =$	$0\,0\,0\,0\,0\,0$

The automaton runs out of active states, so we shift the window by $last = 3$.

1. $\boxed{\text{any\_a}}$ nnealing

Reading a	$1\,0\,0\,0\,1\,0$
$R_0 =$	$1\,0\,0\,0\,1\,0$
$R_1 =$	$1\,1\,1\,1\,1\,1$

$last \leftarrow 4$.

2. any ⌊_anne⌋ aling

Reading e	0 0 0 0 0 0
$R_0 =$	0 0 0 0 0 0
$R_1 =$	1 1 1 1 1 1

last ← 4.

Reading n	0 1 1 0 0 0
$R_0 =$	0 0 0 0 0 0
$R_1 =$	0 1 1 0 0 0

Reading n	0 1 1 0 0 0
$R_0 =$	0 0 0 0 0 0
$R_1 =$	0 1 0 0 0 0

Reading a	1 0 0 0 1 0
$R_0 =$	0 0 0 0 0 0
$R_1 =$	1 0 0 0 0 0

The last bit of R_1 is set, so *last* ← 1.

Reading _	0 0 0 0 0 0
$R_0 =$	0 0 0 0 0 0
$R_1 =$	0 0 0 0 0 0

The automaton runs out of active states, so we shift by *last* = 1.

3. any_ ⌊annea⌋ ling

Reading a	1 0 0 0 1 0
$R_0 =$	1 0 0 0 1 0
$R_1 =$	1 1 1 1 1 1

last ← 4.

Reading e	0 0 0 0 0 0
$R_0 =$	0 0 0 0 0 0
$R_1 =$	1 0 0 1 1 0

The last bit of R_1 is set, so *last* ← 3.

Reading n	0 1 1 0 0 0
$R_0 =$	0 0 0 0 0 0
$R_1 =$	0 0 1 0 0 0

Reading n	0 1 1 0 0 0
$R_0 =$	0 0 0 0 0 0
$R_1 =$	0 1 0 0 0 0

Reading a	1 0 0 0 1 0
$R_0 =$	0 0 0 0 0 0
$R_1 =$	1 0 0 0 0 0

The last bit of R_1 is set and $j = 0$, so we compute edit distance between the pattern and prefixes of the text "**anneali**". Since we find a match ($k \leq 1$) against the prefix "**anneal**", we report the text position 5.
We shift the window by *last* = 3.

4. any_ann ⌊ealin⌋ g

Reading n	0 1 1 0 0 0
$R_0 =$	0 1 1 0 0 0
$R_1 =$	1 1 1 1 1 1

last ← 4.

Reading i	0 0 0 0 0 0
$R_0 =$	0 0 0 0 0 0
$R_1 =$	1 1 1 0 0 0

The last bit of R_1 is set, so *last* ← 3.

Reading l	0 0 0 0 0 0
$R_0 =$	0 0 0 0 0 0
$R_1 =$	0 0 0 0 0 0

The automaton runs out of active states, so we shift by *last* = 3.

Since the window falls out of the text, we stop.

6.5.3 Other filtration algorithms

There are many proposals for filtration. In particular, we have left out some algorithms that are slightly faster than **PEX** and **ABNDM** for a few $(m, k, |\Sigma|)$ combinations [TU93, JTU96, BYN99, CL94, ST95]. In general, however, the differences in performance do not justify the programming effort.

There exist filtration algorithms that are optimal on average. It was proved in [CM94] that a lower bound for the expected time of approximate searching is $O((k + \log_{|\Sigma|} m)n/m)$. In the same paper, a filtration algorithm with that complexity is obtained. The complexity is valid for $\alpha < 1 - e/\sqrt{|\Sigma|}$, a limit shown impossible to improve [BYN99] since at that point there are too many *real* occurrences in the text. Although it is optimal in theory, the algorithm is not fast in practice. Whether a practical algorithm with optimal complexity exists is still an open issue.

On the other hand, most filters achieve $O(k \log_{|\Sigma|}(m)n/m)$ time for $\alpha = O(1/\log_{|\Sigma|} m)$. The central issue is that, in order to break this barrier, it seems necessary to reduce the problem to pieces that are searched with *fewer* errors instead of with *zero* errors. This is precisely what is done in [CM94], as well as in other filters [BYN99] that reach the limit $\alpha < 1 - e/\sqrt{|\Sigma|}$. This last technique does not skip text characters, but it is a reasonable alternative in practice for medium error levels.

6.6 Multipattern approximate searching

A natural extension to the approximate search problem is that of searching multiple patterns simultaneously. Not many algorithms have been proposed for this, and all of them are filters that lose efficiency for high enough error levels.

6.6.1 A hashing based algorithm for one error

A good solution for $k = 1$ proposed in [MM96], which we call **MultiHash**, is based on the observation that if p matches p' with one error, then there are $m - 1$ characters that match. The idea is to obtain m strings from p, which we call "signatures," by removing one character at a time, that is, $\{p_2 p_3 \ldots p_m, \; p_1 p_3 \ldots p_m, \; p_1 p_2 p_4 \ldots p_m, \; \ldots, \; p_1 p_2 \ldots p_{m-1}\}$. We define the j-th signature of a string x of length m as

$$S_{x,j} = x_1 x_2 \ldots x_{j-1} x_{j+1} \ldots x_m$$

For example, for the pattern $p =$"annual" the signatures are $S_{p,1} =$ "nnual", $S_{p,2} = S_{p,3} =$ "anual", $S_{p,4} =$ "annal", $S_{p,5} =$ "annul", and $S_{p,6} =$ "annua".

If we search for r patterns, then we obtain m signatures from each, for a total of rm signatures. All the patterns have to be the same length. If this is not the case, they are truncated to the length of the shortest pattern.

Those rm signatures are stored in a hash table, which will be used for exact searching. To search the text, all m-length windows $t_i t_{i+1} \ldots t_{i+m-1}$ are considered.

For each such window, all m signatures are obtained: $t_{i+2}t_{i+3}\ldots t_{i+m-1}$, $t_{i+1}t_{i+3}\ldots t_{i+m-1}$, ..., $t_{i+1}t_{i+2}\ldots t_{i+m-2}$. We abreviate the notation and call $S_{i,j} = S_{t_i\ldots t_{i+m-1},j}$. Each such signature is searched for in the hash table and, if it is found, an occurrence is reported.

We now show that the method is correct. If p and a text occurrence p' match with one substitution error, so that $p_1 p_2 \ldots p_{j-1} a p_{j+1} \ldots p_m = p'_1 p'_2 \ldots p'_{j-1} b p'_{j+1} \ldots p'_m$, then p' and p are equal after removing a and b, and hence the occurrence will be found because the j-th signatures of p and the text window are the same. If they match with an insertion in p', $p_1 p_2 \ldots p_{j-1} p_j p_{j+1} \ldots p_m = p'_1 p'_2 \ldots p'_{j-1} p'_j b p'_{j+1} \ldots p'_{m-1}$, then since the text windows are of length m there will be a window $x = p'_1 p'_2 \ldots p'_{j-1} p'_j p'_{j+1} \ldots p'_{m-1} c$, and the signatures $S_{x,m} = S_{p,j+1}$ match. Finally, p and p' may match after a deletion in p', $p_1 p_2 \ldots p_{j-1} p_j p_{j+1} \ldots p_m = p'_1 p'_2 \ldots p'_{j-1} p'_{j+1} \ldots p'_m p'_{m+1}$. In this case the text window of interest is $x = p'_1 p'_2 \ldots p'_{j-1} p'_j p'_{j+1} \ldots p'_m$, since $S_{x,j} = S_{p,m}$.

The way to compute the hash function is important. A formula like

$$h(x_1 \ldots x_{m-1}) = \sum_{i=1}^{m-1} x_i d^{i-1} \quad \bmod s$$

for relative primes (d, s), as used in [KR87], is known to distribute the strings fairly uniformly in a table $H[0 \ldots s-1]$. Moreover, it permits computing the hash value of each signature of the new window in $O(1)$ time using those of the previous window. Say that the new window is $t_{i+1}t_{i+2}\ldots t_{i+m}$. Then, its j-th signature is $S_{i+1,j} = t_{i+1}t_{i+2}\ldots t_{i+j-1}t_{i+j+1}\ldots t_{i+m}$, which is obtained from the $(j+1)$-th signature of the previous region $S_{i,j+1} = t_i t_{i+1} \ldots t_{i+j-1}t_{i+j+1}\ldots t_{i+m-1}$ by the formula $S_{i,j+1}t_{i+m} = t_i S_{i+1,j}$. Hence, $h(S_{i+1,j}) = ((h(S_{i,j+1}) - t_i)/d + t_{i+m}d^{m-2}) \bmod s$, which can be computed in constant time.

Since the hash values can be computed in constant time and we have to perform m searches per text window, the search time is $O(mn)$, independent of the number of patterns. We are not accounting for the collision problem in the hashing scheme. On average, the search time remains constant if the size of the hash table is proportional to the number of signatures inserted. Hence the method takes on average $O(mn)$ time and $O(rm)$ space.

The scheme works well in practice even for thousands of patterns. In this respect the method is unbeatable. On the other hand, it is costly to extend to more than one error. For k errors we should consider the $O(m^k)$ alternatives of removing k characters from every pattern and every text window, for a total average cost of $O(m^k n)$ time and $O(m^k r)$ space.

Figure 6.14 shows the algorithm. At any point in the execution it holds $h_j = h(S_{pos,j})$. The time of the preprocessing and the initial filling of h can be reduced by noticing that $S_{x,j+1} = (S_{x,j} + (x_j - x_{j+1})d^j) \mod s$. Hence the algorithm takes time $O(rm + mn)$ plus collisions.

MultiHash $(P = \{p^1,\ p^2,\ \ldots,\ p^r\},\ T = t_1t_2\ldots t_n;\ k = 1)$

1.   Preprocessing
2. $H \leftarrow$ empty hash table
3.   **For** $i \in 1\ldots r$ **Do**
4.   **For** $j \in 1\ldots m$ **Do** insert $(S_{p^i,j}, i)$ in $H[h(S_{p^i,j})]$
5.   Searching
6.   **For** $j \in 1\ldots m-1$ **Do** $h_j \leftarrow h(S_{1,j})$
7.   **For** $pos \in 1\ldots n-m+1$ **Do**
8. $oldh_1 \leftarrow h_1$
9.   **For** $j \in 1\ldots m$ **Do**
10.   **For** $(x, i) \in H[h_j]$ **Do**
11.   **If** $x = S_{pos,j}$ **Then** report pattern p^i at pos
12.   **End of for**
13. $h_j \leftarrow ((h_{j+1} - t_{pos})/d + t_{pos+m}d^{m-2}) \mod s$
14.   **End of for**
15. $h_m \leftarrow oldh_1$
16.   **End of for**

Fig. 6.14. Hashing-based scheme to search for multiple patterns with one error. We assume that H is a hash table where we insert pairs of the form $(key, value)$ and then retrieve the set of pairs associated with a given cell. We also assume that t_{n+1} can be accessed, although its value is irrelevant.

6.6.2 Partitioning into $k+1$ pieces

The algorithm **PEX** described in Section 6.5.1 is easily extended to multiple patterns [BYN97]. We call it **MultiPEX**. Given r patterns, we split each pattern into $k+1$ pieces. Then we proceed exactly as before: We perform a multipattern exact search for all those $r(k+1)$ pieces (Chapter 3), and each time a piece is found we check the corresponding pattern in the candidate text area. If a piece belongs to more than one pattern, then all the owners have to be checked. Hierarchical verification can be used as well.

The algorithm performs well under a wide range of cases. It is shown in [BYN97] that it can be applied whenever basic **PEX** can be applied, that is, $\alpha < 1/\log_{|\Sigma|} m$. The code is basically the same as that of Figure 6.11.

6.6.3 Superimposed automata

A third idea, which we call **MultiBP**, is based on the NFA of Figure 6.4. Given r patterns of the same length to be searched for with k errors, we build the NFA for each of them and then we *superimpose* their automata [BYN97]. Superimposition means that the j-th horizontal arrow can be crossed with the j-th character of *any* pattern. Figure 6.15 shows an example with the patterns "annual" and "binary".

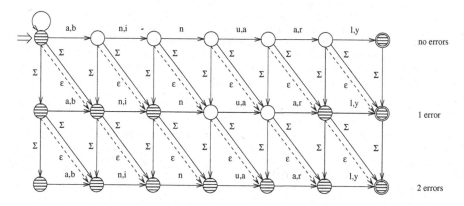

Fig. 6.15. An NFA for approximate string matching of the patterns "annual" and "binary" with two errors. The shaded states are those that are active after reading the text "binual".

In particular we are interested in a bit-parallel simulation of the superimposed NFA. Let $B_i[c]$ be the bit-parallel table for the i-th pattern. Then we build a new table B, where

$$B[c] \;=\; B_1[c] \;\mid\; B_2[c] \;\mid\; \ldots \;\mid\; B_r[c]$$

and apply any of the algorithms suitable for single patterns, such as **BPR**, **BPD**, **BPM**, or **ABNDM**.

The result is equivalent to searching for a single pattern with classes of characters: We convert the search for $\{p^1, p^2, \ldots, p^r\}$ into the search for

$$\{p_1^1, p_1^2, \ldots, p_1^r\} \; \{p_2^1, p_2^2, \ldots, p_2^r\} \; \ldots \; \{p_m^1, p_m^2, \ldots, p_m^r\}$$

So it is not really necessary to use NFAs: Any bit-parallel algorithm can be used, in particular **BPM**.

Of course this is only a filter: If we search for "annual" and "binary", then "binual" will be found with *zero* errors. Each time our relaxed search mechanism reports a match we have to check the area for all the patterns involved.

A new hierarchical verification mechanism is advisable here. If we have superimposed the patterns $\{p^1, p^2, p^3, p^4\}$ and found a possible occurrence, then we can check for $\{p^1, p^2\}$ and $\{p^3, p^4\}$ instead of checking for all four patterns. In many cases we will avoid performing r checks just by testing two superimposed sets. If, say, the superimposed set $\{p^1, p^2\}$ matches, then we have to check for p^1 and p^2 separately.

Compared to **PEX** (Section 6.5.1), this hierarchical verification mechanism is top-down rather than bottom-up. If we find the superimposition of $\{p^1, \ldots, p^r\}$, then we recursively check the relevant text area for the two superimposed sets $\{p^1, \ldots, p^{\lfloor r/2 \rfloor}\}$ and $\{p^{1+\lfloor r/2 \rfloor}, \ldots, p^r\}$. Of course all the $2r-1$ possible superimpositions are precomputed. The process finishes when we do not find the pattern set in the area or when a set of just one pattern is found.

As we superimpose more patterns, it becomes easier to cross the horizontal arrows. Indeed, the probability of crossing raises from $1/|\Sigma|$ to about $r/|\Sigma|$. Therefore, it is not advisable to superimpose too many patterns. The optimal number of patterns to superimpose is shown in [BYN97] to be $r' = |\Sigma|(1 - \alpha)^2$. If there are more patterns, one should split them into groups of r' patterns and search each group separately.

Figure 6.16 shows the preprocessing and Figure 6.17 gives search pseudo-code for this algorithm. The code is independent of how we simulate the bit-parallel search. Our recommendation is to use **BPD** if the patterns fit in a computer word, and **BPM** otherwise. We assume that all the preprocessing information is stored in an object B and that "joining" two such objects produces a new one that reflects their superimposition. For example, "joining" tables B_1 and B_2 into table B (in line 10 of **CreateSuperp**) is translated, for **BPR**, **ABNDM**, and **BPM**, into

For $c \in \Sigma$ **Do** $B[c] \leftarrow B_1[c] \mid B_2[c]$

BPD also needs to reflect these changes in table BB.

6.7 Searching for extended strings and regular expressions

Sometimes one would like to search for complex patterns allowing errors. There are three classes of algorithms addressing this issue: One extends classical dynamic programming for simple strings to regular expressions, a second is based on a Four-Russians approach, and the third uses bit-parallelism. We explain all three approaches but concentrate on bit-parallelism because it is simpler and yields the best results in most cases.

Since classes of characters are trivially solved by either approach, we focus

---

CreateSuperp $(p^i, \ldots, p^j)$
1.   Create new *node*
2.   **If** $i = j$ **Then**
3. $B(node) \leftarrow$ preprocess single pattern p^i
4. $idx(node) \leftarrow i$
5. $left(node) \leftarrow \theta$
6. $right(node) \leftarrow \theta$
7.   **Else**
8. $left(node) \leftarrow$ **CreateSuperp**$(p^i \ldots p^{\lfloor (i+j)/2 \rfloor})$
9. $right(node) \leftarrow$ **CreateSuperp**$(p^{1+\lfloor (i+j)/2 \rfloor} \ldots p^j)$
10. $B(node) \leftarrow$ join $B(left(node))$ and $B(right(node))$
11.   **End of if**
12.   **Return** *node*

Fig. 6.16. Preprocessing for hierarchical verification of the superimposed search for multiple patterns.

Verify $(node, from, to)$
1. $B \leftarrow B(node)$
2.   **For** $pos \in$ occurrences reported with B in $T_{from \ldots to}$ **Do**
3.   **If** $left(node) = \theta$ **Then** report $p^{idx(node)}$ at pos
4.   **Else**
5.   **Verify**$(left(node), pos - m - k + 1, pos)$
6.   **Verify**$(right(node), pos - m - k + 1, pos)$
7.   **End of if**
8.   **End of for**

MultiBP $(P = \{p^1, p^2, \ldots, p^r\}, T = t_1 t_2 \ldots t_n, k)$
9.   **Preprocessing**
10. $tree \leftarrow$ **CreateSuperp**$(p^1 \ldots p^r)$
11.   **Searching**
12.   **Verify**$(tree, 1, n)$

Fig. 6.17. Superimposition scheme to search for multiple patterns with errors.

on more complex extensions such as gaps, optional, and repeatable characters, and regular expressions.

6.7.1 A dynamic programming based approach

This is the oldest solution to the problem [MM89], and a beautiful yet complicated one. To understand it we need to come back to the basic dynamic programming algorithm (Section 6.2).

Consider the graph of Figure 6.18. Each node corresponds to a cell of the dynamic programming matrix of Figure 6.1. The arrows between nodes represent the cost of insertion in the pattern (horizontal), deletion in the pattern (vertical), or matching/substitution (diagonal) among neighboring cells. The cost of the diagonal arrows is 0 or 1, depending on whether the corresponding characters are equal (match) or different (substitution).

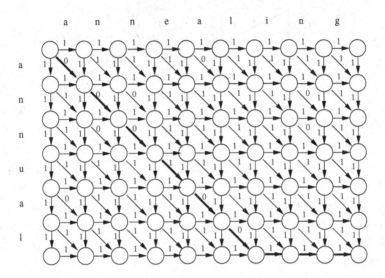

Fig. 6.18. Converting the edit distance problem into a shortest path problem. Bold arrows show the optimum path, of cost 4.

The edit distance problem can be converted into the problem of finding a shortest path from the upper left to the lower right node. If we are interested in approximate searching rather than in computing edit distance, then we assign zero cost to the horizontal arrows of the first row and consider minimum distances to every node of the last row.

Since the graph is acyclic, the optimum path can be computed in $O(mn)$ time. This is just another view of the classical dynamic programming algorithm, but this view is more flexible and can be extended to more complex patterns. In the simplest case, the pattern is represented by the vertical columns of nodes of the graph.

Figure 6.19 shows a graph over the text "baa", where each "vertical" row of nodes has been replaced by the NFA of the regular expression "(a|b)a*" (Thompson's construction; see Section 5.2.1). It can be seen that in this case the distance is zero (i.e., the regular expression matches the text exactly), and that the best path is achieved thanks to an ε-transition.

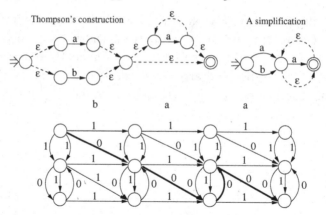

Fig. 6.19. The graph for the regular expression `"(a|b)a*"` on the text `"baa"`. Bold arrows show an optimal path, of cost zero.

The idea of the shortest path can still be applied quite easily if the graph is acyclic, that is, if the regular expression does not contain the "$*$" or the "$+$" operator. On acyclic regular expressions we can find a topological order to evaluate the graph so as to find the shortest paths in overall time $O(mn)$. This requires Thompson's guarantee that there are $O(m)$ edges on an automaton of m nodes.

Cycles in the NFA pose a problem because no suitable order can be found. The problem appears when we combine cycles with deletion (vertical) arrows, because a deletion can propagate through a cycle and influence the departing node. One of the most important results of [MM89] is that those "back edges" coming from the "$*$" or "$+$" operators can be ignored in a first pass, and then a second pass considering the deletion arrows is enough to obtain the correct result. For more details we refer the reader to [MM89].

6.7.2 A Four-Russians approach

We have already seen Four-Russians approaches that deal with regular expression searching without errors (Section 5.3.3) [Mye92] and with simple string matching allowing errors (Section 6.3) [WMM96]. Both methods obtain $O(mn/\log s)$ worst-case time provided $O(s)$ space is available, and the second method obtains $O(kn/\log s)$ average time with the technique of Section 6.2.3.

Both methods are based on similar ideas: An NFA of $O(m)$ states is split into r "regions" of m/r states each. For simple patterns [WMM96] a region is a contiguous pattern substring, while for regular expressions [Mye92] it is some subset of the NFA states. Each region can be represented using $O(m/r)$ bits: For approximate searching of simple patterns we need $2m/r$ bits since each cell differs from the previous one by -1, 0, or $+1$, and hence two bits are enough to represent its value; for exact regular expression searching one bit per state (active or inactive) is enough.

A deterministic automaton, that is, a table storing all the outputs, is precomputed for each region, requiring $2^{O(m/r)}$ space per region. A non-deterministic automaton *of regions* simulates the original NFA arrows that connect different regions. Those arrows are simulated one by one. Either for simple patterns (where there are three arrows leading to each state; recall Figure 6.5) or for regular expressions (where regions are properly chosen and Thompson's construction guarantees $O(m)$ edges), there are $O(r)$ edges across modules. They have to be updated one by one, so the time is $O(rn)$. If we have $s = O(r)2^{O(m/r)}$ space, then we have $O(mn/\log s)$ time.

These ideas can be extended to the more general case of approximate searching for regular expressions [WMM95]. The idea is identical to that of exact searching, except that the states of the NFA are not just active or inactive, but store the minimum error level necessary to make each state active. Since we search with k errors, the value $k+1$ is used to denote any value larger than k. So for each state we need to store a number in the range $0\ldots k+1$, and therefore a deterministic automaton on m/r states needs $O((k+2)^{m/r})$ space. Hence, given $O(s)$ space, the algorithm obtains $O(mn/\log_{k+2} s)$ time.

When faced with approximate searching, a new problem appears that does not exist with exact searching, namely, the problem of dependencies derived from ε-transitions in the regular expression. Just as in Section 6.7.1, a two-sweep algorithm guarantees that all the arrows are considered correctly.

A related work [Mye96] considers "spacers," which are what we have called "gaps" on PROSITE expressions (Section 4.3), except that a spacer can have a negative length. This means that a piece of the regular expression may overlap approximately with the next one in the occurrence. The idea is to search for one of the regular expressions and use its adjacent spacers to define the areas where its neighbor expressions should be searched for. The occurrence is extended until the complete pattern is found. The paper shows an optimal search order that considers the length of the spacers and the probability of matching the regular expressions.

The same work shows that if regular expressions are restricted to "network expressions," that is, no "*" or "+" is permitted, then it is possible to define the regions in increasing distance from the initial state and to apply a technique similar to that of Section 6.2.3 to obtain an $O(kn/\log_{k+2} s)$ average time algorithm.

Note that positive-length gaps can be handled by converting them into regular expressions, but the resulting DFAs are unnecessarily large.

In general, the Four-Russians approach gives the best results for large regular expressions, but they are difficult to implement. A simpler approach that works well on reasonable-sized patterns is presented next.

6.7.3 A bit-parallel approach

Extending the bit-parallel algorithms we have seen in order to handle errors is quite straightforward [WM92b, Nav01b].

If we want to permit wild cards, then only **BPR** and **BPD** are able to handle them efficiently. And only **BPR** is flexible enough to handle all the extensions we are interested in. This is the algorithm we consider now.

Let us go back to Figure 6.4. Each row of the NFA is a replica of the nondeterministic automaton that searches for a single pattern. The replicas are linked together using the rule: "Vertical" arrows link the same states from row i to row $i + 1$; while "diagonal" arrows, either dashed or not, link each state s at row i to the states, in row $i + 1$, that can be reached from s in one transition (the "next" states).

This idea can be generalized to more complex automata [WM92b]. In particular, if we replace each row by the specialized bit-parallel automata developed in Chapters 4 and 5, the result is an NFA that is able to search for the corresponding extended pattern or regular expression with k errors. Moreover, this automaton can be searched in a "forward" manner as in Section 6.4.1 [WM92b] or in a "backward" manner as in Section 6.5.2 [Nav01b]. The only change with respect to the algorithms presented in this chapter is the bit-parallel simulation of the automata; the general mechanism is the same. Figure 6.20 shows an example for a regular expression.

To implement the "diagonal" transitions, we compute a table T_d, which for each state set D gives the bit mask of all the states reachable from D in one step. We have already built this table for regular expression searching (Section 5.4.2). For simple patterns it is simply $T_d[D] = (D << 1)$.

Assume that 1 represents active and 0 inactive. Let $f(c, D)$ be the pattern-type-dependent update function used to search without errors *without* the self-loop, and $f_0(c, D)$ *with* the self-loop.

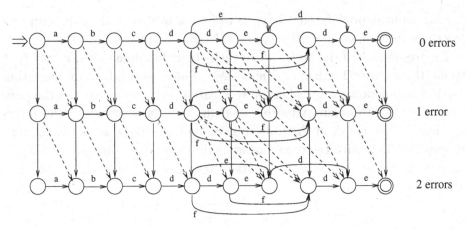

Fig. 6.20. Glushkov's NFAs for the regular expression "abcd(d|ε)(e|f)de" searched with two insertions, deletions, or substitutions. To simplify the figure, the dashed lines represent deletions and substitutions (i.e., they move by $\Sigma \cup \{\varepsilon\}$), while the vertical lines represent insertions (i.e., they move by Σ).

For example, for simple patterns, f corresponds to **Shift-And** (Section 2.2.2) and we have

$$f(c, D) \;=\; (D << 1) \,\&\, B[c]$$
$$f_0(c, D) \;=\; ((D << 1) \mid 0^{m-1}1) \,\&\, B[c]$$

Note that it holds $T_d[D] = |_{c\in\Sigma} f(c, D)$.

Now, to update the rows after reading text character t_{pos}, we use

$R_0' \;\leftarrow\; f_0(t_{pos}, R_0)$
For $i \in 1 \ldots k$ **Do** $R_i' \;\leftarrow\; f(t_{pos}, R_i) \mid R_{i-1} \mid T_d[R_{i-1} \mid R_{i-1}']$

The formula can be plugged into the **BPR** and **ABNDM** algorithms.

It is also possible to deal with very limited cases of multipattern extended searches allowing errors by combining **BPR** or **ABNDM** with the multipattern technique explained in Section 4.6.

6.8 Experimental map

We now present a map of the most efficient approximate string matching algorithms, for single and multiple strings, leaving aside extended patterns and regular expressions.

There exist about 40 algorithms for approximate string searching. The best choices, however, are just a handful of them in most cases. We are leaving aside algorithms that happen to be the best by a slight margin in a few cases in order to present a reasonably simple recommendation.

To give an idea of the areas where each algorithm dominates, Figure 6.21 shows the cases of English text and DNA. Since every filtration algorithm needs a nonfiltration algorithm for verification, we have presented the non-filtration algorithms and superimposed in gray the area where the filters dominate. Therefore, in the grayed area the best choice is to use the corresponding filter with the dominating nonfilter as its verification engine. In the nongrayed area it is better to use directly the dominating nonfiltering algorithm.

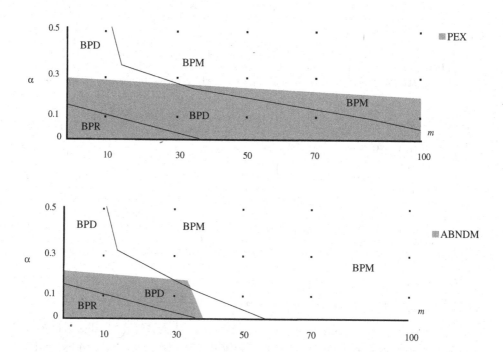

Fig. 6.21. The areas where each single pattern matching algorithm is best. Areas for filtering algorithms are gray. English text is on top and DNA on the bottom. The figures correspond to a word size of $w = 32$ bits. For $w = 64$ bits, the areas of **ABNDM** and **BPD** would grow on the m-axis.

Figure 6.22 shows the case of multipattern searching. On English text, **MultiPEX** is the best algorithm for $\alpha \le 0.3$, **MultiBP** for $0.3 \le \alpha \le 0.4$, and for higher error levels no algorithm is known that improves over sequentially searching all r patterns. **MultiHash** is better for $k = 1$ and a large number of patterns. For longer computer word sizes the area of **MultiBP** would grow to the right along the m-axis.

On DNA there are few choices: For $k = 1$ **MultiHash** is in general the best option, while for $k > 1$ and low α value **MultiPEX** is of some interest. **MultiBP**, on the other hand, is in general not applicable because $|\Sigma| = 4$ and hence superimposing as few as 4 patterns means matching almost every text position.

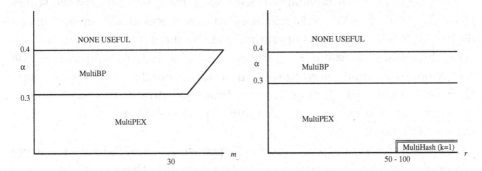

Fig. 6.22. The areas where each multipattern algorithm is best on English text, as a function of α, m, and r. In the left plot (varying m), we have assumed an r less than 50, while in the right plot we have assumed a pattern less than w characters.

6.9 Other algorithms and references

If one is interested in more complex distance functions, then the dynamic programming approach is the most flexible. For example, if the operations have different costs, we add the cost instead of adding 1 when computing $M_{i,j}$, that is,

$$M_{0,0} \leftarrow 0$$
$$M_{i,j} \leftarrow \min(M_{i-1,j-1} + \delta(x_i, y_j), M_{i-1,j} + \delta(x_i, \varepsilon), M_{i,j-1} + \delta(\varepsilon, y_j))$$

where $\delta(x, \varepsilon)$ and $\delta(\varepsilon, y)$ are the cost of inserting and deleting characters.

For distances that do not allow some operations, we just take them out of the minimization formula or, equivalently, we assign ∞ to their δ cost. For transpositions (i.e., permitting $ab \to ba$ in one operation), we introduce a fourth rule that says that $M_{i,j}$ can be $M_{i-2,j-2} + 1$ if $x_{i-1}x_i = y_jy_{j-1}$ [LW75].

The automata approach can handle different *integer* costs for the operations, and some simplifications of the edit distance can be modeled by changing or removing arrows. For instance, if insertions cost 2 instead of 1, we make the vertical arrows go from rows i to rows $i + 2$ in Figure 6.4. Transpositions are more complex but can be modeled as well [Mel96, Nav01b].

All this can be expressed in **BPR** and **ABNDM**. Some restricted cases of different integral costs can be expressed in **BPD**. There is also some very recent work on extending **BPM** to accommodate different costs for the edit operations [BH01], to include transpositions [Hyy01], and to integrate it into **ABNDM** [HN01].

The **PEX** filter can be adapted, with some care, to other distance functions. The main issue is to determine how many pieces an edit operation can destroy and how many edit operations can be made before surpassing the error threshold. For example, a transposition can destroy two pieces in one operation, so we would need to split the pattern into $2k + 1$ pieces to ensure that one is unaltered. A more clever solution [Nav01a] is to leave a hole of one character between consecutive pairs of pieces, so that one transposition cannot alter both.

Readers seeking a deeper coverage of approximate search issues for single patterns are referred to a recent survey [Nav01a]. For those interested in the distances and patterns used in biological applications, see [SK83, KM95].

There are models of approximate searching that deviate significantly from those we have covered. For example, there are totally different distance functions, such as Hamming distance (short survey in [Nav98]), reversals [KS95] (which allow reversing substrings), block distance [Ukk92, LT97] (which allows rearranging and permuting the substrings), swaps [KLPC99] (which are transpositions between nonadjacent characters), and so on. Although Hamming distance is a simplification of edit distance, specialized algorithms exist for it that go beyond our algorithms for edit distance.

With regard to the objects searched, they need not be only sequences of symbols. Extensions such as approximate searching in multidimensional texts (short survey in [BYN00b]) or in graphs [ALL97, Nav00] exist. Approximate searching of context-free grammars also has been pursued [Mye95]. None of these areas is well developed and the algorithms rely on the classical ones.

Finally, there are nonstandard algorithms, such as approximate (not to be confused with our exact algorithms for approximate searching), probabilistic, and parallel algorithms [TU88, AGM$^+$90, LV89]. A good survey on the open theoretical problems in nonstandard stringology, including some results on Hamming distance, is [MP94].

7

Conclusion

Before finishing, we would like to give some extra material that might be of interest.

First, we believe that it is extremely useful to know of freely available tools for on-line text searching, so we cover the existing software of this kind we are aware of.

Second, we give pointers to other books, journals, conferences, and on-line resources one may want to read to enter deeper into the area of text searching. This is also of interest to readers with a specific algorithmic problem not addressed in this book and not solved by the available software.

Finally, we include a section with problems related to combinatorial pattern matching. The section aims at briefing over the different extensions to the basic text searching problem, explaining the main concepts and existing results, and pointing to more comprehensive material covering them.

Up to date information and errata related to this book will be available at http://www.dcc.uchile.cl/~gnavarro/FPMbook.

7.1 Available software

We present in this section a sample of freely available software for on-line pattern matching.

7.1.1 Gnu Grep

What it is GNU (http://www.gnu.org) is an organization devoted to the development of free software. One of its products, *Grep*, permits fast searching of simple strings, multiple strings, and regular expressions in a set of files. Approximate searching is not supported. *Gnu Grep* is twice as fast as the classical Unix *Grep*.

185

Grep reports the lines in the file that contain matches. However, there are many configuration options that permit reporting the lines that do not match, the number of lines that match, whole files containing matches, and so on. The software provides a very powerful syntax that includes operators that go beyond regular expressions.

How it works Simple strings are searched with a **Boyer-Moore-Gosper** search algorithm (similar to **Horspool**; see Section 2.3.2). Sets of patterns are searched using a **Commentz-Walter**–like algorithm (Section 3.3.1). Regular expressions are searched with a lazy deterministic automaton, that is, a DFA (Section 5.3.2) whose states and transitions are built as they are reached while scanning the text using forward scanning. To speed up the search of complex patterns, *Grep* tries to extract their longest necessary factors, which are used as a filter and searched as a set of strings. This technique is explained in Section 5.5.2. It permits *Grep* to decline smoothly in performance as the complexity of the search increases, obtaining in general excellent performance.

Where to get it The current stable version of *Gnu Grep* is 2.4.2 (March 2000). Its source code distribution, in **C** language, can be obtained and used for free from `http://www.gnu.org/software/grep/grep.html`, as well as from `ftp://ftp.gnu.org/pub/gnu/grep/`.

7.1.2 Wu and Manber's Agrep

What it is *Agrep* (for approximate *Grep*) was developed in 1992 by Sun Wu and Udi Manber at the University of Arizona, as the first of a series of tools for on-line and indexed searching that include *Glimpse*, *WebGlimpse* (`http://glimpse.cs.arizona.edu/`), and *Harvest* (`http://www.tardis.ed.ac.uk/harvest/`).

Agrep is an on-line pattern matching software capable of exact and approximate searching for simple strings, extended strings, and regular expressions, as well as exact searching for multiple strings. *Agrep* has a syntax and a set of options similar to *Grep*, albeit less powerful. Extended strings include wild cards and classes of characters. Other extensions are treated as regular expressions. The real novelty of *Agrep* with respect to *Grep* is its approximate searching ability. Also, it has more flexible reporting: Instead of just lines, a "record" delimiter can be defined to report matching records (e.g., whole e-mails in an e-mail archive).

How it works The algorithmic principles of *Agrep* have been described in [WM92b], and the software itself in [WM92a]. It does not use a uniform algorithm but a set of heuristics to deal with the different search problems. As a result, *Agrep* normally chooses the best algorithm, but it experiences sharp changes in its efficiency as a result of slight changes in the complexity of the search patterns. Moreover, there are many restrictions to the length of the patterns and to the combination of options permitted. Despite these shortcomings, *Agrep* is very fast in some very commonly used cases.

Simple strings are searched with a variant of the **Horspool** algorithm (Section 2.3.2) when their length does not exceed 400. Longer strings use a similar technique, but pairs of characters, instead of single characters, are used for building the shift table. Sets of strings are searched with the **Wu-Manber** algorithm described in Section 3.3.3.

For the rest of the patterns, *Agrep* relies on bit-parallelism, more specifically on extensions of **Shift-And** (Section 2.2.2). Classes of characters and wild cards are handled with the techniques described in Chapter 4 to extend **Shift-And**. Similarly, regular expressions are handled with the bit-parallel algorithm **BPThompson** (Section 5.4.1).

Finally, approximate searching is handled in two ways. For simple strings searched with low error levels, *Agrep* uses **PEX** (Section 6.5.1). The other cases are handled using the bit-parallel algorithm **BPR** (Section 6.4.1.1) and its extension to regular expressions (Section 6.7.3).

Where to get it Commercial use requires paying a fee, but *Agrep* can be used for free for academic purposes and by U.S. government organizations. The code is available in source form (**C** language).

Older versions of *Agrep* can be obtained from `ftp://ftp.cs.arizona.edu`. The latest version is 3.0, from 1994, and it can be obtained by downloading *Glimpse* (any version after 1994) from `http://webglimpse.net/download.html`. Look for a top-level subdirectory called `"agrep/"`.

A Windows version of *Agrep* can be obtained from `http://www.tgries.de/agrep`.

7.1.3 Navarro's Nrgrep

What it is *Nrgrep* (for *n*ondeterministic *r*everse *Grep*) is an on-line pattern matching software developed in 2000 by Gonzalo Navarro at the University of Chile. Functionality is similar to that of *Agrep*. Multiple string matching, however, is not supported by *Nrgrep*.

How it works *Nrgrep* is based entirely on the **BNDM** algorithm and its extensions, presented in [NR00, NR99a, NR01a]. A description of the software is given in [Nav01b]. The fact that it is built on a single technique means that its efficiency degrades smoothly with the complexity of the search problem, unlike *Agrep*. The software demonstrates the flexibility of the **BNDM** approach, and it is very fast when searching complex patterns and regular expressions, exactly or allowing errors.

Single strings are searched with the basic **BNDM** algorithm of Section 2.4.2. The software supports extended strings, in particular, classes of characters and optional and repeatable characters, extending **BNDM** as shown in Chapter 4. Regular expressions are searched using **Regular-BNDM** (Section 5.5.3).

Approximate searching is handled, as in *Agrep*, in two possible ways. First, **PEX** can be used as in Section 6.5.1, and the pieces searched using **Multiple BNDM** (Section 3.4.1). Second, **ABNDM** can be used (Section 6.5.2). This permits skipping characters and using the technique not only for simple strings but also for extended strings and regular expressions (Section 6.7.3).

A fact that contributes to the smoothness of the efficiency of *Nrgrep* as a function of the pattern complexity is that it automatically selects the best factor of the pattern for the purpose of filtering the search, and also detects the correct type of pattern regardless of its syntax, in order to apply the simplest possible search algorithm. Finally, if the search cost with **BNDM** is predicted to be too high, it switches to forward scanning (**Shift-And**).

Where to get it *Nrgrep* source code, in **C** language, can be freely downloaded from `http://www.dcc.uchile.cl/~gnavarro/pubcode`. The code is version 1.1 (2001).

7.1.4 *Mehldau and Myers' Anrep*

What it is *Anrep* was built by Gerhard Mehldau and Gene Myers at the University of Arizona in 1993. It is an interactive application for DNA and protein searching, finding exact and approximate matches of patterns ranging from simple strings to network expressions and spacers (Sections 6.7 and 4.3). This includes most patterns of interest in biosequence comparisons. The user specifies such patterns with a declarative, free-format, and strongly typed language called *A*.

How it works *Anrep* is described in [MM91] and its algorithmic principles can be found in [Mye96]. The language is very powerful, as is needed in biological applications, so simple algorithms cannot be used. *Anrep* is based on the algorithm mentioned in Section 6.7.2 for approximate searching with arbitrary costs of network expressions with spacers. This combines dynamic programming for matching network expressions allowing errors and an optimized backtracking procedure to determine which occurrences are at the correct distances from the others.

There is little point in comparing *Anrep* with the previous programs. *Anrep* is much slower because it can search for much more complex patterns.

Where to get it The **C** language source code of *Anrep* can be freely obtained at `http://www.cs.arizona.edu/people/gene/CODE/anrep.tar.Z`.

7.1.5 Other resources for computational biology

Apart from *Anrep*, there are lots of resources available for computational biology applications. We do not cover them all in detail because they focus less on string matching than on statistical problems related to determining relevant subsequences, and use very specific knowledge from computational biology. The algorithms are generally complex variants of approximate searching, with complicated cost functions, gap penalties, and so on. The searching is done with a combination of dynamic programming and filtering approaches (Chapter 6), plus heuristics for handling the gaps. We brielfly review two of the best known systems of this type.

BLAST is an acronym for *Basic Local Alignment Search Tool*. It was created in 1990 by Altschul et al. It consists of a set of similarity search programs for exploring sequence databases for protein or DNA queries. Its main aims are high speed with minimal sacrifice of sensitivity to detect interesting occurrences and a well-defined statistical interpretation of the matches reported. *BLAST* uses a heuristic algorithm that seeks local as opposed to global alignments and is therefore able to detect relationships among sequences that share only isolated regions of similarity. Its algorithmic principles are presented in [AGM+90]. Software executables for different architectures can be freely obtained from `http://www.ncbi.nlm.nih.gov/BLAST/`, where it is also possible to test the system on-line. Its current version is 2.0 (1997).

FASTA was created by Pearson and Lipman in 1988. *FASTA* is another system for searching sequence homology in biosequence databanks, finding optimal local alignment scores. It includes several programs that provide different speed/accuracy trade-offs. *FASTA* has similar aims as *BLAST*, their main differences being in the way they assign significance to the matches [Pea91]. The algorithmic principles behind *FASTA* are presented in [SW81, PL88]. The system sources can be freely obtained from `ftp://ftp.virginia.edu/pub/fasta/`. Its current version is 3.2 (1998).

7.2 Other books

7.2.1 Books on string matching

We present here all the books we are aware of that attempt to cover a reasonably wide area of string matching.

Handbook of algorithms and data structures by G. Gonnet and R. Baeza-Yates, Addison-Wesley, second edition, 1991

This book deals with algorithms in general, but it includes a chapter devoted to exact string matching. The book is organized as a set of recipes. For each algorithm it gives a short explanation of the main idea and then the code and analytical results.

The book is a good reference for somebody in a hurry to find an algorithm to solve a string matching problem, since one can look at the analysis and copy the code. But it probably is not enough for learning why and how an algorithm works. The other problem is that it lacks developments since 1992, as well as approximate search algorithms.

Indeed, there are many books on algorithms that devote one chapter to string matching, for example, [Knu73, AHU83, Meh84, Baa88, Sed88, Man89, CLR90], but in general they cover only **KMP** and **BM**. We chose this book because, among those dealing with general algorithms, it has the best coverage. Some books on compilers or formal languages, such as [ASU86, HU79], explain the classical DFA approach to regular expression searching.

Text algorithms by M. Crochemore and W. Rytter, Oxford University Press, 1994

This book is a good survey of the main techniques used in text searching algorithms. The focus of the book is definitely theoretical; for example, it does not present any bit-parallel algorithms, and it presents many algorithms that we have omitted in this book because they are inefficient in practice. The book is mainly devoted to exact searching.

This book is a good choice for those interested in the theoretical and combinatorial aspects underlying string matching algorithms, but it is definitely not recommended if one needs a practical string matching algorithm and does not want to enter so deep into the field.

String searching algorithms by G. Stephen, World Scientific Press, 1994

This is a fairly complete book on exact and approximate string matching. For exact string matching, it covers more than the usual algorithms, paying special attention to the Boyer-Moore family. Yet it lacks coverage of the BDM family and of bit-parallel algorithms. Multiple and extended string matching are not covered. The coverage of approximate string matching algorithms is quite good, with a long chapter devoted to the different string similarity measures and another chapter with a very complete survey (for 1994) of approximate string matching algorithms. This particular area, however, has evolved a lot since then, so the fastest algorithms today are missing. The book also covers some data structures for indexed text searching, such as suffix trees.

String pattern matching strategies by J. Aoe (Editor), IEEE Computer Science Press, 1994

This book covers the most basic string searching algorithms for single, multiple, approximate, and multidimensional string matching. It lacks coverage of the newer algorithms, which are the fastest.

Pattern matching algorithms by A. Apostolico and Z. Galil (Editors), Oxford University Press, 1997

This book is a collection of chapters written by several researchers. The chapters are well chosen to cover a wide range of issues from on-line exact and approximate pattern matching, to parallel and indexed searching of strings, trees, and matrices. It is highly theoretical, and the same recommendations as for *Text algorithms* apply.

Modern information retrieval by R. Baeza-Yates and B. Ribeiro-Neto, Addison-Wesley, 1999

. This book is mainly on information retrieval, but it is one of the few that pays attention to the algorithmic problems involved, and even includes a chapter devoted to on-line string matching. The chapter is intended to give a reader interested in information retrieval some insight into the string matching problems that lie behind, but it is not enough to solve a string matching problem.

7.2.2 Books on computational biology

A book that lies at the intersection of string matching and computational biology is the following.

Algorithms on strings, trees and sequences: Computer science and computational biology by D. Gusfield, Cambridge University Press, 1997

This book is a survey of the main algorithmic techniques used in computational biology when using data structures like sequences and trees, which actually represent a large part of the field. It gives a complete general view of these techniques, including a large section on indexing, and in particular on the suffix tree and the algorithms built on it.

There are many other books on computational biology that are less related to string matching, so we have chosen three that we consider representative.

Computational molecular biology: An algorithmic approach by P. A. Pevzner, MIT Press, 2000

This recent book presents the main topics in computational molecular biology that involve algorithmic developments. This includes computational gene hunting, restriction mapping, map assembly, sequencing, DNA arrays, sequence comparison, multiple alignment, finding signals in DNA, gene restrictions, genome rearrangements, and computational proteomics.

Introduction to computational biology by M. S. Waterman, Chapman & Hall, 1995

This book presents well-established topics in computational biology on which much research has been performed. Many of those results are now considered as "classical."

Time warps, string edits, and macromolecules: The theory and practice of sequence comparison by D. Sankoff and J. B. Kruskal, Addison-Wesley, 1983

This was one of the first books published in computational biology. It is a collection of texts on different topics, most of them presenting a precise problem in computational biology and the algorithms to solve it. The algorithmic solutions presented are generally too old now to be of real interest, but the problems they solve are still of interest and their presentation is usually clear.

7.3 Other resources

7.3.1 Journals

Articles on pattern matching tend to appear sparsely in different journals. The most commonly chosen are; for tutorials: *ACM Computing Surveys*; for algorithms: *Algorithmica, Journal of the ACM, Journal of Algorithms, Communications of the ACM* (but not recently), *Information and Computation, Information and Control, Information Processing Letters, Information Science, Journal of Computer Systems Science, Nordic Journal of Computing, Random Structures and Algorithms, SIAM Journal on Computing, Theoretical Computer Science*, and the new *Journal of Discrete Algorithms*; for implementations: *Software Practice & Experience, IEEE Trans. on Software Engineering, Information Processing and Management*, and *ACM Journal of Experimental Algorithmics*. In this list we have not considered articles on combinatorial pattern matching, which is a wide area with deep theoretical roots. Indeed, string matching is one of the simplest branches of combinatorial pattern matching.

We also mention a few of the many journals on computational biology: *Bioinformatics* (and its former version, *CABIOS*), *Nucleic Acids Research, Journal of Computational Biology, Genome Research*, and *Journal of Molecular Biology*.

7.3.2 Conferences

There are a few conferences devoted to the field. Among the best are *Combinatorial Pattern Matching (CPM), Computing and Combinatorics*

(COCOON), *ACM Computational Molecular Biology (RECOMB)*, *String Processing and Information Retrieval (SPIRE)*, and *Intelligent Systems for Molecular Biology (ISMB)*.

Other conferences that publish articles on pattern matching are *Data Compression Conference (DCC)*, *European Symposium on Algorithms (ESA)*, *IEEE Foundations on Computer Science (FOCS)*, *Foundations of Software Technology and Theoretical Computer Science (FSTTCS)*, *Automata, Languages and Programming (ICALP)*, *IFIP World Computer Congress*, *Algorithms and Computation (ISAAC)*, *Mathematical Foundations of Computer Science (MFCS)*, *Discrete Algorithms (SODA)*, *Theoretical Aspects of Computer Science (STACS)*, *ACM Theory of Computing (STOC)*, *Scandinavian Workshop on Algorithmic Theory (SWAT)*, *Workshop on Algorithm Engineering (WAE)*, and *Workshop on Algorithms and Data Structures (WADS)*.

7.3.3 On-line resources

Definitely one of the best Web pages on string matching is *Pattern Matching Pointers*, an invaluable directory for searching people, references, books, software, journals, news groups, and discussion boards related to pattern matching in general. The page is maintained by Stefano Lonardi at `http://www.cs.purdue.edu/homes/stelo/pattern.html`.

Other pages are *Pattern Matching and Data Mining Research*, maintained by Mika Klemettinen at `http://www.cs.helsinki.fi/research/pmdm`, and *The Bioinformatics Resources* at `http://hgmp.mrc.ac.uk/CCP11`. Some discussion boards on the subject are available at `http://www.purdue.cs.edu/homes/stelo/pmdb`. Related news groups are `comp.theory`, `comp.theory.info-retrieval`, `comp.text`, and `comp.infosystems`. Finally, relevant mailing lists are `theorynet`, `dbworld` and `dmanet`.

Beware that on-line references may change over time.

7.4 Related topics

We consider finally some topics related to the focus of our book. Any of the related topics cited below could be the subject of an entire volume. We give the main current references for each subject. This list is obviously not exhaustive.

7.4.1 Indexing

Our book is devoted to *on-line* searching in text and sequences, which means that we do not build any structure on the text. For a single search this is an optimal strategy, but for many search operations on the same text we can save time by first building a structure on the text, called an *index*, to speed up queries later.

Typical reasons for preferring on-line searching are (1) size of the text, that is, if the text is too small, an index is not worth maintaining; (2) volatility of the text with respect to the query frequency, that is, there is a cost to build and maintain the index, which to be amortized requires that changes to the text be much less frequent than queries made on it; (3) space unavailability, that is, an index needs extra space on top of the text, which may be too costly or not available. Even when indexes are used, on-line searching is of interest because many indexing techniques use some form of on-line searching inside.

7.4.1.1 General indexes

Indexes permit exact searching of a string of length m in a text of length n in $O(m)$ or $O(m \log n)$ time, after a construction that usually takes $O(n)$ but sometimes $O(n \log n)$ time, and $O(n)$ extra space, with a constant factor that may range from 2 to 30 times the text size. There exist many indexing structures depending on the type of search and the memory available. The most usual ones build on the concept of a *suffix trie* [AG85], which is a trie data structure (Chapter 3) built over all the suffixes of the text. Every text factor is found by descending in this trie following the characters of the pattern.

The most efficient data structures are compacted versions of the suffix trie: the compact suffix tree [AG85, Gus97]; the suffix automaton or DAWG (an automaton that recognizes all text suffixes [CR94]); the compact suffix automaton or CDAWG [CV97a, CV97b, IHS+01]; and the suffix array, an array storing all text suffixes in lexicographical order [MM93, GBYS92].

These structures can also be used for searching extended strings, regular expressions, and for approximate searching [MBY91, BYG96, NBY00]. The search time is either $O(mn^\lambda)$ with $0 \le \lambda \le 1$ or exponential in m (or k for approximate searching with k errors), sometimes multiplied by an extra $O(\log n)$ factor, depending on the data structure.

7.4.1.2 Indexes for natural language

When it comes to natural language texts, a very popular index is the inverted file or inverted index, which is normally just able to retrieve complete words and phrases of the text, not any factor. Inverted indexes consist in general of the set of different words of the text (the vocabulary) and for each such word the list of positions where it appears in the text. This structure is also useful for information retrieval, which involves pattern matching but also concepts such as computing the relevance of a document with respect to a query. Some books dealing extensively with inverted indexes are [WMB99, BYRN99].

There are many variants on this structure, but if we consider the problem of finding words, the most important issue is the *addressing granularity* of the index. The indexes with the finest granularity store the exact positions of each word, and they need about 30% extra space over the text size. Others divide the text collection into documents and point just to the documents where each word appears, needing about 15% extra space. An interesting implementation capable of producing an index as small as 2%–4% over the text size is *Glimpse* [MW94] (`http://glimpse.cs.arizona.edu/`), which divides the text into equal size blocks and points to blocks instead of exact positions. This is called "block addressing." The search on these indexes has to be complemented with sequential searching. An analysis in [BYN00a] shows that the index size can be made sublinear with respect to the text size while keeping the search time sublinear as well. *Glimpse* also introduces techniques for searching extended strings, regular expressions, and approximate searching at the intraword level by scanning the vocabulary of the text, which is of sublinear size.

7.4.2 Searching compressed text

The problem of searching compressed text is that of finding the occurrences of a pattern in a compressed text without decompressing it. The subject has been an active area of research since 1992, motivated by the fact that CPU speed increases much faster than the speed of I/O devices and by the discovery that in some cases it is possible to search the compressed text *faster* than the uncompressed one.

7.4.2.1 Compression algorithms

Compression is a large and active area in computer science and of course we do not attempt to cover it here. Text compression is a subfield that deals with the best algorithms to compress text files. A good book on text compression is [BCW90]. More focused than text compression is the field of compressed text databases, which aims at text compression techniques that permit efficient searching of the compressed text. We briefly cover this area.

Compression formats for text databases must permit efficient decompression and random access to the text. Some of the most popular text compression formats for compressed text databases are Huffman [Huf51] (where each text symbol is replaced by a variable length code, trying to assign shorter codes to more frequent symbols), Ziv-Lempel (where the coder replaces text strings by pointers to previous occurrences already found in the text, without restriction in the LZ77 variant [ZL77] and only permitting a previous repetition plus an extra letter in the LZ78 variant [ZL78]), and Byte-Pair encoding or BPE [Gag94] (where pairs of characters are joined under a new unused code iteratively until no unused codes remain). An important feature of a compression method is the *compression ratio* achieved, which we define as the ratio of the compressed file size to the uncompressed file size. For example, on DNA, Huffman obtains about 25% compression, Ziv-Lempel 25%–30%, and BPE 30%, while on typical natural language text Huffman obtains about 60%, Ziv-Lempel 30%–40%, and BPE 70%.

7.4.2.2 On-line pattern matching in compressed text

The *compressed matching problem* was first defined in the work of Amir and Benson [AB92a] as the task of performing string matching in a compressed text without decompressing it. Given a text $T = t_1 \ldots t_u$, a corresponding compressed string $Z = z_1 \ldots z_n$, and a pattern $P = p_1 \ldots p_m$, the compressed matching problem consists in finding all occurrences of P in T, using only P and Z. A naive algorithm, which first decompresses the string Z and then performs standard string matching, takes time $O(m + u)$. An optimal algorithm takes worst-case time $O(m + n)$.

The most practical methods for on-line pattern matching are based on the BPE algorithm and its variants [Man97, SMT$^+$00, TSM$^+$01]. They are able to search the compressed text faster than the original text. This may be a reason by itself to compress the text. Given the characteristics of the format, however, the compression ratio obtained is poor.

A large line of research is based on Ziv-Lempel compression, which obtains much better compression ratios. The first algorithm for exact searching was [ABF96]. They search LZ78 compressed text in $O(m^2 + n)$ time and space. One of the few techniques for the LZ77 format is [FT98], a randomized algorithm to determine in $O(m + n \log^2(u/n))$ time whether a pattern is present or not in the text.

Later practical improvements appeared in [NR99b, KTSA99, NT00]. Roughly speaking, it is possible to search the compressed text in about half the time necessary for decompressing and then searching it.

Some extensions of the search problem have been pursued for the Ziv-Lempel format. An extension of [ABF96] to multipattern searching was presented in [KTS+98], where they achieved $O(m^2 + n)$ time and space, where m is the total length of all the patterns. Approximate string matching on compressed text was an open problem advocated in [AB92b], and the first theoretical [KNU00, MKT+00] and practical [NKT+01] algorithms for handling it have appeared only recently. All are for the LZ78 format. Regular expression searching over LZ78 was considered in [Nav01c].

A useful search-oriented abstraction of the compression formats used for pattern matching, called "collage systems," was proposed in [KTSA99]. Algorithms designed for collage systems can be implemented for many different formats. In the same paper they design a **KMP** algorithm on collage systems. Later papers of the same group (referenced in the previous paragraphs) develop this concept.

Finally, it is interesting to mention that there are very efficient algorithms able to find complete words and phrases in natural language texts. In [MNZBY00], a word-oriented Huffman coding where the symbols are the text words and separators, not the characters, is used as the basis for very fast algorithms that are able of exact and approximate searching for simple and extended strings. The compression ratio is very good, about 25%–30% on English texts of at least 10 megabytes, and the search on compressed text is as fast as on uncompressed text for simple searching, while it is up to eight times faster when searching for complex patterns and for approximate searching.

7.4.2.3 Indexed pattern matching in compressed text

Building compressed indexes over compressed text is a natural goal on large text databases. Compressed data structures for text searching have been sought for some time [KU96, Kär99, KS98, GV00], but they always used the text in uncompressed form as an integral part of the data structure.

Recently, some very promising structures have appeared which compress the text together with the structure. These data structures are compressed versions of the suffix array [Sad99, Sad00, FM00, FM01], and in some cases they are able to represent index and text in less space than that of the original uncompressed text.

For inverted indexes for word retrieval in natural language text, the text and the index are compressed separately in general. Index compression takes advantage of the fact that the list of occurrences of each word is increasing. Differences are encoded with a coding method that favors small numbers. The larger the addressing granularity, the more effective the compression of the lists of occurrences. A system combining block addressing with index compression on word-based Huffman text compression is described in

[NMN+00]. With respect to file-addressing indexes, the book [WMB99] describes extensively the *MG* system, a compressed inverted index over compressed text (freely available at `ftp://munnari.oz.au/pub/mg`).

7.4.3 Repeats and repetitions

Much research has been undertaken to study and search for repetitions in texts or sequences, since many of them have a biological role. There exist many definitions of a repeat or a repetition. Moreover, it is not clear how to define and take into account the approximate repetitions that are needed in computational biology. Here is a short summary.

7.4.3.1 Exact repetitions

The first notion of a repetition is simply a factor u that is contiguously repeated more than twice, that is, $u^k v$, where $k \geq 2$ and v is a prefix of u. Clearly, a text may contain a quadratic number of repetitions, for example, $T = a^n$. A first form of repetition that has been extensively studied is the square u^2. Many algorithms exist for finding all the square locations (see [CR94] or [KK99] for a survey). If we consider complete repetitions, the notion of a maximal repetition (sometimes called a *run* or a *maximal periodicity*) represents them all it in a compact way. A repetition is maximal if it cannot be extended in the text to the left or to the right without breaking it. There are at most $O(n)$ factors of the text that can be maximal repetitions, and they can be found in $O(n)$ time [KK99].

A second notion is used when considering noncontiguous repetitions. A *repeat* is a factor of the text that occurs at least twice. A *maximal repeat* is a repeat that cannot be extended to the left or to the right without breaking it. There exist at most a linear number of maximal repeats, and they can be enumerated in $O(n)$ time [Gus97]. However, these definitions do not take into account the relative positions of the repeats. A *pair* u is an occurrence of uvu in the text, and a *maximal pair* cannot be extended, similarly to a maximal repeat or a maximal repetition. The most interesting pairs are usually those such that the two occurrences of u are not too close or not too far away, that is, $|v|$ is bounded between $\delta_1 \leq |v| \leq \delta_2$. An $O(n \log n + nocc)$ time algorithm has been proposed to enumerate such a pair (maximal or not) in a text, where $nocc$ is the number of resulting occurrences [BLPS99]. If the upper bound δ_2 is removed, the time reduces to $O(n + nocc)$ [BLPS99].

7.4.3.2 Approximate repetitions

Approximate repetitions are required, for instance, in computational biology, when a sequence rarely matches exactly, and also in musicology, where the problem is to retrieve repeating themes. The concepts are however more fuzzy since the notions used for exact repetitions can be extended in various ways, depending on the approximate relation we want between the repeated parts.

The approximate concept of *repetition* is usually called *tandem repeat*. Originally, this expression was used for two continuous repetitions uv, where v matches approximately u. The algorithmic problem is to find all these factors in a text. An algorithm taking $O(n^2 \log n)$ time and $O(n^2)$ space exists [Sch98]. If the maximal number of errors is bounded by k, then all the nonoverlapping tandem repeats can be found in $O(kn \log k \log(n/k))$ time [KM93]. These algorithms are mainly of theoretical interest, since $O(n^2)$ is generally too large to be of real use on genomic sequences. Moreover, searching for only two repetitions is a strong limitation, for the computational biologist usually looks for more than two continuous parts. One algorithm for this problem permits finding small satellites [SM98], with a more flexible notion of repetitions (some parts can be missing), but with a strong length limitation (less than 40 bases). The idea is to filter the text, and, with an efficient verification algorithm [FLSS92], this idea leads in [Ben98] to a very fast algorithm/software, called *Tandem repeats finder* [Ben99]. The executable files are available on-line for many operating systems (the software is source protected) at `http://c3.biomath.mssm.edu/trf.html`.

The approximate concept of a *pair* is usually called a *nontandem repeat*. When we are interested in nonoverlapping ones, the same algorithm as for tandem repeats can be used [Sch98], but the real problem becomes managing the huge number of occurrences.

Approximate repetitions in computational biology is a recent and moving topic that evolves rapidly. One of the sofware products most used currently is *RepeatMasker* (part of the *Phrap* package, `http://www.phrap.org/`), which masks some repetitive regions of DNA sequences.

7.4.4 Pattern matching in two and more dimensions

Pattern matching in two-dimensional texts, for instance, in images, is a direct extension of string matching. Many of the most efficient algorithms are extensions of those we presented for one-dimensional text. However, many problems are specific to this field. Books partially covering this issue are [Aoe94, AG97].

In this area we speak of a text of $O(n^2)$ size (i.e., $n \times n$ cells), where a pattern of $O(m^2)$ size ($m \times m$ cells) is sought. This is done for simplicity.

Many algorithms can handle general rectangular and even nonrectangular texts and patterns.

7.4.4.1 Two-dimensional pattern matching

Two-dimensional exact string matching was first considered by Bird and Baker [Bir77, Bak78], who obtained $O(n^2)$ worst-case time. Good average-case results are presented by Zhu and Takaoka [ZT89] and Baeza-Yates and Régnier [BYR93]. Karkkäinen and Ukkonen [KU94] achieved $O(n^2 \log_\sigma m /m^2)$ average-case time, which is optimal.

Two-dimensional approximate string matching usually considers only substitutions for rectangular patterns, which is much simpler than the general case with insertions and deletions, because in this case rows and/or columns of the pattern can match pieces of the text of different length.

If we consider matching the pattern with at most k substitutions, one of the best results for the worst case, due to Amir and Landau [AL91], is $O((k + \log \sigma)n^2)$ time using $O(n^2)$ space. A similar algorithm is presented by Crochemore and Rytter [CR94]. Ranka and Heywood [RH91], on the other hand, solve the problem in $O((k + m)n^2)$ time and $O(kn)$ space. Amir and Landau also present a different algorithm running in $O(n^2 \log n \log \log n \log m)$ time. On average, the best algorithm is due to Karkkäinen and Ukkonen [KU94, Par96]. The expected time is $O(n^2 k \log_\sigma m /m^2)$ for $k \leq m^2/(4 \log_\sigma m)$, using $O(m^2)$ space ($O(k)$ space on average). This expected complexity is optimal.

The extension of the classic notion of edit distance is difficult. Krithivasan and Sitalakshmi [KS87] defined the edit distance in two dimensions as the sum of the edit distances of the corresponding row images. Let us call it the KS model. Using this notion they obtain $O(m^2 n^2)$ search time. Krithivasan [Kri87] presents for the same model an $O(m(k + \log m)n^2)$ time algorithm that uses $O(mn)$ space. Amir and Landau [AL91] give an $O(k^2 n^2)$ worst-case time algorithm using $O(n^2)$ space (note that k can be larger than m, so this is not necessarily better than the previous algorithms). Amir and Farach [AF91] also considered nonrectangular patterns, achieving $O(k(k + \sqrt{m \log m}\sqrt{k \log k})n^2)$ time. Finally, Navarro and Baeza-Yates obtain $O(n^2 k \log_\sigma m /m^2)$ average case time for the KS model, for $k < m(m + 1)/(5 \log_\sigma m)$, using $O(m^2)$ space.

For many two-dimensional matching problems, the KS distance does not reflect well simple cases of approximate matching in different settings. New distances and search algorithms have been introduced recently [BYN00b]. In the new models the errors can occur along rows or columns.

7.4.4.2 Other multidimensional matching problems

Other problems related to comparing images are searching allowing rotations [FNU01] and scaling [ABL00].

There are other approaches to matching images that are very different from those cited above (which belong to what is called combinatorial pattern matching). Among them we can mention techniques used in pattern matching related to artificial intelligence, for example, image processing and neural networks, and techniques used in databases, for example, extracting features of the image such as color histograms.

All the previous problems can be generalized to more than two dimensions, and many algorithms running on two-dimensional texts can be extended to run in more dimensions [AL91, KU94, GG97, FU98, BYN00b].

7.4.5 Tree pattern matching

Tree pattern matching is another extension of pattern matching in text. The problem arises in computational biology when we need to compare RNA structures. It also arises when a program is represented during compilation as an instruction tree in which we want to find special patterns, usually to perform some optimizations. Hierarchically structured text databases also require this form of matching.

For exact tree pattern matching there are two ordered trees called the *text* and the *pattern* by extension of string pattern matching, and the problem is to find all the occurrences of the pattern in the text, that is, all nodes of the text rooting a subtree that matches the pattern. We denote by n and m the sizes (in number of nodes) of the text and the pattern. The naive algorithm, which consists of verifying each text node, runs in $O(mn)$ worst-case time.

Several algorithms exist that improve the worst-case bound, but they are mainly theoretical. An $O(nm^{0.75} \log m)$ time algorithm has been proposed in [Kos89], using a connection between this problem and that of searching strings with "don't care" symbols. This in turn has been improved in [DGM94] to $O(nm^{0.5} \log m)$, using the periodicities of the paths of the pattern tree. A major improvement over this has been obtained in several articles by the same authors, leading to an $O(n \log^3 n)$ time algorithm in [CHI99]. A survey on this topic can be found in [ZS97].

The approximate tree pattern matching problem arises in computational biology when comparing and aligning trees. It implies a notion of distance on trees [ZSW94, SZ97]. Many algorithms exist, but this topic is still in development since the notion has to fit exactly the biological properties of the objects that the trees represent, which are generally secondary structures [ZWM99].

A related notion dealing with trees and matching is the maximum subtree agreement problem. Given two rooted trees whose leaves are taken from the same set of items, which for instance represent two phylogenetic trees, the problem is to find the largest subset so that the portions of the two trees restricted to these items are isomorphic. When the two trees are binary, which is usually the case in practice, an $O(n \log n)$ time algorithm exists [CFCH$^+$01].

Finally, structured text databases introduce a concept of tree pattern matching similar to the "extended strings" considered in this book. In this case the pattern is a tree, but each pattern edge can match an arbitrary path in the text tree. It is also possible to force the occurrence to honor the intersibling ordering given in the pattern. Depending on these options, the search complexity goes from polynomial time to NP-complete [Kil92, KM92].

7.4.6 Sequence comparison

Sequence comparison is about determining similarities and correspondences between two or more strings. It is related to approximate searching (Chapter 6) and has many applications in computational biology, speech recognition, computer science, coding theory, chromatography, and so on. These applications look for similarities between sequences of symbols. The general goal is to perform basic operations over the strings until they become equal. Those basic operations have an associated cost, and we seek the minimum-cost sequence of operations that achieves the goal. The reason for preferring the minimum cost is different in each application, but the general idea is that the sequences differ by a series of alterations on one or both of them, and the cheapest series are those of maximum likelihood.

A concept of "distance" between two strings can be defined according to the minimum cost of making them equal. The basic operations considered depend on the application, but the most typical are supressing characters, inserting characters, substituting characters by others, swapping adjacent or nonadjacent characters, reversing substrings, moving substrings to another place of the string, compressing a run of equal characters, expanding a single character to a run of them, and so on. Each operation has a rationale in the model where it is used. The application also gives a rationale for assigning costs to the different operations, for example, the most likely operations cost less. A simple case is to assign a cost that is the logarithm of the probability of this operation occurring in the process that made the strings differ. Hence the sum of the costs corresponds to the logarithm of the product of the probabilities of the operations, which is a good model if they are independent.

Two of the most popular similarity measures are the Levenshtein distance and the "indel" distance. The first one permits character insertions, deletions, and substitutions, all at cost 1. The second one permits only insertions and deletions and is related to the longest common subsequence (LCS) between the two strings. The popularity of these models lies in their simplicity, in the efficiency of the algorithms that handle them, and in the simplicity of their mathematical properties. We devoted Chapter 6 almost entirely to the Levenshtein distance.

In many applications it is also interesting to know how the two sequences differ. In general we speak about *aligning* the two sequences (recall Section 6.2.1). There are several ways to express an alignment. One is to put the strings one on top of the other and space their characters so that similar characters are in the same column. The amount of spacing needed gives an idea of how different the strings are. Another method is to draw a set of *traces*, where lines connect the aligned characters in both strings (Figure 6.1). Yet a third way, less popular but very useful mathematically, is to list the operations made on the strings.

In some cases it is useful to measure the degree of similarity rather than of dissimilarity (i.e., a distance). One example is the LCS, a heavily studied measure. Other examples are the shortest common supersequence (SCS), longest common substring (LCG, different from the LCS because the common string has to be a contiguous substring of both sequences), and shortest common superstring (SCG), as well as their versions on more than two strings.

Most algorithms for sequence comparison rely on dynamic programming, since it is useful to have all previous results precomputed in order to use them. However, backtracking has also been used. The simplest distances such as Levenshtein or indel, even with arbitrary costs for the operations, can be computed in $O(n^2)$ time for two strings of length n. The same holds for computing the LCS or SCS of two strings. For N strings the cost raises to $O(n^N)$ and is NP-complete for arbitrary N. The cost for LCG and SCG is $O(n)$ for two strings. There exist complicated algorithms that improve over the quadratic complexity under diverse assumptions. On the other hand, computing the distance when block moves are involved is NP-complete in some cases. This shows that the nature of the problem depends on the type of distance used.

Another issue in sequence comparison is statistics. How significant is it that the LCS between two binary strings is 80% of their length? Does it mean that they are close, or could it happen perfectly well to two random sequences? There has been much research on the expected length of the LCS between two random strings. It is known that it grows linearly with n, but the exact constant is not yet known; only tight upper and lower bounds exist.

We refer the reader to good books on the subject [SK83] or to the section of books of computational biology (7.2.2).

7.4.7 Meaningful string occurrences

The problem of finding factors that are "unusual" in sequences is a topic that has led to many studies. There are four main underlying points.

First, the sequences have to be considered under a specific probability model, for instance, under a Markov model, to get a comparison point for what should be considered normal.

Next, a formula to get the "normal" occurrence probability or other interesting parameters, for instance, the expected distance between two occurrences, has to be obtained. The expected probability of the approximate occurrences of a string has recently been obtained [RS97]. An algorithm to compute the expected frequency of occurrence of a string, a set of strings, or a regular expression under both the Bernoulli or Markov models exists [NSF01], but evaluating the formula is complicated and computationally time-consuming (the same is true for [RS97]). A *Maple* package implementing the evaluation, called *Algolib*, is available at `http://algo.inria.fr/libraries/software.html`.

Third, given a certain model and a way to compute the interesting parameters of a given factor in that model, one has to decide which factor of the text should be considered as unusual.

Finally, when the three previous problems have been solved for a certain type of sequence, model, and pattern, the algorithmic problem is to find and visualize the unusual factors in an efficient and usable way (for that there could be $O(n^2)$ such factors).

A short survey on these questions can be found in [Pev00], but, to our knowledge, there is no complete survey grouping these questions together. A sofware product called *Verbumculus* [ABLX00] permits visualizing unusual factors under a restricted definition of what a usual factor is. The binaries are available at `http://www.cs.purdue.edu/homes/stelo/Verbumculus`.

Bibliography

[AB92a] A. Amir and G. Benson. Efficient two-dimensional compressed matching. In *Proceedings of the 2th Data Compression Conference*, pages 279–288. IEEE Computer Society Press, 1992.

[AB92b] A. Amir and G. Benson. Two-dimensional periodicity and its applications. In *Proceedings of the 3rd ACM-SIAM Annual Symposium on Discrete Algorithms*, pages 440–452. ACM Press, 1992.

[ABF96] A. Amir, G. Benson, and M. Farach. Let sleeping files lie: Pattern matching in Z-compressed files. *Journal of Computer and Systems Sciences*, 52(2):299–307, 1996.

[ABL00] A. Amir, A. Butman, and M. Lewenstein. Real scaled matching. In *Proceedings of the 11th ACM-SIAM Annual Symposium on Discrete Algorithms*, pages 815–816. ACM Press, 2000.

[ABLX00] A. Apostolico, M. E. Bock, S. Lonardi, and X. Xu. Efficient detection of unusual words. *Journal of Computational Biology*, 7(1/2):71–94, 2000.

[Abr87] K. Abrahamson. Generalized string matching. *SIAM Journal on Computing*, 16(6):1039–1051, 1987.

[AC75] A. V. Aho and M. J. Corasick. Efficient string matching: an aid to bibliographic search. *Communications of the ACM*, 18(6):333–340, 1975.

[ACR01] C. Allauzen, M. Crochemore, and M. Raffinot. Efficient experimental string matching by weak factor recognition. In *Proceedings of the 12th Annual Symposium on Combinatorial Pattern Matching*, number 2089 in Lecture Notes in Computer Science, pages 51–72. Springer-Verlag, 2001.

[AF91] A. Amir and M. Farach. Efficient 2-dimensional approximate matching of non-rectangular figures. In *Proceedings of the 2nd ACM-SIAM Annual Symposium on Discrete Algorithms*, pages 212–223, 1991.

[AG85] A. Apostolico and Z. Galil, editors. *Combinatorial Algorithms on Words*, volume 12. Springer-Verlag, 1985.

[AG97] A. Apostolico and Z. Galil, editors. *Pattern Matching Algorithms*. Oxford University Press, 1997.

[AGM+90] S. F. Altschul, W. Gish, W. Miller, E. W. Myers, and D. J. Lipman. A basic local alignment search tool. *Journal of Molecular Biology*, 215:403–410, 1990.

[AHU83] A. V. Aho, J. E. Hopcroft, and J. D. Ullman. *Data Structures and Algorithms*. Addison-Wesley, 1983.

[AL91] A. Amir and G. M. Landau. Fast parallel and serial multidimensional approximate array matching. *Theoretical Computer Science*, 81(1):97–115, 1991.

[ALL97] A. Amir, M. Lewenstein, and N. Lewenstein. Pattern matching in hypertext. In *Proceedings of the 5th Workshop on Algorithms and Data Structures*, number 1272 in Lecture Notes in Computer Science, pages 160–173. Springer-Verlag, 1997.

[Aoe94] J.-I. Aoe, editor. *String pattern matching strategies.* IEEE Computer Society Press, 1994.

[AR99] C. Allauzen and M. Raffinot. Factor oracle of a set of words. Technical report 99-11, Institut Gaspard-Monge, Université de Marne-la-Vallée, 1999.

[AR00] C. Allauzen and M. Raffinot. Simple optimal string matching. *Journal of Algorithms*, 36:102–116, 2000.

[ASU86] A. V. Aho, R. Sethi, and J. D. Ullman. *Compilers – Principles, Techniques and Tools.* Addison-Wesley, 1986.

[Baa88] S. Baase. *Computer Algorithms – Introduction to Design and Analysis.* Addison-Wesley, 1988.

[Bak78] T. P. Baker. A technique for extending rapid exact-match string matching to arrays of more than one dimension. *SIAM Journal on Computing*, 7(4):533–541, 1978.

[BBE+87] A. Blumer, J. Blumer, A. Ehrenfeucht, D. Haussler, and R. McConnel. Complete inverted files for efficient text retrieval and analysis. *Journal of the ACM*, 34(3):578–595, 1987.

[BBYDS96] V. Bruyère, R. A. Baeza-Yates, O. Delgrange, and R. Scheihing. About the size of Boyer-Moore automata. In N. Ziviani, R. Baeza-Yates, and K. Guimarães, editors, *Proceedings of the 3rd South American Workshop on String Processing*, pages 31–46, Recife, Brazil. Carleton University Press, 1996.

[BCW90] T. Bell, J. Cleary, and I. Witten. *Text Compression.* Prentice Hall, 1990.

[Ben98] G. Benson. An algorithm for finding tandem repeats of unspecified pattern size. In *Proceedings of the 2nd Annual International Conference on Computational Molecular Biology*, pages 20–29. ACM Press, 1998.

[Ben99] G. Benson. Tandem repeats finder: a program to analyze DNA sequences. *Nucleic Acids Research*, 27:573–580, 1999.

[BH01] A. Bergeron and S. Hamel. Vector algorithms for approximate string matching. *International Journal of Foundations of Computer Science*, 2001. To appear.

[Bir77] R. S. Bird. Two-dimensional pattern matching. *Information Processing Letters*, 6(5):168–170, 1977.

[BK93] A. Brüggemann-Klein. Regular expressions into finite automata. *Theoretical Computer Science*, 120(2):197–213, 1993.

[BLPS99] G. S. Brodal, R. B. Lyngsø, C. N. S. Pedersen, and J. Stoye. Finding maximal pairs with bounded gap. In *Proceedings of the 10th Annual Symposium on Combinatorial Pattern Matching*, number 1645 in Lecture Notes in Computer Science, pages 134–149. Springer-Verlag, 1999.

[BM77] R. S. Boyer and J. S. Moore. A fast string searching algorithm. *Communications of the ACM*, 20(10):762–772, 1977.

[Bre95] D. Breslauer. Dictionary matching on unbounded alphabets: uniform length dictionaries. *Journal of Algorithms*, 18(2):278–295, 1995.

[BS86] G. Berry and R. Sethi. From regular expression to deterministic automata. *Theoretical Computer Science*, 48(1):117–126, 1986.

[BY91] R. Baeza-Yates. Some new results on approximate string matching. In *Workshop on Data Structures*, Dagstuhl, Germany, 1991. Abstract.

[BYCG94] R.A. Baeza-Yates, C. Choffrut, and G.H. Gonnet. On Boyer-Moore automata. *Algorithmica*, 12(4/5):268–292, 1994.

[BYG89a] R. A. Baeza-Yates and G. H. Gonnet. Boyer-Moore automata. Report, University of Waterloo, 1989.

[BYG89b] R. A. Baeza-Yates and G. H. Gonnet. A new approach to text searching. In N. J. Belkin and C. J. van Rijsbergen, editors, *Proceedings of the 12th International Conference on Research and Development in Information Retrieval*, pages 168–175. ACM Press, 1989.

[BYG96] R. A. Baeza-Yates and G. H. Gonnet. Fast text searching for regular expressions or automaton searching on tries. *Journal of the ACM*, 43(6):915–936, 1996.

[BYGR90] R. A. Baeza-Yates, G. H. Gonnet, and M. Régnier. Analysis of Boyer-Moore type string searching algorithms. In *Proceedings of the 1st ACM-SIAM Annual Symposium on Discrete Algorithms*, pages 328–343. ACM Press, 1990.

[BYN97] R. A. Baeza-Yates and G. Navarro. Multiple approximate string matching. In *Proceedings of the 5th Workshop on Algorithms and Data Structures*, number 1272 in Lecture Notes in Computer Science, pages 174–184. Springer-Verlag, 1997. Extended version to appear in *Random Structures and Algorithms* (Wiley).

[BYN99] R. A. Baeza-Yates and G. Navarro. Faster approximate string matching. *Algorithmica*, 23(2):127–158, 1999.

[BYN00a] R. Baeza-Yates and G. Navarro. Block-addressing indices for approximate text retrieval. *Journal of the American Society for Information Science*, 51(1):69–82, 2000.

[BYN00b] R. Baeza-Yates and G. Navarro. New models and algorithms for multidimensional approximate pattern matching. *Journal of Discrete Algorithms*, 1(1):21–49, 2000.

[BYR92] R. A. Baeza-Yates and M. Régnier. Average running time of the Boyer-Moore-Horspool algorithm. *Theoretical Computer Science*, 92(1):19–31, 1992.

[BYR93] R. A. Baeza-Yates and M. Régnier. Fast two-dimensional pattern matching. *Information Processing Letters*, 45(1):51–57, 1993.

[BYRN99] R. A. Baeza-Yates and B. Ribeiro-Neto. *Modern Information Retrieval*. Addison-Wesley, 1999.

[CCG+93] M. Crochemore, A. Czumaj, L. Gąsieniec, S. Jarominek, T. Lecroq, W. Plandowski, and W. Rytter. Fast practical multi-pattern matching. Rapport 93-3, Institut Gaspard Monge, Université de Marne-la-Vallée, 1993.

[CCG+94] M. Crochemore, A. Czumaj, L. Gąsieniec, S. Jarominek, T. Lecroq, W. Plandowski, and W. Rytter. Speeding up two string matching algorithms. *Algorithmica*, 12(4/5):247–267, 1994.

[CCG+99] M. Crochemore, A. Czumaj, L. Gąsieniec, T. Lecroq, W. Plandowski, and W. Rytter. Fast practical multi-pattern matching. *Information Processing Letters*, 71(3/4):107–113, 1999.

[CFCH+01] R. Cole, M. Farach-Colton, R. Hariharan, T. Przytycka, and M. Thorup. An $O(n \log n)$ algorithm for the maximum agreement subtree problem for binary trees. *SIAM Journal on Computing*, 30(5):1385–1404, 2001.

[CGR92] M. Crochemore, L. Gąsieniec, and W. Rytter. Turbo-BM. Rapport LITP 92.61, Universités Paris 6 et 7, France, 1992.

[CH97] M. Crochemore and C. Hancart. Automata for matching patterns. In G. Rozenberg and A. Salomaa, editors, *Handbook of Formal Languages*, volume

2: Linear Modeling: Background and Application, chapter 9, pages 399–462. Springer-Verlag, 1997.

[CH98] R. Cole and R. Hariharan. Approximate string matching: A simpler faster algorithm. In *Proceedings of the 9th ACM-SIAM Annual Symposium on Discrete Algorithms*, pages 463–472. ACM Press, 1998.

[CHI99] R. Cole, R. Hariharan, and P. Indyk. Tree pattern matching and subset matching in deterministic $O(n \log^3 n)$-time. In *Proceedings of the 10th ACM-SIAM Annual Symposium on Discrete Algorithms*, pages 245–254. ACM Press, 1999.

[Cho90] C. Choffrut. An optimal algorithm for building the Boyer-Moore automaton. *Bulletin of the European Association of Theoretical Computer Science,* 40:217–225, 1990.

[CL92] W. I. Chang and J. Lampe. Theoretical and empirical comparisons of approximate string matching algorithms. In *Proceedings of the 3rd Annual Symposium on Combinatorial Pattern Matching*, number 664 in Lecture Notes in Computer Science, pages 175–184. Springer-Verlag, 1992.

[CL94] W. I. Chang and E. L. Lawler. Sublinear approximate string matching and biological applications. *Algorithmica*, 12(4/5):327–344, 1994.

[CLR90] T. H. Cormen, C. E. Leiserson, and R. L. Rivest. *Introduction to Algorithms*. MIT Press, 1990.

[CM94] W.I. Chang and T. Marr. Approximate string matching with local similarity. In *Proceedings of the 5th Annual Symposium on Combinatorial Pattern Matching*, number 807 in Lecture Notes in Computer Science, pages 259–273. Springer-Verlag, 1994.

[Col94] R. Cole. Tight bounds on the complexity of the Boyer-Moore string matching algorithm. *SIAM Journal on Computing*, 23(5):1075–1091, 1994.

[CP91] M. Crochemore and D. Perrin. Two-way string-matching. *Journal of the ACM*, 38(3):651–675, 1991.

[CP92] C.-H. Chang and R. Paige. From regular expression to DFA's using NFA's. In *Proceedings of the 3rd Annual Symposium on Combinatorial Pattern Matching*, number 664 in Lecture Notes in Computer Science, pages 90–110. Springer-Verlag, 1992.

[CR94] M. Crochemore and W. Rytter. *Text Algorithms*. Oxford University Press, 1994.

[CR95] M. Crochemore and W. Rytter. Squares, cubes and time-space efficient string-searching. *Algorithmica*, 13(5):405–425, 1995.

[Cro92] M. Crochemore. String-matching on ordered alphabets. *Theoretical Computer Science*, 92(1):33–47, 1992.

[CV97a] M. Crochemore and R. Vérin. Direct construction of compact directed acyclic word graphs. In *Proceedings of the 8th Annual Symposium on Combinatorial Pattern Matching*, number 1264 in Lecture Notes in Computer Science, pages 116–129. Springer-Verlag, 1997.

[CV97b] M. Crochemore and R. Vérin. On compact directed acyclic word graphs. In *Structures in Logic and Computer Science*, number 1261 in Lecture Notes in Computer Science, pages 192–211. Springer-Verlag, 1997.

[CW79] B. Commentz-Walter. A string matching algorithm fast on the average. In

Proceedings of the 6th International Colloquium on Automata, Languages and Programming, number 71 in Lecture Notes in Computer Science, pages 118–132. Springer-Verlag, 1979.

[DGM94] M. Dubiner, Z. Galil, and E. Magen. Faster tree pattern matching. *Journal of the ACM*, 41(2):205–213, 1994.

[FLSS92] V. A. Fischetti, G. M. Landau, J. P. Schmidt, and P. H. Sellers. Identifying periodic occurrences of a template with applications to protein struture. In *Proceedings of the 3rd Annual Symposium on Combinatorial Pattern Matching*, number 664 in Lecture Notes in Computer Science, pages 111–120. Springer-Verlag, 1992.

[FM00] P. Ferragina and G. Manzini. Opportunistic data structures with applications. In *Proceedings of the 41st IEEE Annual Symposium on Foundations of Computer Science*, pages 390–398. IEEE Computer Society Press, 2000.

[FM01] P. Ferragina and G. Manzini. An experimental study of an opportunistic index. In *Proceedings of the 12th ACM-SIAM Annual Symposium on Discrete Algorithms*, pages 269–278. ACM Press, 2001.

[FNU01] K. Fredriksson, G. Navarro, and E. Ukkonen. *Faster than FFT: Rotation Invariant Combinatorial Template Matching*, volume II. Transworld Research Network, 2001. To appear.

[FP74] M. J. Fischer and M. Paterson. String matching and other products. In R. M. Karp, editor, *Proceedings SIAM-AMS Complexity of Computation*, pages 113–125. AMS, 1974.

[FT98] M. Farach and M. Thorup. String matching in Lempel-Ziv compressed strings. *Algorithmica*, 20(4):388–404, 1998.

[FU98] K. Fredriksson and E. Ukkonen. Rotation invariant filters for multidimensional string matching and orientation search. In *Proceedings of the 9th Annual Symposium on Combinatorial Pattern Matching*, number 1448 in Lecture Notes in Computer Science, pages 118–125. Springer-Verlag, 1998.

[Gag94] P. Gage. A new algorithm for data compression. *The C Users Journal*, 12(2), 1994.

[Gal79] Z. Galil. On improving the worst case running time of the Boyer-Moore string searching algorithm. *Communications of the ACM*, 22(9):505–508, 1979.

[GBY90] G. H. Gonnet and R. A. Baeza-Yates. An analysis of the Karp-Rabin string matching algorithm. *Information Processing Letters*, 34(5):271–274, 1990.

[GBYS92] G. Gonnet, R. Baeza-Yates, and T. Snider. *Information Retrieval: Data Structures and Algorithms*, chapter 3: New indices for text: Pat trees and Pat arrays, pages 66–82. Prentice-Hall, 1992.

[GG97] R. Giancarlo and R. Grossi. Multi-dimensional pattern matching with dimensional wildcards: Data structures and optimal on-line search algorithms. *Journal of Algorithms*, 24(2):223–265, 1997.

[Glu61] V-M. Gluskov. The abstract theory of automata. *Russian Mathematical Surveys*, 16:1–53, 1961.

[GP90] Z. Galil and K. Park. An improved algorithm for approximate string matching. *SIAM Journal on Computing*, 19(6):989–999, 1990.

[GS81] Z. Galil and J. Seiferas. Linear-time string matching using only a fixed number of local storage locations. *Theoretical Computer Science*, 13(3):331–336,

1981.

[Gus97] D. Gusfield. *Algorithms on Strings, Trees and Sequences: Computer Science and Computational Biology*. Cambridge University Press, 1997.

[GV00] R. Grossi and J.S. Vitter. Compressed suffix arrays and suffix trees with applications to text indexing and string matching. In *Proceedings of the 32th ACM Symposium on the Theory of Computing*, pages 397–406. ACM Press, 2000.

[Han93] C. Hancart. On Simon's string searching algorithm. *Information Processing Letters*, 47(2):95–99, 1993.

[HBFB99] K. Hofmann, P. Bucher, L. Falquet, and A. Bairoch. The PROSITE database, its status in 1999. *Nucleic Acids Research*, 27:215–219, 1999.

[HM98] C. Hagenah and A. Muscholl. Computing epsilon-free NFA from regular expressions in $O(n \log^2(n))$ time. In *Proceedings of the 23th Symposium on Mathematical Foundations of Computer Science*, number 1450 in Lecture Notes in Computer Science. Springer-Verlag, 1998.

[HN01] H. Hyyrö and G. Navarro. Faster bit-parallel approximate string matching. Technical Report TR/DCC-2002-1, University of Chile, Santiago, Chile, 2002.

[Hor80] R. N. Horspool. Practical fast searching in strings. *Software Practice and Experience*, 10(6):501–506, 1980.

[HSW97] J. Hromkovic, S. Seibert, and T. Wilke. Translating regular expressions into small epsilon-free nondeterministic finite automata. In *Proceedings of the 14th Annual Symposium on Theoretical Aspects of Computer Science*, number 1200 in Lecture Notes in Computer Science, pages 55–66. Springer-Verlag, 1997.

[HU79] J. E. Hopcroft and J. D. Ullman. *Introduction to Automata, Languages and Computations*. Addison-Wesley, 1979.

[Huf51] D. A. Huffman. A method for the construction of minimum redundancy codes. *Proceedings of the Institute of Electrical and Radio Engineers*, 40:1098–1101, 1951.

[Hyy01] H. Hyyrö. Explaining and extending the bit-parallel algorithm of Myers. Technical Report A-2001-10, University of Tampere, Finland, 2001.

[IHS+01] S. Inenaga, H. Hoshino, A. Shinohara, M. Takeda, S. Arikawa, G. Mauri, and G. Pavesi. On-line construction of compact directed acyclic word graphs. In *Proceedings of the 12th Annual Symposium on Combinatorial Pattern Matching*, number 2089 in Lecture Notes in Computer Science, pages 169–180. Springer-Verlag, 2001.

[JTU96] P. Jokinen, J. Tarhio, and E. Ukkonen. A comparison of approximate string matching algorithms. *Software Practice and Experience*, 26(12):1439–1458, 1996.

[Kär99] J. Kärkkäinen. *Repetition-Based Text Indexing*. PhD thesis, Department of Computer Science, University of Helsinki, December 1999.

[Kil92] P. Kilpeläinen. *Tree Matching Problems with Applications to Structured Text Databases*. PhD thesis, University of Helsinki, Finland, 1992.

[KK99] R. Kolpakov and G. Kucherov. Finding maximal repetitions in a word in linear time. In *Proceedings of the 40th IEEE Annual Symposium on Foundations of Computer Science*. IEEE Computer Society Press, 1999.

[KLPC99] D. K. Kim, J. S. Lee, K. Park, and Y. Cho. Efficient algorithms for approximate string matching with swaps. *Journal of Complexity*, 15:128–147, 1999.

[KM92] P. Kilpeläinen and H. Mannila. Grammatical tree matching. In *Proceedings of the 3rd Annual Symposium on Combinatorial Pattern Matching*, number 644 in Lecture Notes in Computer Science, pages 162–174. Springer-Verlag, 1992.

[KM93] S. K. Kannan and E. W. Myers. An algorithm for locating non-overlapping regions of maximum alignment score. In *Proceedings of the 4th Annual Symposium on Combinatorial Pattern Matching*, number 684 in Lecture Notes in Computer Science, pages 74–86. Springer-Verlag, 1993.

[KM95] J. R. Knight and E. W. Myers. Approximate regular expression pattern matching with concave gap penalties. *Algorithmica*, 14(1):85–121, 1995.

[KMP77] D. E. Knuth, J. H. Morris, Jr, and V. R. Pratt. Fast pattern matching in strings. *SIAM Journal on Computing*, 6(1):323–350, 1977.

[Knu73] D. E. Knuth. *The Art of Computer Programming: Sorting and Searching*, volume 3. Addison-Wesley, 1973.

[KNU00] J. Kärkkäinen, G. Navarro, and E. Ukkonen. Approximate string matching over Ziv-Lempel compressed text. In *Proceedings of the 11th Annual Symposium on Combinatorial Pattern Matching*, number 1848 in Lecture Notes in Computer Science, pages 195–209. Springer-Verlag, 2000.

[Kos89] S. R. Kosaraju. Efficient tree pattern matching. In *Proceedings of the 30th IEEE Annual Symposium on Foundations of Computer Science*, pages 178–183. IEEE Computer Society Press, 1989.

[KR87] R. M. Karp and M. O. Rabin. Efficient randomized pattern-matching algorithms. *IBM Journal of Research and Development*, 31(2):249–260, 1987.

[KR95] G. Kucherov and M. Rusinowitch. Matching a set of strings with variable length don't cares. In *Proceedings of the 6th Annual Symposium on Combinatorial Pattern Matching*, number 937 in Lecture Notes in Computer Science, pages 230–247. Springer-Verlag, 1995.

[Kri87] K. Krithivasan. Efficient two-dimensional parallel and serial approximate pattern matching. Technical Report CAR-TR-259, University of Maryland, 1987.

[KS87] K. Krithivasan and R. Sitalakshmi. Efficient two-dimensional pattern matching in the presence of errors. *Information Science*, 43:169–184, 1987.

[KS95] J. Kececioglu and D. Sankoff. Exact and approximation algorithms for sorting by reversals, with application to genome rearrangement. *Algorithmica*, 13(1/2):180–210, 1995.

[KS98] J. Kärkkäinen and E. Sutinen. Lempel-Ziv index for q-grams. *Algorithmica*, 21(1):137–154, 1998.

[KTS+98] T. Kida, M. Takeda, A. Shinohara, M. Miyazaki, and S. Arikawa. Multiple pattern matching in LZW compressed text. In *Proceedings of the 8th Data Compression Conference*, pages 103–112. IEEE Computer Society Press, 1998.

[KTSA99] T. Kida, M. Takeda, A. Shinohara, and S. Arikawa. Shift-And approach to pattern matching in LZW compressed text. In *Proceedings of the 10th Annual Symposium on Combinatorial Pattern Matching*, number 1645 in Lecture Notes in Computer Science, pages 1–13. Springer-Verlag, 1999.

[KU94] J. Kärkkäinen and E. Ukkonen. Two and higher dimensional pattern matching in optimal expected time. In *Proceedings of the 5th ACM-SIAM Annual Symposium on Discrete Algorithms*, pages 715–723. ACM Press, 1994.

[KU96] J. Kärkkäinen and E. Ukkonen. Lempel-Ziv parsing and sublinear-size index structures for string matching. In N. Ziviani, R. Baeza-Yates, and K. Guimarães, editors, *Proceedings of the 3rd South American Workshop on String Processing*, pages 141–155, Recife, Brazil. Carleton University Press, 1996.

[Lev65] V. I. Levenshtein. Binary codes capable of correcting spurious insertions and deletions of ones. *Problems of Information Transmission*, 1:8–17, 1965.

[LT97] D. P. Lopresti and A. Tomkins. Block edit models for approximate string matching. *Theoretical Computer Science*, 181(1):159–179, 1997.

[LV89] G. M. Landau and U. Vishkin. Fast parallel and serial approximate string matching. *Journal of Algorithms*, 10(2):157–169, 1989.

[LW75] R. Lowrance and R. A. Wagner. An extension of the string-to-string correction problem. *Journal of the ACM*, 22(2):177–183, 1975.

[Man89] U. Manber. *Introduction to Algorithms*. Addison-Wesley, 1989.

[Man97] U. Manber. A text compression scheme that allows fast searching directly in the compressed file. *ACM Transactions on Information Systems*, 15(2):124–136, 1997.

[MBY91] U. Manber and R. A. Baeza-Yates. An algorithm for string matching with a sequence of don't cares. *Information Processing Letters*, 37(3):133–136, 1991.

[McC76] E. M. McCreight. A space-economical suffix tree construction algorithm. *Journal of Algorithms*, 23(2):262–272, 1976.

[Meh84] K. Mehlhorn. *Data Structures and Algorithms 1: Sorting and Searching*. Springer-Verlag, 1984.

[Mel96] B. Melichar. String matching with k differences by finite automata. In *Proceedings of the 13th International Conference on Pattern Recognition*, volume II, pages 256–260, Vienna, Austria. IEEE Computer Society Press, 1996.

[MKT+00] T. Matsumoto, T. Kida, M. Takeda, A. Shinohara, and S. Arikawa. Bit-parallel approach to approximate string matching in compressed texts. In *Proceedings of the 8th String Processing and Information Retrieval*, pages 221–228. IEEE Computer Society Press, 2000.

[MM89] E. W. Myers and W. Miller. Approximate matching of regular expressions. *Bulletin of Mathematical Biology*, 51:7–37, 1989.

[MM91] G. Mehldau and E. W. Myers. A system for pattern matching applications on biosequences. *Computer Applications in Biosciences*, 9(3):299–314, 1991.

[MM93] U. Manber and E. W. Myers. Suffix arrays: a new method for on-line string searches. *SIAM Journal on Computing*, 22(5):935–948, 1993.

[MM96] R. Muth and U. Manber. Approximate multiple string search. In *Proceedings of the 7th Annual Symposium on Combinatorial Pattern Matching*, number 1075 in Lecture Notes in Computer Science, pages 75–86. Springer-Verlag, 1996.

[MNZBY00] E. Moura, G. Navarro, N. Ziviani, and R. Baeza-Yates. Fast and flexible word searching on compressed text. *ACM Transactions on Information Systems*, 18(2):113–139, 2000.

[MP70] J. H. Morris, Jr and V. R. Pratt. A linear pattern-matching algorithm. Report 40, University of California, Berkeley, 1970.

[MP94] S. Muthukrishnan and K. Palem. Non-standard stringology: Algorithms and complexity. In *Proceedings of the 26th ACM Symposium on the Theory of Computing*, pages 770–779. ACM Press, 1994.

[MRS96] H. M. Mahmoud, M. Régnier, and R. T. Smythe. Analysis of Boyer-Moore-

Horspool string-matching heuristic. Report 9634, The George Washington University, 1996.

[MW94] U. Manber and S. Wu. GLIMPSE: A tool to search through entire file systems. In *Proceedings of the USENIX Winter 1994 Technical Conference*, pages 23–32, San Francisco, CA. USENIX Association, 1994.

[Mye92] E. W. Myers. A four russians algorithm for regular expression pattern matching. *Journal of the ACM*, 39(2):430–448, 1992.

[Mye94] E. W. Myers. A sublinear algorithm for approximate keyword searching. *Algorithmica*, 12(4/5):345–374, 1994.

[Mye95] E. W. Myers. Approximately matching context-free languages. *Information Processing Letters*, 54(2):85–92, 1995.

[Mye96] E. W. Myers. Approximate matching of network expression with spacers. *Journal of Computational Biology*, 3(1):33–51, 1996.

[Mye99] E. W. Myers. A fast bit-vector algorithm for approximate string matching based on dynamic programming. *Journal of the ACM*, 46(3):395–415, 1999.

[Nav98] G. Navarro. *Approximate Text Searching*. PhD thesis, Department of Computer Science, University of Chile, 1998.

[Nav00] G. Navarro. Improved approximate pattern matching on hypertext. *Theoretical Computer Science*, 237:455–463, 2000.

[Nav01a] G. Navarro. A guided tour to approximate string matching. *ACM Computing Surveys*, 33(1):31–88, 2001.

[Nav01b] G. Navarro. Nr-grep: a fast and flexible pattern matching tool. *Software Practice and Experience (SPE)*, 2001. To appear.

[Nav01c] G. Navarro. Regular expression searching over Ziv-Lempel compressed text. In *Proceedings of the 12th Annual Symposium on Combinatorial Pattern Matching*, number 2089 in Lecture Notes in Computer Science, pages 1–17. Springer-Verlag, 2001.

[NBY99] G. Navarro and R. Baeza-Yates. Very fast and simple approximate string matching. *Information Processing Letters*, 72:65–70, 1999.

[NBY00] G. Navarro and R. Baeza-Yates. A hybrid indexing method for approximate string matching. *Journal of Discrete Algorithms*, 1(1):205–239, 2000. Special issue on Matching Patterns.

[NKT+01] G. Navarro, T. Kida, M. Takeda, A. Shinohara, and S. Arikawa. Faster approximate string matching over compressed text. In *Proceedings of the 11th Data Compression Conference*, pages 459–468. IEEE Computer Society Press, 2001.

[NMN+00] G. Navarro, E. Moura, M. Neubert, N. Ziviani, and R. Baeza-Yates. Adding compression to block addressing inverted indexes. *Information Retrieval*, 3(1):49–77, 2000.

[NR99a] G. Navarro and M. Raffinot. Fast regular expression search. In *Proceedings of the 3rd Workshop on Algorithm Engineering*, number 1668 in Lecture Notes in Computer Science, pages 199–213. Springer-Verlag, 1999.

[NR99b] G. Navarro and M. Raffinot. A general practical approach to pattern matching over Ziv-Lempel compressed text. In *Proceedings of the 10th Annual Symposium on Combinatorial Pattern Matching*, number 1645 in Lecture Notes in Computer Science, pages 14–36. Springer-Verlag, 1999.

[NR00] G. Navarro and M. Raffinot. Fast and flexible string matching by combining bit-parallelism and suffix automata. *ACM Journal of Experimental Algorithmics (JEA)*, 5(4), 2000. http://www.jea.acm.org.

[NR01a] G. Navarro and M. Raffinot. Compact DFA representation for fast regular expression search. In *Proceedings of the 5th Workshop on Algorithm Engineering*, number 2141 in Lecture Notes in Computer Science, pages 1–12, 2001.

[NR01b] G. Navarro and M. Raffinot. Fast and simple character classes and bounded gaps pattern matching, with application to protein searching. In *Proceedings of the 5th Annual International Conference on Computational Molecular Biology*, pages 231–240. ACM Press, 2001.

[NSF01] P. Nicodème, B. Salvy, and P. Flajolet. Motif statistics. *Theoretical Computer Science*, 2001. To appear.

[NT00] G. Navarro and J. Tarhio. Boyer-Moore string matching over Ziv-Lempel compressed text. In *Proceedings of the 11th Annual Symposium on Combinatorial Pattern Matching*, number 1848 in Lecture Notes in Computer Science, pages 166–180. Springer-Verlag, 2000.

[Par96] K. Park. Analysis of two-dimensional approximate pattern matching algorithms. In *Proceedings of the 7th Annual Symposium on Combinatorial Pattern Matching*, number 1075 in Lecture Notes in Computer Science, pages 335–347. Springer-Verlag, 1996.

[Pea91] W. R. Pearson. Searching protein sequence libraries: comparison of the sensitivity and selectivity of the Smith-Waterman and FASTA algorithms. *Genomics*, 11:635–650, 1991.

[Pev00] P. A. Pevzner. *Computational Molecular Biology: An Algorithmic Approach*. MIT Press, 2000.

[Pin85] R. Y. Pinter. Efficient string matching with don't care pattern. In A. Apostolico and Z. Galil, editors, *Combinatorial Algorithms on Words*, pages 11–29. Springer-Verlag, 1985.

[PL88] W. R. Pearson and D. J. Lipman. Improved tools for biological sequence comparison. *Proceedings of the National Academy of Sciences of the U.S.A.*, 85:2444–2448, 1988.

[Raf97] M. Raffinot. On the multi backward dawg matching algorithm (MultiBDM). In R. Baeza-Yates, editor, *Proceedings of the 4th South American Workshop on String Processing*, pages 149–165, Valparaíso, Chile. Carleton University Press, 1997.

[Rég89] M. Régnier. Knuth-Morris-Pratt algorithm: an analysis. In *Proceedings of the 14th Symposium on Mathematical Foundations of Computer Science*, number 379 in Lecture Notes in Computer Science, pages 431–444. Springer-Verlag, 1989.

[RH91] S. Ranka and T. Heywood. Two-dimensional pattern matching with k mismatches. *Pattern Recognition*, 24(1):31–40, 1991.

[RS97] M. Régnier and W. Szpankowski. On the approximate pattern occurrence in a text. In *Proceedings Compression and Complexity of SEQUENCES'97*. IEEE Press, 1997.

[Ryt80] W. Rytter. A correct preprocessing algorithm for Boyer-Moore string searching. *SIAM Journal on Computing*, 9(3):509–512, 1980.

[Sad99] K. Sadakane. A modified Burrows-Wheeler transformation for case-insensitive search with application to suffix array compression. In *Proceedings of the 9th Data Compression Conference*, page 548, 1999. Poster. http://www-imai.is.s.u-tokyo.ac.jp/~sada/papers/Sada99b.ps.gz.

[Sad00] K. Sadakane. Compressed text databases with efficient query algorithms based on the compressed suffix array. In *Proceedings of the 11st International Symposium on Algorithms and Computation*, number 1969 in Lecture Notes in Computer Science, pages 410–421. Springer-Verlag, 2000.

[Sch98] J. P. Schmidt. All highest scoring paths in weighted grid graphs and their application to finding all approximate repeats in strings. *SIAM Journal on Computing*, 27(4):972–992, 1998.

[Sed88] R. Sedgewick. *Algorithms*. Addison-Wesley, 1988.

[Sel80] P. H. Sellers. The theory and computation of evolutionary distances: Pattern recognition. *Journal of Algorithms*, 1(4):359–373, 1980.

[Sim93] I. Simon. String matching algorithms and automata. In R. Baeza-Yates and N. Ziviani, editors, *Proceedings of the 1st South American Workshop on String Processing*, pages 151–157, Brazil. Universidade Federal de Minas Gerais, 1993.

[SK83] D. Sankoff and J. B. Kruskal. *Time Warps, String Edits, and Macromolecules: the Theory and Practice of Sequence Comparison*. Addison-Wesley, 1983.

[SM98] M.-F. Sagot and E. W. Myers. Identifying satellites and periodic repetitions in biological sequences. *Journal of Computational Biology*, 5:539–554, 1998.

[SMT+00] Y. Shibata, T. Matsumoto, M. Takeda, A. Shinohara, and S. Arikawa. A Boyer-Moore type algorithm for compressed pattern matching. In *Proceedings of the 11th Annual Symposium on Combinatorial Pattern Matching*, number 1848 in Lecture Notes in Computer Science, pages 181–194. Springer-Verlag, 2000.

[Sri86] M. A. Sridhar. Efficient algorithms for multiple pattern matching. Technical Report 661, University of Wisconsin-Madison, 1986.

[ST95] E. Sutinen and J. Tarhio. On using q-gram locations in approximate string matching. In *Proceedings 3rd Annual European Symposium*, number 979 in Lecture Notes in Computer Science, pages 327–340. Springer-Verlag, 1995.

[Sun90] D. M. Sunday. A very fast substring search algorithm. *Communications of the ACM*, 33(8):132–142, 1990.

[SV96] S.C. Sahinalp and U. Vishkin. Efficient approximate and dynamic matching of patterns using a labeling paradigm. In *Proceedings of the 37th IEEE Annual Symposium on Foundations of Computer Science*. IEEE Computer Society Press, 1996.

[SW81] T. F. Smith and M. S. Waterman. Identification of common molecular sequences. *Journal of Molecular Biology*, 147:195–197, 1981.

[SZ97] D. Shasha and K. Zhang. Approximate tree pattern matching. In *Pattern Matching Algorithms*, pages 341–371. Oxford University Press, 1997.

[Tho68] K. Thompson. Regular expression search algorithm. *Communications of the ACM*, 11:419–422, 1968.

[TSM+01] M. Takeda, Y. Shibata, T. Matsumoto, T. Kida, A. Shinohara, S. Fukamachi, T. Shinohara, and S. Arikawa. Speeding up pattern matching by text compression: The dawn of a new era. *Journal of the Information Processing Society of Japan (IPSJ)*, 42(3), 2001. To appear.

[TU88] J. Tarhio and E. Ukkonen. A greedy approximation algorithm for constructing shortest common superstrings. *Theoretical Computer Science*, 57(1):131–145, 1988.

[TU93] J. Tarhio and E. Ukkonen. Approximate Boyer-Moore string matching. *SIAM Journal on Computing*, 22(2):243–260, 1993.

[Ukk85] E. Ukkonen. Finding approximate patterns in strings. *Journal of Algorithms*, 6(1–3):132–137, 1985.

[Ukk92] E. Ukkonen. Approximate string matching with q-grams and maximal matches. *Theoretical Computer Science*, 92(1):191–212, 1992.

[Wat96] B. W. Watson. A new regular grammar pattern matching algorithm. In *Proceedings of the 4th Annual European Symposium*, number 1136 in Lecture Notes in Computer Science, pages 364–377. Springer-Verlag, 1996.

[WM92a] S. Wu and U. Manber. Agrep – a fast approximate pattern-matching tool. In *Proceedings USENIX Winter 1992 Technical Conference*, pages 153–162. USENIX Association, 1992.

[WM92b] S. Wu and U. Manber. Fast text searching allowing errors. *Communications of the ACM*, 35(10):83–91, 1992.

[WM94] S. Wu and U. Manber. A fast algorithm for multi-pattern searching. Report TR-94-17, Department of Computer Science, University of Arizona, Tucson, AZ, 1994.

[WMB99] I. Witten, A. Moffat, and T. Bell. *Managing Gigabytes*. Van Nostrand Reinhold, 2nd edition, 1999.

[WMM95] S. Wu, U. Manber, and E. W. Myers. A subquadratic algorithm for approximate regular expression matching. *Journal of Algorithms*, 19(3):346–360, 1995.

[WMM96] S. Wu, U. Manber, and E. W. Myers. A subquadratic algorithm for approximate limited expression matching. *Algorithmica*, 15(1):50–67, 1996.

[Yao79] A. C. Yao. The complexity of pattern matching for a random string. *SIAM Journal on Computing*, 8(3):368–387, 1979.

[ZL77] J. Ziv and A. Lempel. A universal algorithm for sequential data compression. *IEEE Transactions on Information Theory*, 23:337–343, 1977.

[ZL78] J. Ziv and A. Lempel. Compression of individual sequences via variable length coding. *IEEE Transactions on Information Theory*, 24:530–536, 1978.

[ZS97] K. Zhang and D. Shasha. Tree pattern matching. In A. Apostolico and Z. Galil, editors, *Pattern Matching Algorithms*, chapter 11, pages 341–371. Oxford University Press, 1997.

[ZSW94] K. Zhang, D. Shasha, and J. T. L. Wang. Approximate tree matching in the presence of variable length don't cares. *Journal of Algorithms*, 16(1):33–66, 1994.

[ZT89] R. F. Zhu and T. Takaoka. A technique for two-dimensional pattern matching. *Communications of the ACM*, 32(9):1110–1120, 1989.

[ZWM99] K. Zhang, L. Wang, and B. Ma. Computing similarity between RNA structures. In *Proceedings of the 10th Annual Symposium on Combinatorial Pattern Matching*, number 1645 in Lecture Notes in Computer Science, pages 281–293. Springer-Verlag, 1999.

Index